NEWMAN AND THE WORD

LOUVAIN THEOLOGICAL & PASTORAL MONOGRAPHS
—————————— 27 ——————————

NEWMAN AND THE WORD

Edited by

Terrence Merrigan & Ian T. Ker

PEETERS PRESS
LOUVAIN - PARIS - STERLING, VIRGINIA

W.B. EERDMANS

Library of Congress Cataloging-in-Publication Data

Newman and the word / edited by Terrence Merrigan & Ian T. Ker.
    p. cm. -- (Louvain theological & pastoral monograph ; v 27)
    ISBN 9042909218 (alk. paper)
    1. Newman, John Henry, 1801-1890--Congresses. 2. Newman, John Henry,
1801-1890--Contributions in theology of word--Congresses. 3. Word
(Theology)--History of doctrines--19th century--Congresses. I. Merrigan, Terrence. II.
Ker, I. T. (Ian Turnbull) III. Series.

BX4705.N5 N 47 2000
230'.2'092--dc21

                                                                        00-045315

© 2000, Peeters, Bondgenotenlaan 153, 3000 Leuven, Belgium

ISBN 90-429-0921-8 (Peeters Leuven)
D. 2000/0602/126

TABLE OF CONTENTS

INTRODUCTION

Terrence MERRIGAN & Ian KER

The papers collected here were presented at the Second Oxford International Newman Conference, dedicated to the theme of *Newman and the Word*, which was held at Oriel College, Oxford from 10-13 August 1998. The choice of theme for the 1998 conference is easily explained. The 'word' was at the heart of Newman's endeavours as a preacher and writer, while the 'Word made flesh' was the primary object of his faith as a Christian.

The Oxford conferences aim to reflect on the continuing significance of Newman's work as it relates to contemporary developments in religion, theology, philosophy and literature. The papers assembled here, interdisciplinary as they are, clearly fulfill that goal.

Terrence Merrigan reflects on Newman's understanding of the nature of Christian faith in the incarnate Word, by comparing Newman's views to those of the contemporary philosopher of religion, John Hick. Merrigan identifies the religious imagination as the key to Newman's portrayal of faith as essentially a 'lived' relationship to 'persons', and contrasts this with Hick's tendency to 'depersonalise' the transcendent.

Gabriel Daly continues the theme of Newman's understanding of the specificity of Christian revelation by investigating his relationship to the Modernist movement. Daly claims that perhaps the most significant contribution made to the theology of revelation by both Newman and the modernists was their emphasis on experience, especially moral experience, and the crucial role of the imagination in the apprehension and interpretation of experience.

Ian Ker explores the implications of Newman's celebrated claim that the Christian 'faithful', in view of their lived experience of revelation, are qualified to contribute to its articulation. Ker questions whether the traditional distinction between clergy, religious and laity was not 'subverted', as it were, by Newman's recognition that the 'faithful' were not simply equivalent to the laity. He then proceeds to reflect on the significance of Newman's insight in view of the growth of new forms of Christian and apostolic life within the Church.

Alister McGrath challenges Newman's portrayal of a theologian whose life and work were defined by his struggle with the biblical word, Martin Luther. McGrath takes Newman to task for his presentation of Luther's doctrine of faith, claiming to detect in that presentation a foil for Newman's own theological and ecclesiological agenda.

Sheridan Gilley explores that agenda by means of an analysis of Newman's relationship with the editor and owner of the weekly *Spectator*, R.H. Hutton, one of Newman's first biographers. Hutton's interest in Newman commended him to an otherwise suspicious literary public. More importantly, however, the record of Hutton's involvement with Newman throws considerable light on Newman's understanding of the Church and its dogmatic tradition, especially as this relates to its doctrine of the Trinitarian God.

Louis Dupré investigates the roots of Newman's commitment to orthodoxy in his analysis of Newman's debt to the Neoplatonic tradition. Dupré sees this debt reflected in, among other things, Newman's appeal to the *spiritual sense* of Scripture (which he regarded as necessary for a full understanding of the Gospel message), and his view of experience as including spiritual experience. The latter, according to Dupré, means that Newman's theory of experience is more Augustinian than empiricist.

Fergus Kerr continues the reflection on Newman's philosophical credentials by exploring the reception Newman has been accorded among British philosophers, especially those most closely associated with Oxford. Kerr detects in Newman's mature work a near-Derridean skill at locating the repressed other, so to speak, in the mainstream metaphysical tradition, a skill which reflects the empiricist resistance to all rationalistic self-confidence, a sceptical unwillingness to delimit a priori.

William Myers sees this same (postmodern) spirit at work in Newman's reflections on the nature of truth and its representation. According to Myers, Newman anticipates the concerns and questions of contemporary authors like Jacques Lacan, especially in his refusal to fill in the gaps and fissures at the heart of all our thinking, all our feeling, and all our relationships, both political and personal.

T.R. Wright draws a parallel between Newman's approach to the biblical word and the sensitivity to the ambiguity of all discourse displayed in the work of such postmodern thinkers as Jacques Derrida. However, while Newman was acutely aware of the 'indeterminacy' of Scripture and recognized the creative possibilities this brought with it, he looked to the Church and its doctrinal tradition to harnass the power of the word.

THE IMAGE OF THE WORD:
FAITH AND IMAGINATION IN
JOHN HENRY NEWMAN AND JOHN HICK

Terrence Merrigan

1. Introduction: The Problem to be Addressed

The aim of this article is to bring Newman's thought to bear on one of the major issues in contemporary theology, namely, the significance of the traditional Christian portrayal of Jesus as the incarnate Son of God, for *lived* Christian faith. I speak deliberately of 'lived Christian faith', because I wish to focus on the image of Christ around which Christians structure their concrete life of faith - their prayer, their praxis, and their discourse.[1] More specifically, I will be considering Newman's portrayal of the role of the religious imagination in the development of living faith.

I will attempt to do this in three steps: (i) by reflecting on Newman's understanding of this issue; (ii) by comparing Newman's view to a contemporary proposal, namely, that of John Hick, the foremost representative of the so-called pluralist theology of religions; (iii) by reflecting on the relative merits of each proposal.

Let us begin our reflections with Newman.

---

[1] Terrence Merrigan, "Approaching the Other in Faith: A Reply to Paul F. Knitter," *Louvain Studies Studies* 24 (1999) 355-360.

2. John Henry Newman on Christ's Place in Christianity

2.1 Introduction

In the *Grammar of Assent*, Newman claims that "the original instrument" of conversion and the "principle of fellowship" among the first Christians was the "Thought or Image of Christ." Moreover, this "central Image" continues to serve as the "vivifying idea both of the Christian body and of individuals in it." The image of Christ is the principle of Christian fraternity, and the source and soul of Christian "moral life." It "both creates faith, and then rewards it."[2] The whole life of the Church can be conceived as the endeavour to promote and perpetuate this image. Indeed, the whole life of the Church, its narrative tradition, its ethics, and its spirituality, can be regarded as — ideally — the objectification of this image in history.

Newman's concern in the *Grammar* might be described as the attempt to justify the existence and the operation of this image among Christians. His preferred means to this end is an analysis of the process of human perception. A brief presentation of that analysis is essential to any understanding of Newman's thoughts on the 'central image' of Christianity.

2.2 The Nature of Perception

Broadly speaking, Newman distinguishes two sorts of conscious experience, namely, (i) the experience of a world external to oneself, which is made known via sense impressions, and (ii) the experience of one's own inner world, which Newman

---

[2] John Henry Newman, *An Essay in Aid of a Grammar of Assent* (London: Longmans, Green, & Co., 1913) 464-465. Hereafter cited as G.A.

describes as a world of 'mental' impressions.[3] Along with the data of sense experience, mental impressions consti tute the media through which the mind perceives specific objects, distinct from itself.

Moreover, by virtue of their faculty of memory, humans are able to re-experience, as it were, — albeit more faintly — all "those alleged objects" disclosed via mental and sensible impressions. These 'objects' or "things," as Newman calls them, include "mental states and acts," and moral and aesthetical values, as well as material substances.[4]

In the case of "things" they have not directly experienced themselves, individuals can draw on other, "kindred" experiences (for example, the meaning of a fire in London on the basis of our experience of other fires), or on an innate "inventive faculty" (though this latter, known as the "faculty of composition," is "mainly limited, as regards its materials, by the sense of sight").[5]

What unites all these operations is the 'specificity' of their object. In each case, what is involved is, to use Newman's words, "experience or information about the *concrete*." The object of the mind's 'associative act' is "looked upon as something concrete, full of life, as an object of [actual] experience."[6] Newman

---

[3] In fact, there is no absolute separation between these two. Generally, it is the experience of the external world which provokes or elicits the mental impressions. Nevertheless, for Newman, the experience of one's inner world is an irreducible source of information and a vital source of knowledge. See J. H. Newman, *The Philosophical Notebook of John Henry Newman*, Edward Sillem (ed.), 2 vols. (Louvain: Nauwelaerts, 1969-70) 2:23. Hereafter cited as P.N.

[4] John Henry Newman, *The Theological Papers of John Henry Newman on Faith and Certainty*, Hugo M. de Achaval & J. D. Holmes (eds.), (Oxford: Clarendon Press, 1976) 64.

[5] G.A., 27-28.

[6] G.A., 23. (Emphasis ours); Father Zeno, *John Henry Newman: Our Way to Certitude* (Leiden: E.J. Brill, 1957) 123.

described this focussed and vital activity of the mind as "real apprehension." As Henry Habberly Price pointed out, Newman used the word "real" in its etymological sense, as derived from the Latin "res" (thing) - a usage that would have been immediately understood by his nineteenth-century audience in view of their classical education. By "real," then, Newman "means something like 'thingish',"[7] and "real apprehension" is quite simply the mind attending to one, concrete thing.

2.3 *Images, Impressions and Ideas*

Newman uses a variety of terms to describe the mind's 'conception' of those 'things' it has perceived via the data of sensible or mental impressions, or recalled through the medium of memory, or even constructed through the faculty of composition. These included images, impressions and ideas. Each of these terms is possessed of its own philosophical antecedents and much — inconclusive — research has been devoted to tracing the roots of Newman's vocabulary. The empiricist tradition is clearly a source, though Edward Sillem, the editor of Newman's *Philosophical Notebook*, dismisses Locke and Hume as possible sources in favour of the rather obscure Abraham Tucker (1705-1774). Sillem's claim has in turn been dismissed by John Coulson who argues that Newman is most at home in the Romantic, and more specifically Coleridgean, tradition. It would carry us to far to unravel the arguments advanced by various authors in favour of one or other claim. What is clear is that, for all three, the image or idea or impression is the mental counterpart of an object of experience. They *represent* things to the mind.[8]

---

[7] Henry H. Price, *Belief* (London: George Allen & Unwin, 1960) 317.

[8] Indeed, Newman can say that "they are things still, as being the reflections of things in a mental mirror." See G.A., 25, 75, 23.

Newman writes that we "picture" the things to ourselves "*in*" their attendant phenomena, and he relies heavily on the terminology of visual imagery ("picture," "likeness," "the mind's eye," "mental mirror," "an impress") to point up the character of the mind's perceptive activity. However, as David Pailin has pointed out, Newman's mental counterpart of a thing is not "a clearly defined visual representation but an awareness of the reality of the object."[9]

Jan Walgrave claims that Newman tended to call the "total act by which we take hold of a real object" quite simply "imagination," and he perceives a parallel here with the German Romantics for whom imagination is "our entire faculty of knowing the concrete."[10] Indeed, Newman continually equates the 'imaginative' with the 'real', and he initially distinguished 'notional' from 'imaginative' apprehension. Clearly, then, when Newman speaks of imaginative or real apprehension, what he is attempting to express is a vivid realization of a particular object or thing, a realization so intense that the object becomes a fact in the imagination. This carries us to the heart, not only of Newman's epistemological vision, but of his religious sensibility - to the place where the 'objects' of (religious) consciousness are so vividly 'realized' (and so existentially 'charged') as to command the subject's enduring commitment.

[9] David Pailin, *The Way to Faith: An Examination of Newman's 'Grammar of Assent' as a response to the Search for Certainty* (London: Epworth, 1969) 122; Ian Ker, Introduction to *An Essay In Aid Of A Grammar Of Assent*, by J.H. Newman (Oxford: Clarendon, 1985), lx- lxi, lxi n. 7, xli. Hereafter referred to as G.A. (Ker ed.). For Newman's terminology, see, for example, G.A., 103, 23-25.

[10] G.A., 34, 63, 87, 119, 120, 124; T.P., 1:135; G.A. (Ker ed.), 348-349 n. 13.17; J.H. Walgrave, *Newman the Theologian* (London: Geoffrey Chapman, 1960) 110.

2.4 The Idea of Christianity

Of course, the idea or image in the mind of a particular individual does not exhaust the reality of the object represented. Our 'viewing' of an object is always undertaken from a particular 'perspective'. It is aspectual. The achievement of a comprehensive image or idea of a complex reality — such as a university or a religion — is the fruit of a communitarian endeavour. In what is undoubtedly a bow to the Romantic tradition, Newman portrays this comprehensive idea as a dynamic entity, with a life of its own. Speaking of the idea of Christianity, Newman claims that it "takes hold of a thousand minds by its living force," that it "may rather be said to use the minds of Christians, than to be used by them."[11] Coulson comments on the similarity between Newman's use of the term and Coleridge's portrayal of the idea as a "realizing principle," that is, in the poet's words, "a principle existing ... in the minds and consciences of the persons whose duties it prescribes, and whose rights it determines." As such, Coulson continues, the idea represents "a claim made upon us," to which "we must first make a fiduciary response as a whole before we can fully understand its implications."[12] For Newman, the idea of

[11] J. H. Newman, *Fifteen Sermons Preached Before the University of Oxford* (London: Rivingtons, 1872) 316-317. Compare J. H. Newman, *An Essay on the Development of Christian Doctrine*, rev. ed. (London: Longmans, Green, & Co., 1878) 38. Hereafter referred to as Dev.

[12] John Coulson, *Newman and the Common Tradition: A Study in the Language of Church and Society* (Oxford: Clarendon, 1970) 25 quoting Coleridge's *On the Constitution of Church and State*, ed. H.N. Coleridge (London, 1839) 19. See G.A., 464: "[Christ] is found, through His preachers, to have imprinted the Image or idea of Himself in the minds of His subjects individually; and that Image, apprehended and worshipped in individual minds, becomes a principle of association, and a real bond of those subjects one with another, who are thus united to the body be being united to that Image; and moreover that Image, which is their moral life, when they have been already converted, is also the original instrument of their conversion. It is the Image of Him who fulfills the one great need of human nature, the Healer of its wounds, the Physician of the soul, this Image it is which both creates faith, and then rewards it."

Christianity is ultimately nothing other than "God's saving revelation, His self-disclosure in history, which is the 'vital principle' of that Church which is its visible expression."[13]

Nicholas Lash has argued that, in the final analysis, the dynamism and organizing power of the Christian idea is born of its foundation in the risen Christ, God's living Word in history. It is this same rootedness in Christ which accounts for Newman's tendency "to express the transcendence of the 'idea' by hypostasising, or personalizing it."[14]

---

[13] Nicholas Lash, "Faith and History: Some Reflections on Newman's 'Essay on the Development of Christian Doctrine'," *Irish Theological Quarterly* 38 (July 1971) 232. The ecclesiological dimension is all-important here since, as Coulson has shown in his penetrating study, *Newman and the Common Tradition*, it marks the breaking point between Newman and Coleridge. The latter insisted on a real and necessary distinction, indeed a radical dichotomy, between the 'idea' of the Church, which is properly predicable only of the Church universal ("Ecclesia"), and the Church Establishment ("Enclesia"), which is the social and cultural embodiment of the 'idea'. The Ecclesia and Enclesia represent "separate states of the Church," the former, the eschatological assembly, the latter, a visible polity which serves as source and guarantor of a nation's culture, which culture, in turn, becomes the 'form' of religion. For Newman, however, 'ideas' cannot be considered apart from their visible exhibitions. They cannot be treated as "self-subsistent entities." The history of Newman's abandonment of the theory of the 'Via Media' is 'nothing more' than his growing perception of the 'unreality' — that is to say, the unrealized character — of a theological 'idea', and his progressively deepening conviction that the only adequate representation of the 'idea' of the apostolic Church was Roman Catholicism. See Coulson, *Common Tradition*, 62, 63-64; see also pp. 38-51, 66-67, 67-69, 47, 40-42. See J. H. Newman, *Certain Difficulties Felt by Anglicans in Catholic Teaching*, 2 vols. (London: Longmans, Green, & Co., 1850, 1866) 1:364-68. Hereafter referred to as Diff. See also Newman's *The Via Media of the Anglican Church* (Longmans, Green, & Co., 1899) 1:16. Hereafter referred to as V.M.

[14] Nicholas Lash, *Change in Focus* (London: Sheed & Ward, 1973) 92; "Faith and History," pp. 232-233; *Newman on Development: The Search for an Explanation in History* (London: Sheed & Ward, 1975) 74-75, 48. For a list of relevant passages, see Lash, *Development*, 180 n. 60.

The Christian 'idea' exists in the "mind of the Church," as the correlate to the "fact of revelation," in the fashion of the image/impression which the individual mind forms of material objects. The idea is not, properly speaking, the object of faith. It is, however, by means of it that the object of faith is apprehended. We might say that it 'mediates' the object of faith. In the words of Coulson, "an 'idea' is not reality at its most real but an image of what acts upon us in the manner of objects of sense-perception."[15]

The object of faith is prior to the Christian idea and distinct from it, just as the objects 'conveyed' through sense impressions are distinct from the 'ideas' we have of them. The 'idea' which exists in the (church's) 'mind' can come to expression in a variety of forms, in systems of church governance and in systems of thought, in art, literature, forms of conduct, and so forth. This is what Newman means by the 'development' of an idea.[16]

We might say of the Christian *idea* that it lives in the mind of the whole Church, and of *aspects* of that idea that they live in the minds of individual believers, who are (individually) incapable of grasping the whole complex 'fact' of Christianity. The fifteenth University sermon is above all concerned with aspects of the Christian idea in the minds of individual believers, and considers development from a *psycho-epistemological* point of view. The *Essay on Development*, while it retains traces of the empiricist "object _ impression _ idea" schema is above all concerned with the idea's own inherent dynamism and the exhibition of this in a social and historical context. Its point of view is accordingly *socio-epistemological*.[17] It would be wrong, however, to divorce

---

[15] U.S., 331; Coulson, *Common Tradition*, 64.

[16] Dev., 42-54. Newman speaks of "political," "logical," "historical," "ethical," and "metaphysical" exhibitions of the idea.

[17] The categories "psycho-" and socio-epistemological" are used by J.H. Walgrave, *J.H. Newman: His Personality, His Principles, His Fundamental*

the two considerations from one another. As Walgrave rightly points out, even in the sermon Newman views the development of the idea in the individual mind against the broader background of its evolution in society. Indeed, the case of the individual is but a microcosm of the idea's societal evolution. Moreover, the idea is imparted to the individual within a communal context, namely, the living tradition of the Church.

Newman acknowledges that "religious impressions" may be made on the mind by "supernatural" operations on the part of the Divine, such as those presumably manifest in the process of "inspiration," or by "illuminating grace" at baptism. However, in keeping with his general principle that God usually acts "through, with, and beneath those physical, social, and moral laws, of which our experience informs us," Newman insists that the "secondary and intelligible," means by which one receives the "impression of Divine Verities," are, for instance, "the habitual and devout perusal of Scripture ..., the gradual influence of intercourse with persons those who are in themselves in possession of sacred ideas, ... the study of Dogmatic Theology ..., a continual round of devotion, or again, sometimes, in minds both fitly disposed and apprehensive, the almost instantaneous operation of a keen faith."[18]

Doctrines - Courses Delivered by Professor J.H. Walgrave, Katholieke Universiteit Leuven, 1975-1976-1977 (Leuven, Belgium: By the Author, 1981) 182-183. See also pp. 203-204. Regarding the "object-impression-idea" schema, see James Cameron, Introduction to *An Essay on the Development of Christian Doctrine: The Edition of 1845*, by John Henry Newman, J.M. Cameron (ed.), (Harmondsworth, Eng.: Penguin Books, 1974) 40; Coulson, *Common Tradition*, 59.

[18] J.H. Newman, *Essays Critical and Historical*, 2 vols. (London: Longmans, Green, & Co., 1871) 2:190, 192. Hereafter cited as Ess.; U.S., p. 333. See also T.P., 138; 132-133. See also J.H. Newman, *Parochial and Plain Sermons*, 8 vols (London: Rivingtons, 1873-1877) 3:160-161, 169. Hereafter referred to as P.S. See also G.A., pp. 118-119. See Robert Holyer, "Religious Certainty and the Imagination," *The Thomist* 50 (1986) 415-416. See p. 415: "For Newman, one important effect of living a religious life is that it schools the imagination." See

2.5 The Religious Imagination and the Image of Christ

Newman, convinced of the living presence of the risen Christ in the church and the world, has woven the Romantic and empiricist traditions into a perspective peculiarly his own. The link between both traditions is the imagination, that is to say, the faculty by which we are enabled to bring home to ourselves the objects of experience. A comparative analysis of the *Grammar* and Newman's writings on development reveals a 'dual' understanding of imagination in Newman, or, more accurately, allows one to isolate two separate, though not distinct, functions accorded by Newman to the imaginative faculty. These can be identified, for the sake of convenience, by the terms 'realizing imagination', and 'prehending imagination'. In the case of realizing imagination, attention is focussed on the fact as grasped or apprehended ('imaged'). Viewed in this respect, imagination is primarily an 'evocative' power. In the case of 'prehending' imagination, what is at stake is the synthetic operation by means of which imagination's object is grasped, or, as it were, set before the mind's eye. Viewed in this respect, imagination is a 'synthetic' power.

Of course, the distinction of 'realizing' and 'prehending' imagination does not imply a division of these, as if there were two imaginative 'faculties'. There is one 'faculty' which grasps its object as a concrete fact.[19] The prehensive function of the imagination is Newman's chief concern in the works on doctrinal development, and in the discussion of conscience in the *Grammar*. The

also M. Jamie Ferreira, "Newman and William James on Religious Experience: The Theory and the Concrete," *Heythrop Journal* 29 (1988) 51-52. See finally, H.D. Weidner, "Introduction" to John Henry Newman, *The 'Via Media' of the Anglican Church*, (ed.) H.D. Weidner (Oxford: Clarendon, 1990) lxxii.

[19] To speak of the imagination and other 'faculties', is not necessarily to advocate what Hick describes as a "discarded faculty psychology." See John Hick, *Faith and Knowledge*, 2d ed. (Ithaca, N.Y.: Cornell University Press,

realizing imagination is the subject of Newman's reflections in the
first half of the *Grammar* in particular, and in his occasional considerations on 'modern' threats to religious consciousness.[20]

In light of the distinction we have proposed, it is interesting to note that Newman, in a letter of 1852, spoke of "the intellectual difficulty of imagining and realizing Emmanuel."[21] While
one ought not make more of this remark than the text itself can
bear, the juxtaposition is at least instructive. In the first place,
Newman connected the imagination to the task of 'realizing' the
great mystery of faith. In the second place, he did this in the context of a reflection on the existence of the conflicting, and seemingly contradictory, elements which go to make up the believer's
idea of Christ. In so doing, he indicated the second function of
imagination, its prehensile role.

Newman had already treated the problem of the difficulty of
combining conflicting elements into a comprehensive idea of

1966), 76 In the final analysis, however, as Warnock points out in her study,
Imagination, "it is very hard to find a substitute for the vocabulary of faculty
psychology." She is perhaps correct when she maintains that "in fact ... such
vocabulary is steadily becoming more innocuous as we more and more clearly
recognize it as metaphorical." See Mary Warnock, *Imagination* (London: Faber
& Faber, 1976) 196. As the notes preparatory to the *Grammar* indicate, Newman
used the terms 'faculty' and 'power' interchangeably as early as 1868. Writing in
1885, he observed that: "A faculty .... is the exercise of a power of the mind
itself, and that *pro re nata*; and, when the mind ceases to use it, we may almost
say that it is nowhere. Of course, for convenience, we speak of the mind as pos-
sessing faculties instead of saying that it acts in a certain way and on a definite
subject-matter; but we must not turn a figure of speech into a fact." T.P., 155,
135. Note the title of these reflections (p. 154): "On the Mind's Faculties existing, not 're', but 'ratione', and therefore only abstract names for its operations."

[20] Ian Ker, *John Henry Newman: A Biography* (Oxford: Oxford University
Press, 1990) 729; Terrence Merrigan, *Clear Heads and Holy Heart: The Religious and Theological Ideal of John Henry Newman*, Louvain Theological and
Pastoral Monographs, 7 (Leuven: Peeters; Grand Rapids, W.B. Eerdmans, 1991)
48-81.

Christ in a sermon preached in 1835 and entitled, "The Humilia-
tion of the Eternal Son." Newman's aim in the sermon, he
declared, was "to facilitate your *conception* [emphasis Newman]
of Him who is the subject of [a mystery], to help you towards contemplating Him as God and man at once." To this end, Newman
adduces several instances of apparent contradictions that are the
stuff of daily life, such as, for example, an individual's momentary
inability to recall what he nevertheless has not actually forgotten.
Might we not say of such a one, Newman asks, that "in one sense
he knows it, [while] in another he does not know it." The purpose
of such examples, Newman indicates, is "to appease [the] imagination, if it startles at the mystery."[22] Newman was acutely aware
that it might very well "startle." After all, "what is *strange*, is to
the imagination *false*," and, for it, "experience is the measure of
truth." The provision of analogous instances of the mind's balanc-
ing of conflicting data is, then, a necessary propaedeutic to the
contemplation of the fullness of the mystery of Christ. In this
regard, long familiarity with the religious tradition is a decided
advantage:

> The picture of our Lord in the gospels may be to some men unreal and
> untrue, it being so strange to their imaginations, as being so unlike
> any thing they ever met with. But the Christian has a reflexion of it in
> his own mind to help him, and a Catholic is familiar with multiplied
> and recent copies of it in the *Lives of the Saints*.[23]

[21] See *The Letters and Diaries of John Henry Newman*, C. S. Dessain et al.
(eds.), vols. 1-4 (Oxford: Clarendon Press, 1978-1984); 11-22 (London: Oxford
University Press, 1961-1972); 23-31 (Oxford: Clarendon Press, 1973-1977). See
15:57. Hereafter referred to as L.D.

[22] P.S., 3:166-167. See L.D., 13:82 for another instance of Newman's use of
the analogy of memory.

[23] T.P., 47 (emphasis Newman); P.N., 2:171. Note that the unitive power of
the imagination breaks down when the Trinity is involved. See G.A. (Ker ed.),
88: "But the question is whether a real assent to the mystery [of the Trinity], as

Given some analogous experience then, the imagination is apparently able to balance conflicting claims — in the case at hand, that Jesus "possessed at once a double assemblage of attributes, divine and human" — and thereby to realize the object of whom or which they are predicated — in the case at hand, the "Object of faith." We can only be truly said to "know" Jesus "if our idea of Him be ... such as to take up and incorporate into itself the manifold attributes and offices which we ascribe to Him." Our idea of Him — Newman also speaks of "the *image* of the Incarnate Son in our hearts" — is "one true and simple vision" when it facilitates "the [holding] together in our minds" of those "distinct notions" involved in the dual affirmation that Jesus is at once human and divine.[24]

The creation of such an 'idea' is the task of the 'prehending' imagination. Its supreme achievement consists in the 'construction' of an 'image' of Christ that reconciles conflicting descriptions or "truths ... which often appear to diverge from each other," in "one representative."[25]

Newman develops this line of thought in the fifteenth university sermon where he argues that "the ideas which we are granted of Divine Objects under the Gospel, from the nature of the case and because they are ideas, answer to the Originals so far as this, that

such, is possible; and I say it is not possible, because though we can image the separate propositions, we cannot image them altogether. We cannot, because the mystery transcends all our experience; we have no experiences in our memory which we can put together, compare, contrast, unite, and thereby transmute into an image of the Ineffable Verity ..." See also p. 89: "We know one truth about Him and another truth, — but we cannot image both of them together." See also pp. 90, 92. Se also pp. 81-82. See also Gerard Magill, "Moral Imagination in Theological Method and Church Tradition: John Henry Newman," *Theological Studies* 53 (1992) 459.

[24] P.S., 3:166, 169, 170-171. See also P.S., 3:129.

[25] John Coulson, *Religion and Imagination: 'in aid of a grammar of assent'* (Oxford: Clarendon Press, 1981) 65-66; G.A., 446; U.S., 27.

they are whole, indivisible, substantial, and may be called real, as being images of what is real."[26] In the *Essay on Development*, Newman observes that:

> *Religious* men, according to their measure, have an idea or vision of the Blessed Trinity in unity, of the Son Incarnate and His Presence, not as a number of qualities, attributes, and actions, not as the subject of a number of propositions, but as one, and individual, and indepen dent of words, as an impression conveyed through the senses.[27]

The 'object' of Christian faith is, then, apprehended in all its dizzying complexity by the religious imagination. It is this 'power' of the mind which both 'creates' the object and 'pro-poses' it for the contemplation (and animation) of the human spirit. It is the imagination which, to use Newman's words, both creates faith and then rewards it.

In his study, *Religion and Imagination*, John Coulson argues that, "in making an appeal to the imagination in the full sense, Newman was obliged to modify or abandon the precise vocabu-lary of philosophical usage for that of literary criticism," and especially, for such criticism in the Coleridgean mould. Coulson is of the opinion that "the real assent made to primary forms of reli-gious faith (expressed in metaphor, symbol, and story), [and treated by Newman] is of the same kind as the imaginative assent we make to the primary forms of literature." Newman's decision to explore religious faith in terms of imaginative apprehension and assent was born of his conviction that "all beliefs — religious, secular and political — must first be credible to imagination," the faculty which enables us to relate to an object as a 'whole', that is to say, as something with a claim on us. In this vision, imagination is, in the words of Kierkegaard, "what providence uses to get men

---

[26] U.S., 330-331.
[27] U.S., 319, 331.

into reality, into existence, to get them far out, or in, or down into existence." Newman's achievement, according to Coulson, was twofold: in the first place, his perception of, and attention to, the "crucial difficulty for succeeding generations," namely, the demand for the rational justification of faith before faith is allowed; and secondly, his elucidation of principles by which the "proper priority may still be exercised," namely, that faith be grounded on imagination and supported by rational inferences, which inferences authenticate our imaginative assents and allow us (in view of the accumulation of probabilities) to become certain of what we cannot absolutely prove.[28]

Newman is in no doubt that Christian life and Christian discourse must take their lead from the imaginative apprehension of Christianity's founding event — the life, death, and resurrection of Jesus of Nazareth — what theologians call the 'Christ-event'. This imaginative apprehension, which is necessarily a communal process, gives rise to the 'idea' of Christianity. Doctrine is one expression of this living idea. But doctrine is only comprehensible within the framework of the communal and imaginative apprehension of the founding event. Newman's priorities are clear. The systems or creeds which are the fruit of theological reason must be grounded in and cohere with what is at first "an impression on the imagination."[29]

The time has come to examine an alternative vision, one which inverts Newman's priorities. Let us now reflect on John Hick's proposal regarding the place of the incarnate Word in Christianity.

---

[28] Coulson, *Religion and Imagination*, 51-52, 145, 45. Coulson is quoting from Kierkegaard's *The Journals*, ed. E.T.A. Dru (New York: Harper Torchbooks, 1959) 243.

[29] U.S., 329.

3. John Hick on Christ's Place in Christianity

3.1 Hick and the Pluralist Theology of Religions

The theology of religions can perhaps best be described as that branch of Christian theology which reflects on the nature and function of non-Christian religious traditions, in the light of Christianity's own faith in the salvific character of the Christ-event. There is a tendency to distinguish three major schools of thought in the contemporary theology of religions. These are as follows: (i) the *exclusivist* school which insists that salvation is only possible through an explicit faith in the Christ; (ii) the *inclusivist* school, which acknowledges the positive role played by other religious traditions, but regards Christ as the normative source/symbol of all salvation, and conceives of explicit Christian faith as the completion of every religious system;[30] and, (iii) the *pluralist*

---

[30] For Catholic inclusivism, Christ is always implicated in the salvific process, either as the *font* of saving grace (including that grace which is operative in the non-Christian religions), or as the *goal* of all of humanity's religious striving (in which case he is the norm against which all religious systems are to be measured) or as the *catalyst* for the operation of "the Spirit of truth" who fills all of creation and draws all women and men to the Father (via diverse religious traditions). As example of these three approaches, one thinks of Karl Rahner, Hans Küng and Gavin D'Costa respectively. See, for example, Karl Rahner, "Christianity and the Non-Christian Religions," in *Theological Investigations*, vol. 5 (Baltimore: Helicon, 1966), pp. 115-134; Hans Küng, "The World's Religions in God's Plan of Salvation," in J. Neuner (ed.), *Christian Revelation and World Religions*, (London: Burns & Oates, 1967), pp. 25-66; Gavin D'Costa, "Towards a Trinitarian Theology of Religions," in C. Cornille, V. Neckebrouck (ed.), *A Universal Faith? Peoples, Cultures, Religions and the Christ*, Louvain Theological and Pastoral Monographs, vol. 9 (Grand Rapids: W.B. Eerdmans / Leuven: Peeters, 1992), pp. 139-154. See Terrence Merrigan, "Exploring the Frontiers: Jacques Dupuis and the Movement 'Toward a Christian Theology of Religious Pluralism'," *Louvain Studies* 23 (1998) 338-359; "'For us and for our salvation'. The Notion of Salvation History in the Contemporary Theology of Religions," *Irish Theological Quarterly* 64 (1999) 339-348.

school which argues for the essential parity of the world's great religious traditions as "authentic and valid contexts of salvation/liberation."[31] John Hick is the foremost representative of the pluralist school.

The pluralist insistence on the essential parity of the great world faiths extends beyond the matter of their salvific efficacy to the question of their origins and their claims to uniqueness. According to Hick, each of the world's religions embodies "different perceptions and conceptions of, and correspondingly different responses to, the

---

[31] John Hick, *Disputed Questions in Theology and the Philosophy of Religion* (London: Macmillan, 1997) 143. For an analysis of the epistemological framework of pluralist thought, see Terrence Merrigan, "Religious Knowledge in the Pluralist Theology of Religions," *Theological Studies* 58 (1997) 686-707. See also Terrence Merrigan, "The Anthropology of Conversion: Newman and the Contemporary Theology of Religions," in Ian T. Ker (ed.), *Newman and Conversion*, ed. Ian T. Ker (Edinburgh: T. & T. Clark, 1997) 119-123, 125-126; "The Challenge of the Pluralist Theology of Religions and the Christian Rediscovery of Judaism," in Didier Pollefeyt (ed.), *Jews and Christians: Rivals or Partners for the Kingdom of God?*, Louvain Theological and Pastoral Monographs, 21 (Leuven: Peeters; Grand Rapids: Eerdmans, 1997) 95-132. Paul Knitter describes the pluralist theology of religions as "a project that is not yet complete and that has various proposed versions." See his *One Earth Many Religions*, 23. See also p. 29: "Such a theology is still very much a growing, changing, often ambiguous phenomenon." Keith Yandell observes that the pluralist school itself is characterized by a plurality of approaches. See his "Some Varieties of Religious Pluralism," in J. Kellenberger (ed.), in *Inter-Religious Models and Criteria* (London: Macmillan, 1993) 187-211. In "Five Misgivings," in L. Swidler, P. Mojzes (ed.), *The Uniqueness of Jesus: A Dialogue with Paul F. Knitter* (Maryknoll, NY: Orbis, 1997) 80, John Hick chides Knitter for describing pluralism as recognizing only the "probability" of other true and valid religions. According to Hick, religious pluralism involves "the affirmation not merely of a possible or probable but of an actual plurality of authentically true-and-salvific religious traditions." In a response ("Can our 'one and only' also be a 'one among many'?: A Response to Responses," 54 n. 2), Knitter acknowledges that "practically and experientially" he does in fact agree with Hick. The basis for this agreement is Knitter's observation of the "the ethical and spiritual fruits" manifest among the adherents of other traditions.

Transcendent, from within the different cultural ways of being human."[32] "Christianity," he insists, "is one among a plurality of authentic responses to the divine reality,"[33] what Hick calls the Real, which is postulated as the source of humankind's religious experience.[34]

In the course of history, particular religious traditions have advanced absolutist claims regarding both their founders and their doctrines. This is the almost inevitable outcome of religious enthusiasm for the founder and the tradition.[35] As long as the absolutist claims of a particular tradition were not challenged by the actual experience of, or encounter with, other traditions, they could remain both culturally and religiously self-evident. But this is no longer the case. In the words of one prominent pluralist theologian, "the contemporary context [is] pressing Christians toward a new pluralist approach to other religions."[36] The encounter with the depths and richness of other world faiths is "pushing our cultural consciousness toward the simple but profound insight that *there is no one and only way.*"[37]

[32] John Hick, *Problems of Religious Pluralism* (Basingstoke: Macmillan, 1985) 91. See also John Hick, *An Interpretation of Religion: Human Responses to the Transcendent* (London: Macmillan, 1989) 240.

[33] John Hick, *Metaphor of God Incarnate* (London: SCM, 1993) 104, 160.

[34] Hick, *An Interpretation of Religion*, 243, 249; see also John Hick, *The Rainbow of Faiths: Critical Dialogues on Religious Pluralism* (London: SCM, 1995) 68. Of course, this is perfectly in keeping with Hick's Kantian epistemology according to which a distinction must be made between the divine *noumenal* Reality *an sich*, which exists independently of and outside our perception of it, and the "phenomenal manifestations" of that reality which occur "within the realm of religious experience." See John Hick, *God Has Many Names* (London: Macmillan, 1980) 105. Hick sometimes speaks of the world's religious traditions as 'faiths'. See, for example, *Rainbow of Faiths*, 32.

[35] See Hick, *God has Many Names*, 59-70; *Rainbow of Faiths*, 96, 82-103; see also John Hick, *God and the Universe of Faiths* (London: Macmillan, 1973) 172, 178.

[36] Paul Knitter, "Preface," *The Myth of Christian Uniqueness*, John Hick, Paul Knitter (ed.), (Maryknoll, NY: Orbis, 1988) ix.

[37] Paul Knitter, *No Other Name? A Critical Survey of Christian Attitudes Toward the World Religions* (Maryknoll: Orbis, 1985) 5 (emphasis Knitter).

Pluralist theologians insist that this insight does not lead to the relativization of particular religious traditions. The world faiths provide the forums within which religious experience becomes possible, and the categories which allow believers both to express that experience and, most importantly, to name its source or its ground.[38] Nevertheless, in line with the Liberal Protestant tradition represented by Schleiermacher,[39] the pluralists insist that the grounding religious experience is ineffable and that no particular religious tradition can ever do it justice.

It is clear that, within this framework, the doctrinal traditions or truth-claims of the world's religions need to be reassessed. As the culturally-conditioned expressions of culturally-determined religious experiences, their role is essentially a functional one.[40] They promote the particular religious experience which characterizes a particular tradition. Their aim is not to provide information, but to encourage the transformation of the believer in the direction indicated by the religious tradition as a whole.[41]

Hick recounts how his views were moulded by his experience of life in multi-cultural Birmingham (England), and his personal contacts with people of other faiths. See John Hick, *Problems of Religious Pluralism*, 5-10; *Disputed Questions*, 139-141.

[38] See, for example, Paul Knitter, *One Earth Many Religions: Multifaith Dialogue and Global Responsibility* (Maryknoll, NY: Orbis, 1995) 115 where Knitter speaks about religious experience "illuminating the language" of religion at the same time that "the language is forming the experience."

[39] Merrigan, "Religious Knowledge in the Pluralist Theology of Religions," 693-697.

[40] See Merrigan, "Religious Knowledge in the Pluralist Theology of Religions," 698-702, 706-707; "The Challenge of the Pluralist Theology of Religions and the Christian Rediscovery of Judaism," 103-111; Paul J. Griffiths, "The Uniqueness of Christian Doctrine Defended," in Gavin D'Costa (ed.), *Christian Uniqueness Reconsidered: The Myth of a Pluralistic Theology of Religions* (Maryknoll, N.Y.: Orbis, 1990) 159-160.

[41] In his most recent work, Paul Knitter has endorsed George Lindbeck's view that religious doctrines are best understood as "rules" of life, that is to say,

Among pluralist thinkers, Hick has insisted with most force on
the necessity of relativizing truth-claims in view of the practical
goal of humanity's religious quest. Hick describes that goal as
"human transformation from natural self-centeredness to a new
centering in the Real, the Ultimate."[42] The actual differences
among the world's religious traditions (whether these concern
questions of history, metaphysics or doctrine)[43] are only "penulti-
mately important" as far as the realization of this goal is concerned. Hence, they ought to be "de-emphasized" in the interreli-
gious encounter. What counts is the process of transformation
from "self-centeredness to Reality-centeredness,"[44] a transformation that "is most readily observed by its moral fruits, which can
be identified by means of the ethical ideal, common to all the great
traditions, of ... love/compassion."[45] Within the world's religious
traditions, Hick continues, those who bear such fruits are regarded
as "authentic mediators" of the transcendent reality (Hick's
'Real').[46] For Christians, Jesus is the mediator par excellence.

as "communally authoritative rules of discourse, attitude and action," rather than
as fixed, propositional formulae. See George Lindbeck, *The Nature of Doctrine:
Religion and Theology in a Postliberal Age* (Philadelphia: Westminster, 1984)
18; Paul Knitter, *Jesus and the Other Names: Christian Mission and Global
Responsibility* (Maryknoll, N.Y.: Orbis, 1996) 168 n. 6. See Merrigan, "The
Challenge of the Pluralist Theology of Religions and the Christian Rediscovery
of Judaism," 110-111.

[42] Hick, *Rainbow of Faiths*, 106. See especially *An Interpretation of Religion*,
343-376.

[43] See John Hick, "On Conflicting Religious Truth-Claims," *Religious Studies* 19 (1983) 75-80, reprinted as chapter 6 of *Problems of Religious Pluralism*
(London: Macmillan, 1985) 89-95; *An Interpretation of Religion*, 362-376. Hick
resumes the discussion in his *Metaphor of God Incarnate*, 140-149, where he
employs the terms, "conceptions of the ultimate, sets of metaphysical beliefs,
and historical questions," and where he reverses the order of presentation (i.e.,
by beginning with conceptions of the ultimate).

[44] Hick, *Problems of Religious Pluralism*, 91; *Rainbow of Faiths*, 114-116

[45] Hick, *An Interpretation of Religion*, 14.

[46] Hick, *An Interpretation of Religion*, 326.

Hick's reflections on Jesus' mediatory role are the subject of the following section.

3.2 Hick on the Myth/Metaphor of Incarnation

The tendency of religious traditions to absolutize their founders and their doctrines finds its most striking expression, in the case of Christianity, in the divinization of Jesus, that is to say, "in the exaltation ... of the man of Nazareth into the divine Christ,"[47] the object of Christian worship. This process culminated in the christological dogmas of the councils of Nicea (325) and Chalcedon (451) which affirmed, in Hick's words, that Jesus of Nazareth was "God the Son, second person of a divine Trinity, incarnate in two natures, one human and the other divine."[48]

While Hick is able to appreciate the origins of this doctrine and its religious significance for previous generations of Christians, he formulates three objections to the continued insistence on its literal interpretation. The first of these is the lack of dominical authority for the teaching.[49] The second is the failure of the church or theology to provide any intelligible explanation of the content of the doctrine, understood literally.[50] In this regard, Hick returns often to what he calls the problem of the "incompatible attributes" ascribed to Jesus, namely, divinity and humanity. The third objection posed by Hick is the historical fallout, so to speak, of the church's insistence that Jesus is Son of God in a unique sense. In Hick's words, "the literally understood doctrine" has "literal implications" which have 'damaged' Christianity's relationship

[47] Hick, *God has Many Names*, 60.

[48] Hick, *Rainbow of Faiths*, 94-95.

[49] Hick, *Rainbow of Faiths*, 95: "It [the doctrine of the incarnation] was not taught by Jesus himself but is a creation of the church."

[50] See especially Hick, *God and the Universe of Faiths*, 165-179; *Metaphor of God Incarnate*, 99-111.

with people of other faiths, and been invoked to justify "terrible human injustices and cruelties."[51] The doctrine of the incarnation means that Christianity regards itself as "the only religion to have been founded by God in person." This "singles it out as having a uniquely central, normative, final status among the religions of the world, constituting it a more effective context of salvation than any other."[52] According to Hick, this Christian self-understanding was grist for the mill of all sorts of exploitative movements, including anti-Semitism, colonialism, and patriarchalism.[53]

As an alternative to the literal interpretation of the traditional doctrine, Hick proposes that we approach incarnation as a myth or metaphor. He uses these terms more or less interchangeably, a practice which he defends by explaining that a myth is simply "an expanded metaphor," i.e., that "whereas a metaphor usually operates within a single sentence, a myth is a more or less developed story based on a metaphor." However, both the myth and the metaphor "function to help us see something in a new light and so to react to it in a new way."[54] Or, as Hick puts it elsewhere, the myth/metaphor aims both "to express a valuation and [to] evoke an attitude."[55] In the case at hand, the myth/metaphor of incarnation "expresses the religious significance of Jesus in a way that has proved effective for nearly two millennia. It thus fulfills its function, which is to evoke an appropriate response of faith in Jesus. The response is the attitude to Jesus as saviour."[56] According to Hick, this response is not dependent on the confession of a metaphysical doctrine concerning the union in Jesus of a divine

---

[51] Hick, *Rainbow of Faiths*, 99-100.

[52] Hick, *Disputed Questions*, 143-144; *The Metaphor of God Incarnate*, 162.

[53] Hick, *Rainbow of Faiths*, 99-100; *Disputed Questions*, 144.

[54] Hick, *Rainbow of Faiths*, 102; *Metaphor of God Incarnate*, 105, 106.

[55] Hick, *God has Many Names*, 71 (*The Myth of God Incarnate*, 178).

[56] Hick, *God and the Universe of Faiths*, 172; *The Metaphor of God Incarnate*, 104-105.

and a human nature. The salvific significance of Jesus, for Hick, is the subject of the following section.

3.3 The Religious Imagination and the Image of Christ

Along with other pluralists, Hick equates Jesus' saving significance quite literally with the history of his effects. In other words, Jesus can be described as "saviour" because of the concrete, salutary effects that his personality and his story have had on human history. He is saviour to the degree that his history, which has been recycled in dogmatic myth and ecclesiastical tradition, makes a difference in the lives of particular men and women. To put it another way, Jesus' relationship to God's saving power is contingent rather than ontological, or representational rather than constitutive. Jesus does not belong to the definition of God. Instead, he belongs to the history of God's encounter with particular men and women; he is an instance of God's saving presence, not its source or its cause.[57]

Pluralist theologians have sought to develop this understanding of Jesus' salvific role — and remain within the framework of traditional Christian discourse — by appealing to what can best be described as a form of Spirit Christology (or, as it is sometimes called, inspiration christology).[58] For better or worse, this is a notoriously vague notion.[59] In its most orthodox form, it consists

[57] For my understanding of the soteriology of Liberal Protestantism, I am indebted to Alister McGrath, *The Making of Modern German Christology* (Oxford: Basil Blackwell, 1986) 53-68, especially his discussion of Adolf von Harnack (pp. 59-64).

[58] Both words are used interchangeably by G.W.H. Lampe. See his *God as Spirit* (Oxford: Clarendon, 1977) 34, 96; "The Holy Spirit and the Person of Christ," in S.W. Sykes, J.P. Clayton (ed.), *Christ, Faith and History* (Cambridge: Cambridge University Press, 1972) 123, 125.

[59] See Harold Hunter, "Spirit Christology: Dilemma and Promise (1)," *Heythrop Journal* 24 (1983) 127-140, esp. pp. 127-128. This article was contin-

in the affirmation that the human person, Jesus of Nazareth, was totally imbued by the divine Spirit.[60] As a theological device, however, it is often used to redress the perceived inadequacy of the classical doctrine of the hypostatic union. As is well known, that doctrine gave rise to the idea of the *anhypostasis*, namely, the view that the personal identity of Jesus is determined by the presence of the divine Logos.[61] Advocates of Spirit christology wish to undo this apparent denial of Jesus' full humanity by portraying his life and ministry as an instance of a cooperative endeavour between God, conceived as Spirit, and Jesus, understood as a fully human and historical person

The appeal of Spirit christology for pluralist theologians is obvious. It allows the 'domestication' of Jesus as one inspired religious leader among others. As far as this use of Spirit christology is concerned, it is important to note a distinction between the earliest proponents of the theory and the pluralists. The former were apparently convinced that while Jesus was 'only' different in degree, he had no equal. The latter appear to be convinced of the probability (and perhaps even the actuality) of an equal to Jesus.[62]

---

ued as "Spirit Christology: Dilemma and Promise (2)," *Heythrop Journal* 24 (1983) 266-277.

[60] See Lampe, "The Holy Spirit and the Person of Christ," 111-130. "This union might be envisaged as 'indwelling', or as the descent of 'Spirit' from heaven and its incarnation as man" (p. 118); Lampe also speaks of Spirit-Christology as follows: "the 'possession' of a man by God" (120); "God-in-man and man-in-God" (p. 127); "Christ was a man indwelt by the Spirit" (p. 128); "Christ's possession by the Spirit" (129); "the perfection of his [Christ's] unity with God" (p. 129); "Jesus of Nazareth, the man fully possessed by the Spirit and thus united with God" (p. 130).

[61] For a discussion of the evolution of this doctrine, see Dennis Ferrara, "'Hypostatized in the Logos': Leontius of Byzantium, Leontius of Jerusalem, and the Unfinished Business of the Council of Chalcedon," *Louvain Studies* 22 (1997) 311-327.

[62] John Hick, "An Inspiration Christology for a Religiously Plural World," in S.T. Davis (ed.), *Encountering Jesus: A Debate on Christology* (Atlanta: John Knox, 1988), 21-22; *The Metaphor of God Incarnate*, 109-110.

For Hick, Jesus is best understood as a "a man living in a startling degree of awareness of God and of response to God's presence."[63] "He was a soul liberated from selfhood and fully open to
the divine Spirit."[64] In so far as Jesus was "responsive to God's
loving presence" and thus reflected the divine love on earth in a
"humanly limited way" — albeit "to an eminent degree" — Jesus
can be described as *incarnating* God's love. However, it must be
borne in mind that "the 'incarnation' of divine love occurs in all
human lives" in so far as these constitute responses to and reflections of the divine love.[65]

The most that can be claimed for Jesus is that he incarnated
God's love to an "eminent degree."[66] This leaves open the question of how the particular "exemplification" of God's love which
found place in Jesus "stands in relation to other exemplifications,
such as those in some of the other great religious traditions"[67] —

[63] Hick, *The Metaphor of God Incarnate*, 106.

[64] Hick, *God and the Universe of Faiths*, p. 115. Roger Haight points out that
in his earlier writings (Haight mentions "Jesus and the World Religions," which
dates from 1977), Hick preferred "the symbol of Logos in a way analogous to
[Raimundo] Panikkar." This is certainly the case. However, the passage quoted
here dates from 1972. Moreover, in an article first published in 1966 and
reprinted in *God and the Universe of Faiths*, Hick (p. 161) quoted Tertullian's
remark (*Apology*, ch. 21) that "Christ is Spirit of Spirit, and God of God, as light
is kindled of light." See Roger Haight, "Jesus and World Religions," *Modern
Theology* 12 (1996) 344 n. 51.

[65] Hick, *The Metaphor of God Incarnate*, 76-77, 106, 108. Of course, it is difficult to imagine what this divine love can be said to consist of, independently of
the history of Jesus' life, death and resurrection. This is a constant problem for
pluralist theology. The 'democratic' approach to all traditions makes it nearly
impossible to deploy particular religious categories outside the confines of one's
own tradition. See Hick, *Rainbow of Faiths*, 136.

[66] Ibid., p. 77; see also John Hick, Edmund S. Meltzer (ed.), *Three Faiths -
One God: A Jewish, Christian, Muslim Encounter* (London: Macmillan, 1989)
208.

[67] Hick, "An Inspiration Christology for a Religiously Plural World,"21.

and, presumably, in any and every human life.[68]

In Hick's hands, the Trinitarian symbol becomes "three ways in which the one God is humanly thought and experienced," namely "as creator, as transformer, and as inner spirit."[69] The doctrine of the Trinity is not to be understood "as a literal claim with universal implications, but as internal Christian metaphorical discourse."[70] It is a form of God-talk shaped by the theistic culture of the ancient Judaeo-Hellenistic world.[71] As such, it is an obstacle to the meaning it was originally intended to convey, namely, that in Jesus of Nazareth we are confronted with "the ideal of humanity living in openness and response to God."[72]

Christians can continue to regard Jesus as their saviour, if by this they mean that the memory of him effects in them the sort of fruitful encounter with the divine presence which was manifest in his life. To approach Jesus as saviour is to follow his lead in align-

---

[68] See Hick, *The Metaphor of God Incarnate*, 154 where Hick observes that "the way to salvation/liberation [for the followers of religious giants, like Jesus] involves a gradual or sudden conversion to [the] new way of experiencing" the self and the world, disclosed by the founder though, in the case of "ordinary believers, the new mode of experiencing usually occurs only occasionally and is of only moderate intensity." See also pp. 109-110.

[69] Hick, *The Metaphor of God Incarnate*, pp. 149, 152-153. See Hick, *Rainbow of Faiths*, 136.

[70] Ibid., pp. 88, 79. It is interesting to note that Hick's language here comes very close to George Lindbeck's description of doctrinal formulations as "communally authoritative rules of discourse, attitude and action." For Lindbeck, doctrines function primarily as rules governing the way in which members of a given faith-community speak, feel and act. They are primarily "regulative devices," and not first-order truth claims. See Lindbeck, *The Nature of Doctrine*, 8. Of course, Lindbeck's confessionalism is far removed from Hick's pluralism.

[71] Hick, *God and the Universe of Faiths*, 116.

[72] Hick, *The Metaphor of God Incarnate*, pp. 12-13. See Hick, *Rainbow of Faiths*, p. 94: "The term 'son of God' was not intended literally but as a metaphor, indicating that he was close to God, open to God's presence, doing God's will. It was only later, in the different context of the Gentile world, that the familiar metaphor was transformed into a metaphysical doctrine."

ing our lives with the "ultimate referent" of his own life and praxis, whom he identified as his heavenly Father. The truth of Christian claims about Jesus is, therefore, "a practical truthfulness," insofar as they evoke in us a "dispositional response that is appropriate to .... the Transcendent, the eternally Real."[73]

The eternal and unfathomable Real is at the heart of Hick's pluralistic vision. Indeed, in what can only be described as an inversion of the traditional way of thinking, Hick appears to hold that one must approach the mediator through the mediated. The character and mission of Jesus are defined in function of Hick's understanding of the Transcendent *in se*. Ironically, the most consistent feature of Hick's many discussions of the Transcendent or the Real is his insistence on its ineffability.

Hick appeals to a Kantian-inspired distinction between, on the one hand, "the divine noumenon," the "ultimate transcendent reality," what Hick calls "the Real *an sich*," and, on the other hand, the "divine phenomena," the "deities and absolutes" which are the object of human religious experience.[74] Elsewhere, Hick explains that "the simplest and most satisfactory way to draw this distinction is ... between, on the one hand, God *a se*, in God's eternal self-existent being, 'before' and independently of creation, and on the other hand, God in relation to God's creation and thus as thought of and encountered by human beings."[75]

The Real "cannot be directly experienced by us as it is in itself but only as it appears in terms of our various human thoughtforms."[76] As the history of religions makes clear, the available

[73] Hick, *The Metaphor of God Incarnate*, 161, *An Interpretation of Religion*, 348, 352-353.

[74] Hick, *Metaphor of God Incarnate*, 140-141; *An Interpretation of Religion*, 240-249; 350-351. See also John Hick, *Rainbow of Faiths*, 42-43.

[75] Hick, *Disputed Questions*, 158.

[76] Hick, *Metaphor of God Incarnate*, 140. See Hick, *An Interpretation of Religion*, 249: "But if the Real in itself is not and cannot be humanly experi-

thought-forms can be grouped into two major categories, namely, "first, the concept of <u>God</u>, or of the Real <u>as personal</u>, which presides over the various theistic forms of religious experience; and second, the concept of the <u>Absolute</u>, or of the Real <u>as non-personal</u>, which presides over its various non-theistic forms."[77] Hick proposes that "the relation between these two very different ways of conceiving and experiencing the Real, as personal and non-personal, is perhaps a complementarity analogous ... to that between the two ways of conceiving and registering light, namely as waves and as particles."[78]

Nevertheless, Hick insists that "the Real, *an sich*, is not the object of a cult. It is the ultimate reality that we postulate as the ground of the different forms of religious experience and thought insofar as these are more than human projections."[79] What religious men and women worship, then, is not the Real *an sich*, but the Real as it is "thought of and experienced through the 'lens' of [their] own tradition."[80] In Hick's words, "Every human concept of God, in terms of which worship is directed, is a finite image, or mental picture, of the infinite divine reality that exceeds all human thought .... Indeed <u>all our concepts of God are 'images' of the infinite divine reality</u>: <u>Christ is the Christian's image of God</u>."[81] Like each and every conception of the Transcendent, this image, too, is "a joint product of the universal divine presence and a particular historically formed mode of constructive religious imagination."[82]

---

enced, why postulate such an unknown and unknowable *Ding an sich*? The answer is that the divine noumenon is a necessary postulate of the pluralistic religious life of humanity."

[77] Hick, *An Interpretation of Religion,* 244-245.

[78] Hick, *An Interpretation of Religion*, 245; *Disputed Questions*, 24-25.

[79] Hick, "An Inspiration Christology for a Religiously Plural World," 32-33

[80] Hick, *Disputed Questions*, 159.

[81] Hick, *God and the Universe of Faiths*, 178.

[82] Hick, *Disputed Questions*, 159.

The question which Hick and his fellow pluralists raise concerns the place which this particular imaginative construction —
and its subsequent theological elucidation — should occupy in the
religious life of Christians. In the final section of this presentation,
I would like to compare the views of Newman and Hick with
regard to this issue.

4. John Henry Newman and John Hick on the Image of the Word

4.1 Introduction

At the outset of this paper, I indicated that I wished to focus on
the image of Christ as the object around which Christians structure
their concrete life of faith. I also suggested that the life of faith
might be seen to involve three essential components, which I identified as prayer, praxis, and speech or discourse. One could
express the same thing by saying that Christianity, as a lived and
living faith, consists of a spirituality or mystagogy (to use Rahner's term), an ethic and a narrative. Jesus is central to each of
these elements. He is the object of Christian worship, the paradig-
matic teacher of Christian ethics, and the focus of the Christian
story. Within the framework of traditional Christian faith, this centrality is justified by the appeal to Jesus' substantial unity with the
Godhead, that is to say, his status as the unique Son of God. The
Jesus whom Christians approach in prayer, who animates their
ethical praxis, and who encounters them as the protagonist of the
Christian story is not a penultimate figure, a stepping stone on
their journey towards the truly Real, but the Real in person, God
incarnate. Within the framework of traditional Christianity, we
might say, Jesus, the mediator, provides immediate access to God

Self. This notion of 'mediated immediacy' is at the heart of incarnational christology. And, as we shall see, it is at the heart of the
divide between Newman and Hick regarding the role of the religious imagination.

4.2 The Operation of the Religious Imagination

In the first part of our presentation, we quoted Walgrave's
claim that Newman employed the term, "imagination," for the
"total act by which we take hold of a real object." We also
recalled Coulson's assertion that, for Newman, as for Kierkegaard,
the imagination is "what providence uses to get men into reality,
into existence, to get them far out, or in, or down into existence."
Coulson and Walgrave are agreed, then, that Newman regarded
the imagination as a means to knowledge of things as they are.

This is no less true of the religious imagination. According to
Newman, the religious imagination or, perhaps more accurately,
the imagination deployed on religious matters, is capable of bringing home to us both *that* something is and *what* it is. It both creates and evokes its object.

Of course, Newman was sensitive to the fact that the presence
of even vivid 'images' in the mind was "no warrant for the existence of the objects which those images represent."[83] The dema-
gogue can be as convinced of the legitimacy of his imaginative
constructions as is the hero or the saint, Newman observes in the
Grammar.[84] For Newman, the task of determining the legitimacy
of claims to knowledge of the religious object ultimately falls to
the community of faith. That community is, ideally, characterized
by a vigorous internal life and a division of labour among three
indispensable offices, the priestly or sacramental, the kingly or

[83] G.A., 80. See also p. 76.
[84] G.A., 88.

organizational, and the prophetic or theological. In matters relating to the content of faith, i.e., revelation, Newman looks to the prophetic office to "regulate" affairs. This is perfectly in keeping with his conviction, expressed in the *Grammar*, "that in religion the imagination and affections should always be under the control of reason."[85]

Of course, the reason Newman has in mind is the reason which is grounded in the communitarian apprehension of the religious object. As he also insists in the *Grammar*, "no theology can start or thrive without the initiative and abiding presence of religion."[86] Those who exercise the prophetic office are, ideally, possessed of "clear heads and holy hearts."[87]

The church which Newman relies upon to determine the legitimacy of claims to religious knowledge is a thinking church, a church engaged in a ceaseless quest to articulate the inexhaustible richness of the originating idea which is its possession. When necessary, it fixes its certitudes in the language of dogmatic propositions. But it only does this after a process of rigorous reflection nourished by a present intuition of the originating idea. In all its theologizing it represents the ideal which, according to Coulson, was embodied by Newman himself, namely, "the practice of the saintly intellect."[88]

At the conclusion of *The Metaphor of God Incarnate*, Hick describes his pluralist version of Christianity in terms which recall Newman's juxtaposition of religion (imagination) and reason (the-

[85] G.A., 98-99. See also p. 121. See Merrigan, *Clear Heads and Holy Hearts*, 229-254; Ian Ker, *John Henry Newman: A Biography* (Oxford: Oxford University Press, 1990) 639-640; 729.

[86] G.A., 98. See P.N., 2:169.

[87] V.M., 1:lxxv. See also p. xlviii; Ker, *John Henry Newman*, 351-352.

[88] J. H. Newman, *On Consulting the Faithful in Matters of Doctrine*, John Coulson (ed.), (London: Geoffrey Chapman, 1961) 48. Hereafter referred to as Con.

ology) as the joint sources of Christian life. According to Hick, the pluralist version of Christianity, which moves beyond the metaphysical understanding of incarnation to a metaphorical one, constitutes the "Christian form" of a "basic religious faith." Pluralist Christianity represents "our human response to the mystery of the universe, powered by religious experience and guided by rational thought."[89]

As the earlier discussion of Hick has made clear, however, the experience at stake here cannot be invoked to justify the distinctive confessional formula which has characterized traditional Christianity. Religious experience is inevitably 'contaminated', as it were, by the cultural filters which make it possible. The Real remains hidden behind — or within — the culturally-determined experience of even the most religious men and women. It must not be identified with any particular mediation. The most that one can say is that "the transcendent Reality ... postulated by a religious [as opposed to a naturalistic] understanding of religion is experienced in a variety of ways which have become enshrined in the different religious traditions."[90] Keith Ward has summarized Hick's position in this regard as amounting to the claim that "there is a spiritual reality of supreme power and value; but [that] we are unlikely to have a very adequate conception of it."[91]

[89] Hick, *The Metaphor of God Incarnate*, 163.

[90] Hick, *Disputed Questions*, 21.

[91] Keith Ward, "Divine Ineffability," in A. Sharma (ed.), *God, Truth and Reality: Essays in Honour of John Hick* (New York: St. Martin's Press, 1993) 219. Of course, as Ward points out (p. 215), Hick's own reflections on the Real belie his theoretical agnosticism. Hick claims that the Real "is a supremely valuable reality; that it is one cause of everything other than itself; that it manifests to human experience in a number of ways which are not wholly misleading." Moreover, Ward continues, Hick "does wish to rule out some experiences as inadequate - experiences of the Real as malevolent, as having no causal effects on the future, or as entailing no ontological claims about how the world is. So he does work with a criterion of adequacy, embodying ideas of moral demand and

In the final analysis religious experience yields little. What then of rational thought? Here, too, we are far removed from Newman and his understanding of theological reason grounded in the church's communal life. However, whereas Hick's distillation of religious experience yields only a meagre residue of deity, his application of rational thought to the Christian tradition promises remarkable variety.

Where Newman turns to the living tradition of the church to forge his image of Jesus, Hick turns to the fruits of historical-critical research. While both explicitly acknowledge the contribution of the "imagination" to the process of image-making, it is clear that Hick understands by this faculty something more akin to Coleridge's "fancy."

The poet had described 'fancy' as an "assembling" or "aggregating power," "a mode of memory emancipated from the order of time and space," which, in the words of one commentator, "is modified by the conscious selecting powers of the mind."[92] Already in his contribution to *The Myth of God Incarnate* (1977), Hick had pointed out that "modern New Testament scholarship has shown how fragmentary and ambiguous are the data available

promise for the future; and with a concept of the Real as one supreme cause. Bluntly, he is a theist who is concerned to show how God may be experienced in many traditions, which partially show aspects of the Divine being." See Hick, *An Interpretation of Religion*, 350-351.

[92] I.A. Richards, *Coleridge on Imagination*, 2d ed. (London: Routledge & Kegan Paul, 1950), p. 76; Samuel Taylor Coleridge, *The Collected Works of S.T. Coleridge*, (ed.) K. Coburn, Bollingen Series LXXV, 16 vols. (Princeton: Princeton University Press; London: Routledge & Kegan Paul, 1969-). See vol. 7:1 — *Biographia Literaria*, p. 304; Richard Holmes, *Coleridge*, Past Masters, (ed.) Keith Thomas (Oxford: Oxford University Press, 1982) 52; *G.A.*, 28. See Hick, *An Interpretation of Religion*, 355, where he speaks of the various conceptions of the afterlife, in the world's religions, as "imaginative pictures of the ultimate state, produced to meet our need ... for something to which our minds can cling as we contemplate our own finitude."

to us as we try to look back across nineteen and a half centuries, and at the same time how large and how variable is the contribution of the imagination to our 'pictures' of Jesus."[93] Indeed, he argues that in offering his own "impression" of Jesus, he is "doing what ... everyone else does who depicts the Jesus whom he calls Lord: one finds amidst the New Testament evidences indications of one who answers one's own spiritual needs."[94] Ten years later, Hick answered the question, "Where should we begin?" in christology, i.e., with "the man Jesus of Nazareth," or with the Second Person of the Trinity, by declaring that: "I propose to resolve the methodological dilemma by beginning with the historical Jesus." Hick explains that this involves an act of the "imagination," which will be influenced by "our knowledge of other religiously impressive people," our choice of historical data, and "our own varying spiritual needs."[95]

The image of Jesus which emerges from this combination of historical research and 'imaginative' reconstruction need bear little resemblance to the incarnate Son dear to traditional Christianity. Indeed, in a logical application of his basic methodology, Hick has declared that "it can no longer be an *a priori* dogma that Jesus is the supreme point of contact between God and humankind. This is now a matter of historical judgement, subject to all the difficulties and uncertainties of such judgements."[96]

[93] Hick, *God Has Many Names*, 59.

[94] Hick, *God has Many Names*, pp. 64-65. See also Hick, "An Inspiration Christology for a Religiously Plural World," 5-6 where Hick answers the question, "Where should we begin?," i.e., with "the man Jesus of Nazareth," or with the Second Person of the Trinity, by declaring that: "I propose to resolve the methodological dilemma by beginning with the historical Jesus." Hick explains that this involves an act of the "imagination," which will be influenced by "our knowledge of other religiously impressive people," our choice of historical data, and "our own varying spiritual needs."

[95] Hick, "An Inspiration Christology for a Religiously Plural World," 5-6.

[96] *Hick, Metaphor of God Incarnate*, 110.

Clearly, the religious imagination operates very differently in the case of Newman and of Hick. According to Newman, the imagination takes its lead from the living faith of the church and produces an image of the deity which is coherent with that faith. According to Hick, the imagination selects and arranges the data of historical-critical research, in the light of present needs, both personal and social (for example, the need to accommodate the new situation of pluralism), and produces images of Jesus which are as variegated as the contexts within which they emerge. Not surprisingly then, each author credits the imagination with a very different function as regards the conduct of the religious life. The function of the religious imagination is the subject of the following section.

4.3 The Function of the Religious Imagination

We have indicated that, for Newman, the imagination serves to bring home to the individual the reality of an object. The imagination is the place where the 'objects' of (religious) consciousness, in all their paradoxical complexity, are so vividly 'realized' (and so existentially 'charged') that they are able to command the subject's enduring commitment. As such, the imagination is vital to the practice of religion.

In the *Grammar*, Newman argues that a religious truth-claim (such as, 'The Son is God') can be held "either as a theological truth, or as a religious fact or reality." In the first instance, "the proposition is apprehended for the purposes of proof, analysis, comparison and the like intellectual exercises." That is to say, it is regarded "as the expression of a notion." In the second instance, the proposition is apprehended "for the purposes of devotion." In this case, it is "the image of a reality."[97]

---

[97] G.A., 119. See Ker, *John Henry Newman*, 704.

According to Newman, religion "lives and thrives in the contemplation" of images. It is this which provides the believer with "motives for devotion and faithful obedience." Precisely because it is "an image living within us," precisely because it occupies "a place in the imagination and the heart," a dogmatic proposition, such as the claim that 'the Son is God', is able to "work a revolution in the mind," to inflame the heart, and to shape our conduct.(140; 126)

This is not — and need not — be the case where the same proposition is looked upon as the expression of a notion and subjected to critical scrutiny. Indeed, Newman observes that the application of the intellect to religious issues may well issue in a diminishment of lively faith. "In the religious world," he observes, "no one seems to look for any great devotion or fervour in controversialists, ... theologians, and the like, it being taken for granted, rightly or wrongly, that such men are too intellectual to be spiritual, and are more occupied with the truth of doctrine than with its reality."[98]

That being said, however, Newman's religious and theological ideal was a tensile or polar unity between both activities — "religion using theology, and theology using religion."[99] Newman insisted that, to be effective, the theologian must engage in what he called a "theology of the religious imagination,"[100] that is to say, a theology which unites the concern for the notional elaboration of faith with a profound respect for, and immersion in, its fundamental symbols and images.

We have already seen that the image of Christ which Hick proposes for the contemplation of Christians is far removed from the one Newman found mediated in the church's dogmatic tradition. Hick's

[98] G.A., 216.
[99] VM, 1:xlvii.
[100] G.A., 117.

understanding of the function of the traditional image and its notional
expression in the doctrine of incarnation, is rather ambiguous.

On the one hand, he often gives the impression that the myth or
metaphor of the incarnate Son can be translated into a formal
proposition, such as, for example, the assertion that the Real is
especially present to, and may even be said to act in, receptive
human beings. The sense of the religious metaphor is then no
more opaque than it is when one asserts that "Joan of Arc incarnated, or personified, the resurgent spirit of France." Hick even
speaks in this regard of a "self-explanatory metaphor."[101]

On the other hand, he also argues that metaphorical speech is
resistant to such translation. Indeed, he reproaches theologians
throughout the ages for having sought to provide a physical or
psychological or metaphysical hypothesis which would make
sense of the traditional doctrine. Incarnation, he goes on to insist,
"cannot be so translated without destroying its metaphorical character."[102] "Metaphorical speech," he writes, "is ... akin to poetry,
and shares its non-translatability into literal prose."[103]

How are we to explain this tension?[104] The answer may be
found in Hick's discussion of myth in *An Interpretation of*

---

[101] John Hick, "Incarnation and Atonement: Evil and Incarnation," in
Michael Goulder (ed.), *Incarnation and Myth: The Debate Continued* (London:
SCM, 1979), 83-84. See also Hick, *God and the Universe of Faiths*, 71-72 where
Hick reflects that the myth of incarnation "gives definitive expression to [Jesus']
efficacy as saviour from sin and ignorance and as giver of new life; it offers a
way of declaring his significance to the world; and it expresses a disciple's commitment to Jesus as his personal Lord." It is striking that this explanation of the
'myth' follows immediately upon the declaration that "the doctrine of the incarnation is not a theory which ought to be able to be spelled out but — in a term
widely used throughout Christian history — a mystery."

[102] Hick, *Metaphor of God Incarnate*, 106.

[103] Hick, *Metaphor of God Incarnate*, 100.

[104] The tension is especially evident in Hick, *Metaphor of God Incarnate*, 100
where Hick insists that "a metaphor's central thrust can be literally translated,

Religion (1989). There he distinguishes between what he calls the "expository" use of myths and the use of myths in response to "mysteries," that is to say, "questions to which no answer is possible in a literal use of language."

An expository myth is a myth which "say(s) something that can also be said non-mythologically, though generally with less imaginative impact." An example of such a myth would be the biblical story of the Fall. This story expresses the truth that "ordinary human life is lived in alienation from God and hence from one's neighbours and from the natural environment." It is striking that Hick appears to locate the value of the expository myth in the fact that it "engraves [the truth] in the imagination."[105] In a similar fashion, in *The Metaphor of God Incarnate* (1993), he asserts that though "a metaphor's central thrust can be literally translated ... its ramifying overtones and emotional colour are variable and changing and thus are not translatable without remainder into a definitive list of literal propositions."[106] There, too, he affirms the "positive value" of myth "in touching the more poetic and creative side of our nature, and then allowing our imagination and emotion to resonate to myth as myth."[107] It would seem that Hick is using the notion of non-translatability with reference to the variegated reactions evoked by myth, i.e., the dispositions it produces, rather than with respect to its essential content. This would explain how it is that he can portray the metaphor of incarnation as resistant to translation while proceed-

---

but its ramifying overtones and emotional colour are variable and changing and thus are not translatable without remainder into a definitive list of literal propositions."

[105] Hick, *An Interpretation of Religion*, 349; *Metaphor of God Incarnate*, 160. See also *God and the Universe of Faiths*, 168-169.

[106] Hick, *Metaphor of God Incarnate*, 100.

[107] Hick, *Metaphor of God Incarnate*, 160.

ing to unpack its essential meaning as speech about Jesus' significance for Christians.[108]

Hick's understanding of the second use of myth is inextricably bound up with his Kantian-inspired epistemology. The Real, as the noumenal ground of "the varied realm of religious phenomena" is, by definition, beyond the scope of human language which originates within, and is only literally applicable to, "the phenomenal or experienceable realm." The noumenal reality *an sich* is quite simply "outside the scope of our cognitive capacities." It can only be 'postulated' as the "ultimate ground" of our variegated religious experience. Hence, we can only talk about it "indirectly and mythologically," on the basis of its phenomenal manifestations in the various personae and impersonae which are the objects of the world's religions. In short, when the object of our discourse is the Real *an sich*, mythological or metaphorical language is our only option.[109]

At first glance, it would appear that this second use of myth or metaphor does not apply in the case of the man of Nazareth. But things are not that simple. The doctrine of the incarnation impinges not only on the historical person of Jesus, but on the Christian understanding of the Real as such. It is, at one and the same time, a claim about the nature of Jesus and about the nature

[108] As Nicholas Lash rightly points out, Hick is of the opinion that "the fathers of Nicea unwittingly taught meaningless nonsense," since they intended the doctrine to be interpreted literally, though it made no literal sense. See Lash, "Interpretation and Imagination," in *Incarnation and Myth*, 22. See, for example, Hick, *Metaphor of God Incarnate*, 101-102.

[109] Hick makes a distinction between "substantial properties, such as 'being good', 'being powerful', 'having knowledge', and purely formal and logically generated properties such as 'being a referent of a term' and 'being such that our substantial concepts do not apply'." Substantial concepts do not (literally) apply to the Real, Hick insists. Elsewhere, Hick writes that the religious language "is mythological throughout in the sense that it constitutes discourse in human terms which is ultimately about that which transcends the literal scope of human lan-

of the deity. It would appear that Hick regards it as an expository
myth when its referent is Jesus, and as a metaphor in the second
— and truer sense — when its referent is God or the Real. In other
words, when it is applied to Jesus, the doctrine of incarnation is
perfectly susceptible of translation into a formal proposition. It is
an expository myth. However, when it is applied to God — the
agent of incarnation in Jesus and elsewhere — it is a myth in the
second sense of the term. That is to say, it represents an inevitably
figurative attempt to articulate what must remain a mystery, the
manner of God's presence in the world and in religiously gifted
men and women like Jesus. In the first instance, the metaphor is
ultimately dispensable; in the second instance, it is indispensable
although the particular metaphor of incarnation, as the product of
a specific cultural context, was by no means inevitable.

As it is, the doctrine of the incarnation represents the distinc-
tively Christian contribution to humankind's religious language.
For Hick, though, as we have seen, this language and its historical
referent have no more claim to authority or authenticity than the
doctrines and symbols of the other great religious traditions.
Strictly speaking, Jesus is not the image of God and intellectual
integrity demands that we draw the inevitable consequences born
of this insight. Accordingly, Hick declares that Christians must
eventually give up their practice of worshipping Jesus. After all,
as Hick points out, "only the ultimate — in Anselm's formula,
that 'than which no greater can be conceived' — is to be worshipped, and the worship of any lesser reality is idolatry."[110]

Hick is prepared to tolerate a gradual phasing out of the Christian worship of Jesus. Indeed, in his earlier writings he seems
almost to acknowledge the inevitability of such worship. "In prac-

guage - except ... when that language is purely formal and devoid of descriptive
content." See *An Interpretation of Religion*, 239, 352.

[110] Hick, *God and the Universe of Faiths*, 177.

tice," he observes, "we are only able to worship the ultimate under some more proximate, and indeed anthropomorphic, image." In the case of Christianity, Jesus, regarded as the incarnate Son of God, has served in this capacity.[111]

In his most recent writings, however, Hick acknowledges that where the "pluralistic vision" triumphs, worship will be "explicitly directed to God, rather than to Jesus, or to the Virgin Mary or the saints." Moreover, "God's goodness and mercy" will no longer be "sought 'for Jesus' sake' but on the ground of the eternal divine nature."[112] Where the pluralistic vision takes hold, the classical doctrine that Jesus is the incarnate Son of God will be understood for what it is, namely, "a metaphorical way of speaking about openness and obedient response to God — so that whenever a man or a woman freely does the divine will, in that action God becomes incarnate on earth." Though Jesus' life will be "seen as an outstanding occasion of divine incarnation," it will no longer be regarded as an unsurpassable and incomparable revelatory event.[113] In short, Jesus will be 'returned' to his proper place as one culturally- and historically-determined mediator, alongside others, of the unfathomable mystery of the omnipresent Real.

Clearly, the religious imagination serves very different functions in the case of Newman and of Hick.

According to Newman, the imagination provides believers with 'real' access to the object of their faith, Emmanuel, God with us. Fed by the biblical narrative and the church's teaching, and strengthened by the practice of devotion, the imagination serves as a medium for the encounter with the living Christ, the image of the invisible God — the God who acquires a name and a face in

---

[111] Hick, *God and the Universe of Faiths*, 177-178.

[112] Hick, *Rainbow of Faiths*, 136-137.

[113] Hick, *Rainbow of Faiths*, 136; *Metaphor of God Incarnate*, 109-111.

Jesus. That image, in turn, serves as the vivifying and controlling focus for Christian devotion, discipleship and discourse.

For Newman, the idea of God-incarnate expresses a truth that cannot be expressed in other terms. To use the words of Newman in the *Oxford University Sermons*, "the meaning [of the image of the God-man] is coincident and identical with the idea."[114] This is what Coulson calls the opaque or dense use of metaphor. As he explains it, one speaks as one does because "there are no further expressions for which these are the expression."[115]

In contrast to the opaque use of metaphor, there is also what Coulson calls the "translucent" use of metaphor. Here, a metaphor is, as in the later plays of Shakespeare, the expression of a "common theme."[116] In this case, the metaphor stands for "a meaning expressible in other, perhaps more specifically theological terms." Here, "we must first comprehend in order to apprehend." The metaphor "seems to invite, even demand, interpretation or paraphrase." It is this use of metaphor which seems to characterize Hick's discussion of the incarnation."[117]

According to Hick, the imagination, fed by historical-critical research, provides believers with a provisional and personal image of Jesus, which is useful to the degree that it directs the individual towards the unmediated and ineffable Real. In the final analysis, this image is dispensable. Indeed, it may well be an impediment to

---

[114] U.S., 338; see Coulson, *Religion and Imagination*, 27: "Such statements as 'the taking of manhood into God' have, as Newman reminds us, either a very abject or human meaning, or none at all. There is, he says, 'no inward view' of these doctrines, because the metaphors by which they are signified 'are not mere symbols of ideas which exist independently of them, but their meaning is coincident with and identical with the ideas'. In other words, there are no further expressions for which these are the expression."

[115] Coulson, R*eligion and Imagaination*, 27.

[116] Coulson, *Religion and Imagination*, 24.

[117] Coulson, *Religion and Imagination*, 25. See also p. 26 where Coulson says of these metaphors that they "seek completion in some more reflective mode of

authentic worship of the Real and authentic communion with people of other faiths. For Hick, then, the religious imagination must yield to historical-critical research and the principles of pluralist episte-mology. In short, if the image of God incarnate is to have a future, it cannot be confined to the fragmentary past of the man of Nazareth.

4. Concluding Reflections

One might enquire whether it is fair to either John Henry Newman or John Hick to pit them against one another, against the background of a problematic — religious pluralism — which Newman did not consider and Hick cannot avoid. Clearly, I do not think that it is unfair. The reason is because the issue at stake is not ultimately the response of Christianity to other religions but the identity of Chris-tianity itself, understood as a living religion. It seems to me that the pluralist understanding of Christian faith, especially as regards the position of Jesus Christ, represents a complete rupture with the whole tradition of Christian self-understanding. Pluralist Christianity cannot sustain and, as Hick makes clear, is not interested in sustain-ing, the tradition of narrative, praxis, and worship which have defined the Christian religion. In an article written some years ago, Brian Hebbelthwaite suggested that the refusal to contemplate the incarnation of God in Jesus Christ — the linchpin of Christian iden-tity and the main target of pluralist theology — represented "a poverty of both imagination and theological grasp."[118] When Hick is compared to Newman, this claim looks very plausible indeed.

discourse, and cannot be convincingly apprehended, until they have first been successfully explained or authenticated."

[118] Brian Hebbelthwaite, "The Propriety of the Doctrine of the Incarnation as a Way of Interpreting Christ," *The Incarnation: Collected Essays in Christology* (Cambridge: Cambridge University Press, 1987) 66. The article was first pub-lished in 1980 in the *Scottish Journal of Theology*.

NEWMAN, DIVINE REVELATION,
AND THE CATHOLIC MODERNISTS

Gabriel DALY

Maisie Ward, Wilfrid Ward's daughter and biographer, in her book, *Insurrection versus Resurrection*,[1] relates the story of how her father and George Tyrrell had a serious falling out over an article that Tyrrell had published in *The Month*, January 1904, under the title "Semper Eadem."[2] Maisie Ward describes Tyrrell's article, which was a review of Wilfrid Ward's *Problems and Persons*, as "a declaration of the basic principle of Modernism. Catholic theology and modern science could not be reconciled."[3] The statement can of course be taken to imply either 'so much the worse for Catholic theology', or 'so much the worse for modern science'. Either way it held true only if one identified Catholic theology with mandatory neo-Scholasticism. That was the constant and consistent complaint of most of the Modernists.

The immediate effect of Tyrrell's article was to create the impression that he was arguing the conservative case while Wilfrid Ward was made to appear liberal. The true situation was of course the reverse, and Ward was extremely touchy on such matters. Tyrrell claimed that the article was intended ironically but was widely misunderstood. The whole business merely demonstrates the instability and imprecision of the terms 'liberal' and 'conservative': in this area context is all. By 'Catholic theology'

---

[1] Maisie Ward, *Insurrection versus Resurrection* (London, 1937)164-70.

[2] Republished in George Tyrrell, *Through Scylla and Charybdis: Or the Old Theology and the New* (London, Longmans, Green, & Co., 1907) 106-32.

Tyrrell meant the neo-Scholasticism which characterized mainline Catholic theology at that time. In a letter to Ward Tyrrell said:

> I have carefully (very) studied John Henry Newman's sermon on *Theological Development* and have no doubt whatever that he held the pre-scholastic and patristic idea of the *permanence* of revelation in the mind of the faithful, and never quite twigged the school theory of a mere formula of a long-past revelation as the subject matter of theology... [Newman's theology] formulates certain subjective immanent *impressions* or *ideas* exactly analogous to sense impressions which are realities of experience by which notions and inferences can be criticised. *In principle* (with one or two unimportant modifications) this is *Liberal* theology.[4]

This letter, together with the article to which it referred, marked the parting of the ways between Tyrrell and Ward. The word 'liberal' was explosive at the time. To imply (however ironically) that Ward was a liberal was bad enough; but to state that John Henry Newman's theology was 'liberal' was far worse. Ward would very soon be tormenting himself and others with the obsessive worry that Newman was included retrospectively among those condemned as 'Modernists'.

The passage from Tyrrell's letter which I have just quoted contains material which is central to my topic. My plan in this paper is to reflect briefly on (1) the theology of revelation; (2) Newman's 'pre-scholastic and patristic' view of it; and (3) the nature of Catholic Modernism with particular reference to pre-linguistic thought. There will be considerable overlap between these three sections.

---

[3] Ward, *Insurrection versus Resurrection*, 166.

[4] M. J. Weaver (ed.), *Letters from a 'Modernist': The Letters of George Tyrrell to Wilfrid Ward 1893-1908* (Shepherdstown, VA: Patmos, 1981) 92-93.

1. Revelation

Revelation was not a prominent category in medieval theology. When it was used, the word 'revelation' tended to convey St Augustine's idea of illumination, which placed the emphasis on what happens to the person receiving the illumination. This view of revelation was modified by the contribution to Western theology made by Albert the Great and Thomas Aquinas, whose utilization of Aristotle's philosophy made a more didactic approach to revelation possible. Thomism makes a firm distinction between the revelation given to the prophets and the apostles and its mediated transmission to the rest of believing humankind. The model of teacher and pupil is prominent in Aquinas's conception of revelation, and it was exploited to the full, and beyond, in 19th and 20th century Roman Catholic Church teaching. The irony is that in the 13th century the Thomistic view of revelation was the radical and innovative one, while the Augustinian-Franciscan view was the conservative and traditional one. Thus the Franciscan Alexander of Hales, Bonaventure's teacher, while teaching that theology is a science, adds tartly "but not in Aristotle's sense." Theology, according to Alexander, "is not a rational or demonstrative science, but one which is affective, moral, experiential, and religious."[5] Alexander was fortunate to have lived in the age of Innocent III. He would hardly have survived under Pius X.

If we move forward to the period between the two Vatican Councils, we find a complete reversal of these positions, with Thomism (or rather, neo-Thomism) putting down all the conservative markers, while Augustinianism is viewed by the guardians of orthodoxy as potentially if not actually dangerous.

[5] Y. Congar, *A History of Theology* (Garden City, NY: Doubleday, 1968) 116.

In 1879, in the encyclical letter, *Aeterni Patris*, Pope Leo XIII imposed Thomism on the entire Roman Catholic Church. As a result, Catholics were to be bound not merely by the creeds, conciliar dogmas, papal pronouncements, and the 'ordinary magisterium' — a phrase created in 1863;[6] they were from now on to practise a command theology which prescribed *method* as well as substance in theology. This distinction is of capital importance in any consideration of both Newman and the Modernists. In 1898 Leo wrote to the Minister General of the Franciscans informing him that the Order was not free to follow St Bonaventure and Scotus, if it meant departing from the mind of St Thomas.[7] The Jesuit General received a similar, though secret, warning about the teaching of Suarez — a fact which for a very brief period put Tyrrell on the side of the angels, since he had been teaching pure Thomism rather than Suarezianism to the Jesuit scholastics in Stonyhurst, much to the disedification of his professorial colleagues.[8]

In 1847 Newman, in his anxiety to test whether his theory of doctrinal development accorded with Roman Scholastic notions of orthodoxy, tightened the argument, reduced it to its bare essentials, cast it into Latin and sent it off to Giovanni Perrone who was one of the leading Roman theologians of the period.[9] Perrone's response was basically one less of disagreement than of simple incomprehension. For Perrone revelation was identified with the *depositum fidei*. As Perrone saw it, Newman appeared to be say-

---

[6] See J.P. Boyle, "The 'Ordinary Magisterium': History of the Concept," parts 1 and 2, *The Heythrop Journal* 20 (1979) 380-98; 21 (1980) 14-29.

[7] L. Barmann, *Baron Friedrich von Hügel and the Modernist Crisis in England* (Cambridge: Cambridge University Press, 1972) 140 n.

[8] D. Schultenover, *George Tyrrell: In Search of Catholicism* (Shepherdstown, VA: Patmos, 1981) 36-37.

[9] The paper was published for the first time in 1935: T. Lynch (ed.), "The Newman-Perrone Paper on Development," *Gregorianum* 16 (1935) 402-447.

ing that the deposit grew, and this was totally unacceptable to him. The subtleties of Newman's 'idea', as an impression made on the imagination, were totally lost on a neo-Scholastic accustomed to dealing with essences which by definition do not and cannot change or grow. Tyrrell put his finger unerringly on the nub of the matter when he pointed out the incompatibility of Newman's model of revelation as something permanently present in the mind of the faithful with the Scholastic concept of revelation as the divinely privileged, and hence immutable, record of a *past* event. Tyrrell may have been a trifle mischievous, but he knew exactly what he was doing when he described Newman's theory as "liberal," where 'liberal' was understood to mean non-Scholastic.

In or about 1905 the term 'Liberal' began to be replaced by the term 'Modernist'. I shall return later to the necessary, if difficult, task of defining Modernism.

The Scholastic manuals of theology became one of the most effective instruments for ensuring the uniformity of Catholic theology down to the meeting of the Second Vatical Council. It may help if I summarize manual teaching on revelation in the period between the two Vatican Councils.

The manuals treated revelation under the heading of 'fundamental theology', which, in the period between the two Vatican councils, was strongly apologetical in character. Fundamental theology was seen as the link between philosophy and dogmatic theology. The philosophy of God undertook to study the divine existence and aspects of the divine nature, allegedly from the standpoint of natural reason alone. In practice, officially sanctioned philosophy of God was radically shaped by the theology for which it was designated as a preparation. The manual theology of revelation was divided into two parts, and the argument was deployed in strict logical sequence. Revelation was first proved to be possible (i.e., that there is no valid rational argument against the notion that God *can* communicate with human creatures). Then the question was raised, again at a purely theoretical level and in a radically a priori manner: if God were to communicate with creatures, how would the divine origin of the communication be known without error? The answer to this question was unambiguous: miracles and fulfilled prophecies would offer clear testimony to the divine origin of whatever a prophet might put before his listeners as coming from God. Miracles were then in a similarly *a priori* manner proved to be possible: God can suspend the laws which God himself has given to nature.

The argument then moves from possibility to actuality. Jesus Christ claimed to be speaking in the name of God. He vindicated his claim as divine legate by working many miracles of which the greatest was his resurrection from the dead. The fact that the resurrection was treated in fundamental rather than in dogmatic theology is characteristic of neo-Scholasticism.

In manual theology analysis of the act of faith followed the same clinical pattern. The would-be Christian believer considers the evidence in favour of belief in Jesus Christ. In the 'preambulatory' stage the only aim is to remove any reasons for 'prudent doubt'. Having satisfied oneself (i) that revelation is possible, (ii) that Jesus Christ claimed to be speaking in God's name, and (iii) that he supported his claim by working miracles, one is ready to make one's submission of faith to what God has revealed, not because of any intrinsic reasons (which would be rationalism) but because it is God who reveals it, and God cannot deceive.

Paradoxically the neo-Scholastic system was both rationalist and positivist. Its rationalism, which was more methodological than substantive, resulted from its propositional view of revelation and its deductive method of argument. It neglected and, after the condemnation of Modernism in 1907, repudiated, any experiential, affective, or intuitive mode of thought. It was positivist in that its approach to Scripture was innocent of any hermeneutical awareness of the literary character of the text. History was what really happened, and the documents which bore witness to these happenings shared in their objective givenness.

2. Newman's Method

In the *Apologia* Newman tells us that in or about 1826-1827, "The truth is, I was beginning to prefer intellectual excellence to moral; I was drifting in the direction of liberalism."[10] In an appendix on Liberalism in the *Apologia* Newman describes the truths of revelation as "the most sacred and momentous" of first principles. He continues

> Liberalism then is the mistake of subjecting to human judgement those revealed doctrines which are in their nature beyond and independent of it, and of claiming to determine on intrinsic grounds the truth and value of propositions which rest for their reception simply on the external authority of the Divine Word.[11]

Perrone would not merely have concurred whole-heartedly with those words; perhaps more to the point, he would actually have fully understood them and found them methodologically sound into the bargain. How one can square them with the University Sermon on development, with the *Essay*, and especially with the *Grammar of Assent* is not immediately clear.

Tyrrell saw this difficulty and fully accepted the importance of distinguishing between the substance of Newman's thought and the philosophical method which Newman used in deploying that thought. According to Tyrrell, Newman "used the liberal method in defence of the conservative position ... he was a liberal in intel-

---

[10] *Newman's Apologia pro Vita Sua: The Two Versions of 1864 and 1865, Preceded by Newman's and Kingsley's Pamphlets* (Oxford, 1913) 116.

[11] Ibid., 493.

lect and conservative in sentiment."[12] When Tyrrell came to write the Introduction to Henri Bremond's *The Mystery of Newman*, he expressed the view that the Modernists had taken Newman's notion of an 'idea' as a spiritual force or impetus "and turned [it] against much of that system in whose defence he had framed it." "Newman's incontestable abhorrence of doctrinal liberalism does not at once prove that he may not be the progenitor of it."[13] "If scholasticism is essential to Catholicism, Newman must go overboard."[14]

I have emphasized the role of neo-Scholasticism in Rome's setting up of ever more demanding and restrictive criteria of orthodoxy between 1860 and 1910, because those exceedingly limited criteria were invoked in Rome's condemnation of Modernism. They could also have been invoked against Newman, if the guardians of orthodoxy were so minded.

Newman was very restrained in his public reaction to neo-Scholasticism, but his rejection of Paley's rationalism is an implicit rejection of Roman fundamental theology, especially its rationalistic approach to the theology of revelation. Blondel and Laberthonnière would later describe this approach as extrinsicist, i.e., lacking in inner preparation and receptivity. Newman, in the spirit of Coleridge, found it mechanical and deeply impersonal. As he put it in the *Grammar of Assent*, he did not wish to be converted by a smart syllogism or to convert others by overcoming their reason without touching their hearts.

And how, after all, is a man better for Christianity, who has never felt the need of it or the desire? On the other hand, if he has

[12] M. J. Weaver (ed.), *Letters from a 'Modernist'*, 72.

[13] G. Tyrrell, Introduction to Henri Bremond, *The Mystery of Newman* (London: Williams & Norgate, 1907) xv.

[14] G. Tyrrell, "The Prospects of Modernism," *The Hibbert Journal* 6 (1908) 243.

longed for a revelation to enlighten him and to cleanse his heart, why may he not use, in his inquiries after it, that just and reasonable anticipation of its probability, which such longing has opened the way to his entertaining?[15]

True revelation, then, enlightens and cleanses the heart. The preparatory longing for this enlightenment and cleansing is a strong pointer to its probability. Blondel's 'method of immanence', though coming from a different background — that of French personalist philosophy going back to Maine de Biran — was equally concerned with the inner dimension of the revelatory process. Newman's target was Paley and, by extension, Bentham,[16] while Blondel's was neo-Thomism.

In terms of the content of revelation to be found in the *Essay on Development*, 'revelation' is more or less identical with the 'idea' of Christianity which is impressed on the imagination. Paul Misner and Nicholas Lash claim that the notion of a 'living, real idea' demands a concept of revelation far wider and richer than anything that was current in 19th century theology.[17] Since Newman believed that revelation was definitively and exhaustively given from the very beginning, he had to hold that it was all present in some way in the original idea impressed on the imagination. In the *Essay* he says that "the holy Apostles would *without words* know all the truths concerning the high doctrines of theology, which controversialists after them have piously and charitably reduced to formulae, and developed through argument."[18]

---

[15] J.H. Newman, *An Essay in Aid of a Grammar of Assent* (London: Longmans, Green & Co., 1895) 425.

[16] John Coulson, *Newman and the Common Tradition: A Study in the Language of Church and Society* (Oxford: Clarendon, 1970) 3-13.

[17] Nicholas Lash, *Newman on Development: The Search for an Explanation in History* (London: Sheed & Ward, 1975) 98.

[18] John Henry Newman, *An Essay on the Development of Christian Doctrine*, rev. ed. (London: Longmans, Green & Co., 1878) 5.4.3.

The phrase "without words" in Newman's description of the apostles' knowledge of subsequent doctrines is worth noting together with the fact that he distinguishes between the truths and the doctrines which express them. This was of course a major concern of the Modernists. In Newman's case it reflects his insistence on distinguishing carefully between conscious and unconscious, and between explicit and implicit, reasoning. First principles may lie deep in the unconscious and not be explicitly recognized for what they are; though they can be brought to consciousness and owned with real assent if they have become existentially real to the person concerned.[19]

3. Modernism

Defining modernism is a political act, in that it commits one, if not to a position, at least to a perspective from which to launch one's investigations: and this can have ideological implications. Attempts at historical objectivity are as commendable as claims to have achieved it are illusory.

There has been a suggestion that "the most manageable description of Modernism is to be found in the document which condemns it."[20] It is well to reflect on what this piece of advice would entail. *Pascendi's* definition of modernism is notorious: "And now, with Our eyes fixed upon the whole system, no one will be surprised that We [*scil*. Pius X] should define it to be the synthesis of all [the] heresies."[21] The condemnation of modernism

---

[19] See Ian T. Ker, *The Achievement of John Henry Newman* (Notre Dame, IN: Notre Dame University Press, 1991) 60.

[20] J. Fitzer (ed.), *Romance and the Rock: Nineteenth-Century Catholics on Faith and Reason* (Mineapolis: Fortress Press, 1989) 347. This view had already been expressed by J.J. Heaney: "Any definition of Modernism must be drawn mainly from *Pascendi*, the most solemn Church condemnation," in *The Modernist Crisis: Von Hügel* (London: Chapman, 1969) 232.

[21] *Encyclical Letter ("Pascendi Gregis") of Our Most Holy Lord Pius X by Divine Providence Pope on the Doctrines of the Modernists* (London: Burns & Oates, 1907) 48.

cannot be allowed to set the agenda, for the very good reason that it is itself a major part of the problem to be resolved. Rome did much to create the monster it slew. Allowing *Pascendi* to define modernism leads to the intrinsically ridiculous business of deciding who was and who was not a modernist by reference to an artificial criterion: there is a considerable measure of agreement among scholars that no single modernist conforms to the systematic profile depicted in *Pascendi*.

Any worthwhile definition of Catholic modernism will incorporate a value judgement. Part of the problem stems from the instability of the term itself. Friedrich von Hügel, writing to Maude Petre in 1918, distinguished between two 'modernisms'. The first modernism is the never ending attempt to interpret the old faith "according to what appears the best and the most abiding elements in the philosophy and the scholarship and science of the later and latest times." The second modernism is "a strictly circumscribed affair ... that is really over and done," namely, that which took place during the pontificate of Pius X.[22] Von Hügel's distinction is of course open to being seen as a not altogether creditable attempt to distance himself from "those terrible years," when he was at the heart of all that was going on. From the perspective of today's postmodernity his distinction appears more plausible than it seemed to Maude Petre or would have seemed to George Tyrrell.

Although the term 'modernism' was first used by its Roman opponents, Tyrrell had no problem accepting and working with it as a label for the conviction that Catholic faith is compatible with modern culture. In chapter 16 of *Medievalism* he writes: "Medievalism is an absolute, Modernism a relative term. The former will always stand for the same ideas and institutions; the meaning of the latter slides on

---

[22] B. Holland (ed.), *Baron Friedrich von Hügel: Selected Letters, 1896-1924* (London: Dent, 1928) 248.

with the times."[23] On this evidence Tyrrell would not have cared much for our contemporary term 'post-modern'. As Malcolm Bull has put it, "Contrary to Tyrrell's expectations, modernity proved unable to keep up with itself, and modernism has now become as much an absolute as medievalism."[24] That does not affect Tyrrell's argument, since cultural relevance is what he is seeking, whether or not one calls it modernity. His protest is not against medieval theology as such but only against its imposition upon the modern church as a timeless absolute. He delighted in the thought that St Thomas Aquinas was a thirteenth century modernist.

In the light of these points I define Modernism as follows: 'Modernism' was the term employed by Pius X and his curial advisers in their attempt to describe and condemn certain liberal, anti-scholastic, and historico-critical forms of thought occurring in the Roman Catholic Church between c.1890 and 1914. It can be reasonably said to have begun with Maurice Blondel's doctoral thesis for the Sorbonne entitled *L'Action*. According to Blondel, action, or human dynamism, when reflected upon philosophically, reveals a sense of insufficiency and incompleteness which cannot be satisfied by philosophical reflection. Philosophy, in reflecting upon its own incapacity, delivers the enquirer at a point where he or she is forced to ask whether God is in actual fact speaking to human beings. The similarity to Newman is palpable here.

In 1904 Blondel published his *Letter on Apologetics* which argued that prevailing Scholastic apologetics relied on extrinsic arguments and evidence for the existence of relevation. These

[23] George Tyrrell, *Medievalism: A Reply to Cardinal Mercier* (Tunbridge Wells: Burns & Oates, 1994) 133.

[24] M. Bull, "Who was the First to Make a Pact with the Devil?," *London Review of Books*, 14 May, 1992, p. 22. This short review-article raises a number of thought-provoking ideas on the relationship (or absence of it) between modernity and postmodernity in the arts and in theology.

arguments totally lacked any interior resonance. One has to remind oneself that Blondel knew little or nothing about Newman or his writings when he wrote in the *Letter on Apologetics*: "If the revelatory fact is to be accepted by our minds and even imposed on our reason, an interior need, and, as it were, an ineluctable appetite must prepare us for it."[25]

Blondel's friend and philosophical colleague, Lucien Laberthonnière, was an Oratorian priest who explicitly invoked Newman in support of his observation that the meaning we give to revelation is conditioned by the sort of persons we are.[26] Laberthonnière believed that his own philosophy was an attempt to link up again with the Augustinian tradition that had been disrupted by the Aristotelianism of Albert and Thomas in the 13th century, with the consequent divorce between intellect and will, between reason and experience, and between knowledge and faith. "We do not set out from knowledge so that faith may follow. We believe as we know and we know as we believe. The outcome is a complete transformation of the soul."[27] Revelation, for Laberthonnière, is not an extrinsically delivered package of divine truths extrinsically notarised by miracles, as it was for the neo-Thomists. God's self-disclosure is resplendently present, together with God's authority, in the *fait intérieur*, the experienced givenness of God's revelatory presence within the believer's mind and heart. The authority comes with the experience and does not need to be extrinsically imposed. Laberthonnière's philosophy of revelation

[25] Maurice Blondel, *Les Premiers Écrits de Maurice Blondel*, vol 2 (Paris: Presses Universitaires de France, 1956) 15. There is an English translation in A. Dru and I. Trethowan (eds.), *Maurice Blondel: The Letter on Apologetics and History and Dogma* (London: Harvill Press, 1964).

[26] See G. Daly, "Laberthonnière and Newman," in A.H. Jenkins (ed.), *John Henry Newman and Modernism* (Sigmaringendorf: Glock und Lutz, 1990) 41-55.

[27] Lucien Laberthonnière, *Essais de philosophie religieuse* (Paris: Lethielleux, 1903) 84.

has been well described as 'critical mysticism'. By his interioriz-
ing of revelation he drew down upon himself the wrath of the
right-wing neo-Thomists in France and Rome, who accused him
of substituting experience for dogma. In their eyes he was no different from the liberal Protestants. Wearily Laberthonnière com-
mented: "With the liberal Protestants you have faith without
belief; with the neo-Thomists you have belief without faith."[28]

Henri Bremond noted the similarity between the method of
immanence of Blondel and Laberthonnière and Newman's religious philosophy. There is the same rejection of extrinsicism, the
same concern for interior truth which is a prerequisite for the fruitful reception of revelation, and the same regard for the mind functioning as intuition and imagination which Pascal had called the
esprit de finesse, and Newman the illative sense. Newman's per-
sonalism expressed itself in his preoccupation with conscience.
"For him," says Bremond, "to listen to the voice of conscience is
to hear directly the voice of God; and not the God of natural religion, but the God of revelation."[29] In other words, the experience
of conscience, when analysed, is not merely an indication of the
existence of an infinite and transcendent Being; conscience is the
voice of the triune God of revelation. It is in human moral experience that God's presence and revelation can be found. Bremond
begins from the premise that conscience "is the grand principle
upon which rests, in whole and in detail, the philosophy of Newman" and "the whole religious edifice."[30] He differs from "so
many other Christian thinkers who require religion to be, so to

[28] Lucien Laberthonnière, "Dogme et théologie," in *Annales de philosophie chrétienne* 5 (1908) 511.

[29] Bremond, The Mystery of Newman, 334 (emphasis added). See Roger Haight, "Bremond's Newman," in M. J. Weaver (ed.), *Newman and the Modernists* (London: University Press of America, 1985) 119-137.

[30] Bremond, *The Mystery of Newman*, 336, 333.

speak, the foundation of conscience." Newman reverses this by making conscience the foundation of religion. Bremond then quotes aptly from the second University Sermon: "Now in the first place, it is obvious that Conscience is the essential principle and sanction of Religion in the mind."

For Newman the passage from natural to revealed religion is free of the discontinuity which characterized Scholastic theology with its sharp disjunction between fundamental and dogmatic theology. This is so because unlike the Scholastics his approach to revelation is non-foundational, and the conscience which is active in natural religion does not declare its own insufficiency in the presence of the Church's dogmas, as Blondel's philosophy does in the presence of revelation. Conscience for Newman remains to be enriched by revelation and forms part of the indelible impression made upon the imagination. Benjamin Jowett, in a letter to Margot Tennant in 1891, said, startlingly, of Newman: "His conscience had been taken out, and the Church put in its place."[31] It is a grotesque allegation; yet one would like to know how the Master of Balliol could have come to make it.

The whole of the *Grammar of Assent*, says Bremond, "is nothing but a long definition of the 'illative sense', and this 'illative sense' is the name taken by the conscience when in quest of religious truth."[32] Bremond freely concedes that "It is possible, indeed, that Newman succeeded but imperfectly in reconciling logically the principle of the primacy of conscience with that of dogmatic Catholicism."[33] George Tyrrell put it more bluntly than that when he said that Newman had never really tried to reconcile his teaching on conscience with his teaching on the Church.

---

[31] *The Autobiography of Margot Asquith*, vol. 1 (London: Penguin Books 1936) 107.

[32] Bremond, *The Mystery of Newman*, 333.

[33] Ibid., 332.

Tyrrell was seriously disillusioned by this failure. He felt a genuine debt to Newman, especially to the *Grammar of Assent*, which had helped him greatly following his break with Scholasticism in the mid 1880s. He was also irritated by Ward's attempt to set up an authentic Newman who would preside over Ward's notion of 'mediating liberalism'. Tyrrell had become utterly convinced that there was simply no median position between Scholastic dogmatism based on a severely propositional view of revelation, on the one hand, and, on the other, a view which took personal experience, history, and scientific criticism seriously. He opposed Ward because he came to believe that Ward's position lacked intellectual honesty and integrity.

Tyrrell's second and deeper reason for rejecting 'mediating liberalism' was a conviction, shared with Bremond, that Newman had failed "to work the static idea of a deposit and the dynamic idea of development into one system."[34] "It is not the articles of the Creed, but the word 'Credo' that needs adjustment."[35]

What is the revelation which the believer embraces in the act of believing, if one rejects the notion that it is word, or statement or even event? In a formal lecture, entitled "Revelation as Experience" and delivered in King's College London four months before his death, George Tyrrell marshalled his final thoughts on revelation.[36]

He begins by distinguishing carefully between primary and secondary revelation. Primary, or "first-hand" revelation is "the direct and immediate illumination of the mind by God." Secondary or transmitted revelation must obviously be mediated by statement,

---

[34] Letter to von Hügel, February 1905, cited in M.D. Petre, *Autobiography and Life of George Tyrrell*, vol. 2 (London: Arnold, 1912) 220.

[35] Ibid.

[36] The lecture was first published and edited by Thomas M. Loome in *The Heythrop Journal* 12 (1971) 117-149.

though the statement is always to be carefully distinguished from the revelation itself. Tyrrell focuses on primary revelation, which, he says, is given not in words but "in felt promptings and guidings of the finite by the infinite will, and not in man's spontaneous or reflex interpretations of those promptings."[37] "Divine truth ... is revealed to us, not as statement but as a thing — just as beauty or love is revealed to us." To be transmitted it must be coded in notional form. In this form it is latent or virtual until it becomes the occasion of actual revelation in the receiver of the coded message, and assent moves from notional to real.

Tyrrell then fuses Newman on conscience with Matthew Arnold on the divine as "a Power not ourselves that makes for righteousness." "Newman rightly maintained that the world apart from man's inner moral experience might give us the idea of a vast though scarcely infinite power and intelligence, but not of God."[38]

Tyrrell freely conceded that he had not solved the problem he had set himself. Perhaps the problem is intrinsically insoluble like the problem posed in quantum mechanics by the Uncertainty Principle. As G. E. Moore claimed about consciousness, "The moment we try to fix our attention upon consciousness and to see *what*, distinctly, it is, it seems to vanish."[39] Perhaps the same can be said about primary revelation.

Friedrich von Hügel postulated a "theory of spiritual dynamics" for diagnosing the presence of the transcendent in human experience. "Stop the machinery to look, and you must not expect to see it moving; there is no such thing as a science of statics for the living forces of the soul ..."[40] Von Hügel tried to meet the

[37] Ibid., 135-136.

[38] Ibid., 144.

[39] Cited in Fergus Kerr, *Theology after Wittgenstein* (Oxford: Blackwell, 1986) 6.

[40] See J.J. Kelly (ed.), "Von Hügel on Authority," in *The Tablet*, 6 May, 1978, 446.

problem by making a careful distinction between clear and explicit knowledge, on the one hand, and 'dim experience', on the other. 'Dim experience' for him is intuitional, impressionistic, in soft focus. He attributes this interpretative perspective to Leibniz;[41] but it probably owes as much to Newman's idea impressed on the imagination as it does to Leibniz's distinction between dim experience and reflex knowledge. After Newman's death von Hügel remarked in a letter to Ignatius Ryder, "I talk Newman even oftener than I know."

4. Conclusion

Perhaps the most significant contribution made to the theology of revelation by both Newman and the Modernists is their emphasis on experience, especially moral experience, and on the crucial role played by the imagination in the apprehension and interpretation of experience. These issues are as alive today as they were then; with the important difference that 'modernity' has taken on an historically fixed reference. The appeal to experience in liberal theology of all kinds, including that of the Modernists, was intended as a corrective to essentialism and extrinsicism. Today there is a widespread reaction against the Enlightenment project and the turn to the subject. The appeal of both Newman and the Modernists to wordless and conceptless mental experience as the initial moment in the reception of revelation is open to challenge from a variety of postmodernists; but challenge, as Newman pointed out, is one of the ways through which great ideas are developed. What matters is that a philosophical justification be found for recognizing, with Coleridge, that religious and poetic

---

[41] Friedrich von Hügel, "Experience and Transcendence," *The Dublin Review* 138 (1906) 358.

truth is to be found primarily in "the radiance of the eternal in the particular."[42]

This thought was centrally important to that fine Newman scholar, John Coulson, who contributed so gracefully to the bringing together of religion, literature, and the imagination. There is considerable agreement today that experience is always interpreted experience. There is also widespread recognition that the interpretative process entails a complex relationship between the author, the text and the reader. Hermeneutics plays a role in today's revelation theology which was absent in that of Newman and the Modernists. This has implications for the concept of church teaching.

John Coulson, believed that the essential difference between Newman and a Modernist like George Tyrrell was that whereas Tyrrell despaired of coordinating the forms of faith — metaphor, analogy and symbol — with the dogmatic language of belief, Newman refused to create a dichotomy between them. I cannot help thinking that Dr. Coulson was perhaps too lenient on Newman in this matter. I believe, however, that he was correct about Tyrrell's despair; but one has to remember that Tyrrell saw no prospect of Rome's rescinding its imposition of Scholasticism on the entire Roman Catholic Church as a badge of orthodoxy; and, unlike Alfred Loisy, Tyrrell never left the Church. He died happy in the thought that God, not the rulers of his Church, would be his judge.

And what of today? Rome no longer insists on subscription to the Scholasticism which it employed to centralize and enhance its power in the period between the two Vatican Councils. Yet it continues to proclaim and exercise that power in a painfully negative manner. "It was not the Modernists but Newman who referred to

---

[42] Richard Holmes, *Coleridge* (Oxford: Oxford University Press, 1982) 49.

the 'Nihilism in the Catholic body', whose rulers 'forbid, but they do not direct or create'."[43] The Catholic theology of revelation cannot be detached from ecclesiology and especially from the claim of Church rulers to act in the name of God's Word. But that is a topic for another occasion.

---

[43] J. Coulson, *Religion and Imagination: 'In aid of a grammar of assent'* (Oxford: Clarendon, 1981) 80. See also James Gaffney, "Newman's Criticism of the Church," *The Heythrop Journal* 29 (1988)1-20.

NEWMAN ON THE *CONSENSUS FIDELIUM* AS 'THE VOICE OF THE INFALLIBLE CHURCH'

IAN KER

The quotation in the title of this paper comes from Newman's celebrated article, "On Consulting the Faithful in Matters of Doctrine." (1859). This article, which got its author into so much trouble with the authorities in Rome, has become a classic theological text on the laity. Newman writes: " ... The body of the faithful is one of the witnesses to the fact of the tradition of revealed doctrine, and ... their *consensus* through Christendom is the voice of the Infallible Church."[1] In a private letter of 1875, written five years after the definition of papal infallibility, Newman referred to "the *passive infallibility* of the whole body of the Catholic people," that is, "the 'universitas' of the faithful," as opposed to the "active infallibility" of "the Pope and Bishops."[2] Similarly, in its Constitution on the Church, <u>*Lumen Gentium*,</u> the Second Vatican Council declared (omitting Scriptural references in the text) :

> <u>The whole body of the faithful </u>who have an anointing that comes from the holy one <u>cannot err in matters of belief.</u> This characteristic is shown in the supernatural appreciation of the faith (*sensus fidei*) of the whole people, when, "from the bishops to the last of the faithful" they manifest a universal consent in matters of faith and

[1] John Henry Newman, *On Consulting the Faithful in Matters of Doctrine*, John Coulson (ed.), (London: Geoffrey Chapman, 1961) 63. Hereafter cited as Cons.

[2] *The Letters and Diaries of John Henry Newman*, (eds.) Charles Stephen Dessain et al. (London: Nelson, 1961-72; Oxford: Clarendon Press, 1973~) 27:338. Hereafter cited as LD.

morals. By this appreciation of the faith, aroused and sustained by
the Spirit of truth, the People of God, guided by the sacred teaching
authority (*magisterium*), and obeying it, receives not the mere word
of men, but truly the word of God ... (art. 12)

In this paper I propose (1) to examine Newman's use of the
word "faithful" and to ascertain whether it coincides with this
usage in *Lumen Gentium* where the whole body of the
faithful means *all* the members of the Church including the bishops; (2) to examine how far *Lumen Gentium* and Newman are
consistent in their usage; and (3) to discuss the implications for
the ecclesiology of both Vatican II and Newman.

1

As an Anglican who had discovered the Greek Fathers, Newman conceived of the Church as primarily the communion of
those who have received the Holy Spirit in baptism. While the
Church "is a visible body," it is nevertheless "invested with, or ...
existing in invisible privileges," for "the Church would cease to
be the Church, did the Holy Spirit leave it," since "its outward
rites and forms are nourished and animated by the living power
which dwells within it." Thus the Church is the Holy Spirit's
"especial dwelling—place." For while Christ came "to die for us;
the Spirit came to make us one in Him who had died and was
alive, that is, to form the Church." The Church, then, is "the one
mystical body of Christ ... quickened by the Spirit"[3]
- and is "one" by virtue of the Holy Spirit "giving it life."[3]

Towards the end of his life Newman wrote a very lengthy new
preface (1877) to his Anglican *Lectures on the Prophetical Office*

---

[3] John Henry Newman, *Parochial and Plain Sermons*, 3:224; 5:41; 3:270;
4:170, 174, 171. Except where otherwise stated, all references to Newman's
works are to the Longmans uniform edition.

of the Church viewed relatively to Romanism and Popular Protes-
tantism (1837). He wanted, he explained, to account for the apparent discordance between the Roman Catholic Church's "formal
teaching and its popular and political manifestations;" the other
charge which he had brought against Rome in these lectures published nearly half a century before - "the contrast which modern
Catholicism is said to present with the religion of the Primitive
Church" — had been answered in his *Essay on the Development
of Christian Doctrine* (1845).[4] It is striking how Newman takes as
his starting point not the institutional but the sacramental understanding of the Church as Christ's "mystical Body and Bride ...
and the shrine and organ of the Paraclete."[5] Given the Tridentine
conception of the Church as first and foremost the hierarchical
Church militant, one might have supposed that Newman would
explain these apparent corruptions in Catholicism in a very different way. Having dealt with the so-called doctrinal corruptions in
1845, he now had to account for the superstitions end abuses of
power which notoriously alienated the average Englishman from
Rome. And surely the most obvious explanation would have been
to point out that the Catholic belief that the pope and bishops were
the successors of Peter and the Apostles, in whose apostolic ministry the ministerial priesthood shared, meant that inevitably such
divine power was open to corruption in a way that the Protestant
ministry was not. It was, Newman might have argued, the
unavoidably clerical and hierarchical nature of the Church which
led unavoidably to such abuses. A Catholic as opposed to a
Protestant clergy were naturally tempted to abuse their supernatural authority to keep the laity in submission by tolerating, even

---

[4] *Via Media*, 1:xxxvii. Hereafter cited as VM.

[5] VM, 1:xxxix. Cf. Avery Dulles, "Newman's Ecelesiology," in Ian Ker &
Alan G. Hill (eds.) *Newman after a Hundred Years*, (Oxford: Clarendon Press,
1990) 377.

encouraging, superstition, just as episcopal and papal authority could easily be misused in the laudable desire to extend the Church's influence.

Now the striking thing about the 1877 Preface is that Newman makes no such attempt. Far from speaking about the Church in terms of clergy and laity, as he might so easily have done, the Preface instead begins with the Church as the body of Christ as Newman wants to argue that since the Church therefore shares in the three offices of Christ as prophet, priest, and king, it is in fact the difficulty of exercising this "triple office" simultaneously which accounts for the discrepancies between the theory and practice of Catholicism.[6] The Preface as a whole simply does not consider the Church in terms of the usual clerical-lay description. Even the regal office, which is seen by Newman as belonging preeminently to "the Papacy and its Curia" (no doubt because of Vatican I and the papalism of the nineteenth-century Church), is not regarded as shared by the bishops, let alone the clergy.[7] Of the other two offices, the prophetical is assigned to the theologians, but nothing is said about whether they are clergy or laity. And, even more significantly, as Avery Dulles has noted, the priestly office "is not particularly assigned to the ordained, as one might have expected." Instead, "initially" Newman "attributes this office to the "pastor and flock," but in the main body of the Preface he focuses almost entirely on popular religion and on the beliefs of the simple faithful."[8] Thus, rather than distinguishing clergy and laity, Newman says that the Church as "a religion" has "its special centre of action" in "pastor and flock."[9] Catholicism, then, from the point of view of its devotion and worship is not

---

[6] VM, 1:xl.

[7] VM, 1:xl.

[8] Dulles, "Newman's Ecclesiology," 380.

[9] VM, 1:xl.

only not conceived as regulated or misregulated by the clergy but is regarded as belonging to priests and people together in the first place.

If Newman has the same sacramental conception of the Church in 1877 as he had in the 1830s, what do we find in the essay "On Consulting the Faithful in Matters of Doctrine"? Do we find the Church discussed in the usual institutional terms of clergy and laity? If you look at John Coulson's introduction to his edition of the essay (1961), you will find it taken for granted that the faithful are synonymous with the laity: "... not only is the existence of a lively and educated laity fundamental to his conception of the Catholic Church and to his theology, but ... the most fruitful approach to his work is to see it as a developed theology of the laity in all its ramifications."[10] In the course of his remarks Coulson alternates between the word "faithful" and the word "laity."[11] Nor does he distinguish the bishops, with whom Newman's article is concerned, from the clergy, as when he speaks of Newman's asking "for the fullness of the Church to be made manifest, for that fullness which is not in the priests alone, but only in the conspiratio of priests and faithful laity."[12] In his *Newman and the Common Tradition: A Study in the Language of Church and Society* (1970), where he reproduces the substance of this introduction, Coulson sees Newman as protesting against the Church's being "conceived as divided into two castes - the clerical or dynamic element; and the lay or passive element."[13] Coulson's emphasis is on the descriptive terms "dynamic" and "passive," but the question is whether Newman did in fact conceive of the Church as fun-

---

[10] Cons., 20.

[11] See, for example, Cons., 24.

[12] Cons., 34; cf. p. 49.

[13] John Coulson, *Newman and the Common Tradition: A Study in the Language of Church and Society* (Oxford: Clarendon Press, 1970) 129.

damentally divided into the clerical and lay castes - as certainly
Coulson does.

I believe that <u>Newman</u>, like *Lumen Gentium* (as we shall see),
<u>equivocated,</u> or rather sometimes spoke scriptural and patristic lan-
guage and sometimes the language of a clerical, institutional Church.
In the 1875 letter referred to, his thought and language seem to coin-
cide remarkably with that of article 12 of *Lumen Gentium*, which,
since it breathes the same air as that of Newman's theological world,
may reasonably be used to interpret Newman's words. According to
the letter, "the whole body of the Catholic people" enjoy "passive"
infallibility, while "active" infallibility is reserved to the pope and
bishops. The Council's "whole body of the faithful," who explicitly
contain the bishops (and therefore presumably the pope who is the
head of the college of bishops), "cannot err in matters of belief," but
this "supernatural appreciation of the faith" which comes from the
Holy Spirit and is shared by all the faithful members of the church is
distinguished from the magisterial guidance of the "teaching authority" of pope and bishops (Newman's's "active" infallibility).

On the other hand, however, Newman was living in the Tridentine
Church of the nineteenth century, where the Church was divided into
the teaching (*docens*) and taught (*docta*) Church, a Church in which
"the 'faithful' do not include the 'pastors'."[14] Newman is here quoting the Roman theologian Perrone and uses the distinction for his
own purposes: if the Church has to be seen as divided between
clergy end laity, then in a highly clericalized Church it is necessary
at least to insist that the laity do possess the *sensus fidelium* traditionally recognized by theologians as one of the witnesses to the
Apostolic tradition. And so Newman seizes on the words in the bull
of 1854 defining the doctrine of the immaculate conception, in which
Pope Plus IX referred to the importance of the belief of the "faithful" as well as that of the bishops: *"Conspiratio*; the two, the

---

[14] Cons., 65.

Church teaching and the Church taught, are put together, as one twofold testimony, illustrating each other, and never to be divided."[15]

Nevertheless two points need to be made about Newman's language. First, the distinction drawn is not so much between clergy and laity as between *bishops* and laity. Here is the crucial passage in which Newman summarizes his argument:

> It is not a little remarkable, that, though, historically speaking, the fourth century is the age of doctors, illustrated, as it was, by the saints Athanasius, Hilary, the two Gregories, Basil, Chrysostom, Ambrose, Jerome, and Augustine, and all of these saints bishops also, except one, nevertheless in that very day the divine tradition committed to the infallible Church was proclaimed and maintained far more by the faithful than by the Episcopate.

In the passage of explanation that follows, Newman does refer to the clergy as opposed to the bishops, but it is noticeable that the clergy are on the side of the laity:

> ... I must explain: — in saying this, then, undoubtedly I am not denying that the great body of the Bishops were in their internal belief orthodox; nor that there were numbers of clergy who stood by the laity, and acted as their centres and guides; nor that the laity actually received their faith, in the first instance, from the Bishops and clergy; nor that some portions of the laity ware ignorant, and other portions at length corrupted by the Arian teachers, who got possession of the sees and ordained an heretical clergy; but I mean still, that in that time of immense confusion the divine dogma of our Lord's divinity was proclaimed, enforced, maintained, and (humanly speaking) preserved, far more by the "Ecclesia docta" than by the "Ecclesia docens;" that the body of the episcopate was unfaithful to its commission, while the body of the laity was faithful to its baptism ...[16]

---

[15] Cons., 71.
[16] Cons., 75-76.

Later on the essay, when Newman sets out his historical evidence, we learn that in Nicopolis, the metropolis of Armenia, "'there was a remarkable unanimity of clergy and people in rejecting'" the Arian bishop.[17]

The second aspect of Newman's terminology that is noteworthy is his use of the word "laity." When he comes to give his documentary "proofs of the fidelity of the laity," it is striking that his very first text, a quotation taken from Athanasius about the Alexandrian church, speaks about the Arian bishops physically attacking the "'holy virgins and brethren'." In the terminology of Newman's day these "virgins" would have had to be classed as "religious" — would they also have been seen as lay women? (I shall be returning to the significance of this modern canonical uncertainty later). In the same example from Athanasius there is another reference to "'virgins'" in a later quotation. Incidentally, it should be noted that in each of these two instances, as in the ones that follow, the words are italicized by Newman to indicate that the words in question are proofs of the fidelity of the laity. The same is true of the proof text offered at the end of the preceding point about Newman's distinction being between laity and bishops rather than clergy: the words "'clergy and people'" in that happy example of lay-clerical harmony at Nicopolis are also italicized. Similarly, in the third of Newman's examples of the fidelity of the laity, the references to "'monasteries'" and "'monks'" are also italicized as though religious were indistinguishable from lay people. Again, in the fifth example of the church of Antioch, "'Flavian and Diodorus, who had embraced the ascetical life'" are explicitly described as being "'in the ranks of the laity','" since "'they were not as yet in the sacred ministry'."[18]

[17] Cons., 94.
[18] Cons., 86-88, 90.

But as we have seen, for Newman's purposes it does not very much matter if Flavian and Diodorus had been priests - for the issue is really about bishops not clergy. Newman is perfectly happy to class the clergy with the laity so long as they are upholding the Catholic faith against the Arian bishops. Indeed, he openly admits this to be the case in a note he added in the appendix to the third edition of *The Arians of the Fourth Century* when he republished it in 1871 in the uniform edition of his works. This note contains part of the article "On Consulting the faithful in Matters of Doctrine," together with some amendments and some additions, which include in the first paragraph a sentence which should surely have sounded alarm bells in John Coulson's ears: "And again, in speaking of the laity, I speak inclusively of their parish-priests (so to call them), at least in many places; but ... we are obliged to say that the governing body of the Church came short ..."[19] — in other words the bishops. We might note (I shall return to this point at the and of the paper) that apologetic parenthesis "so to call them" - Newman of course is referring to people who would have been called "presbyters" in a Church which did not know the parochial system.

To conclude, then, "On Consulting the Faithful in Matters of Doctrine" is not a learned tract or manifesto defending the rights of the laity against the clergy, as Coulson and many others have imagined. On the contrary, the "faithful" turn out to include both priests and religious. If it is a tract against any part of the Church, it is against the bishops. We need to recall that the origins of the article lay in Newman's concern about the way in which the English bishops had failed to hold any consultations with the laity before refusing to co-operate with a Royal Commission into the state of primary education.[20] At the deeper theological level he wanted to

---

[19] Newman, *The Arians of the Fourth Century*, 445.
[20] Ian Ker, *John Henry Newman: A Biography* (Oxford: Clarendon Press, 1988) 474, 477- 478, 480.

point out that the faith did not belong to the bishops alone but to the whole people of God, a fact which was dramatically highlighted in the greatest crisis ever to face Christianity when that very part of the Church whose responsibility it was to proclaim and teach the faith substantially failed to do so. But since the faith was not their property alone, it was saved by the body of the faithful. I have shown that for Newman the faithful in fact included both priests and religious. But his use of the word laity, who naturally constituted the largest part of the faithful, can be misleading. However, Newman was living in a highly clericalized Church which saw itself as essentially consisting of clergy and laity, and in such a situation he had to protest in favour of the rights of the laity. But when he is true to the scriptural and patristic sources he knew so well, I think he is not really talking about the "laity" but about what *Lumen Gentium* calls "the whole body of the faithful," "the whole people ... 'from the bishops to the last of the faithful'."

2

It is well known that the turning-point in the Second Vatican Council came early in its proceedings when the Council Fathers decided to reject the draft constitution on the Church prepared by the Roman Curia, which followed the usual Tridentine line of Bellarmine in beginning with the Church as the Church militant before describing the Church in its hierarchical character. The constitution *Lumen Gentium* which the Council eventually adopted was the most significant achievement of a Council predominantly occupied with the nature of the Church and its relationship with the world, other Christian bodies, and other religions. If there is a crisis in the Catholic Church today and if the period of history in which we are living is above all a time of realizing and developing Vatican II, then the interpretation and understanding, or alternatively the misinterpretation and misunderstanding, of *Lumen Gentium* must surely be crucial for reading the signs of the times, to use the favourite expression of the Pope who convened that Council.

But having said that, one has to recognize that conciliar documents inevitably reflect both the contemporaneous state of theology and also the compromises and tensions that lie behind the final text. The Council of Trent had set an agenda for the Church which had lasted four centuries; the first two chapters at least of *Lumen Gentium* set a very different agenda, but if other parts of the Constitution still breathe the atmosphere of the old Church that should not surprise us, particularly if we understand the life of the Church in terms of Newmanian development. Anyone who had read the *Essay on the Development of Christian Doctrine*, should have known better after the Council than to have supposed that all that remained was simply to "implement" (to use the word then in vogue) the conciliar texts. Newman knew that the life of the Church is not so simple as that. As he had often remarked after Vatican I, the texts have to be interpreted by the theologians. Not only was Newman not a fundamentalist Catholic, but the author of the *Essay on Development* also knew that Christian doctrine and practice develop and grow within the life - and not least the tensions - of the whole Church, and not just the theological community. After Vatican I Newman had to contend with the exaggerations of both Döllinger and Manning, diametrically opposed to each other theologically but united in their determination to exaggerate as much as possible the force and scope of the definition of papal infallibility. Knowing history as he did, Newman could have prophesied the rise of both Lefebvre and Küng after Vatican II. He would have been delighted by *Lumen Gentium*, but he would also have recognized that because the revolutionary nature of its first two chapters in particular was setting the Church on a new course, there was bound to be a rough passage ahead as four and more centuries of history could not be undone in a moment, especially as the signals from the Council's conclusions were not totally unambiguous. I want now to turn to one central ambiguity in *Lumen Gentium*, which, as I have already indicated, was also an unresolved ambiguity in the key Newmanian text we have been looking at.

My impression is that there is a popular assumption, if only implied, that *Lumen Gentium* begins with "the People of God," which is in fact the subject of chapter II. If I am also correct in suspecting that "the People of God" is generally supposed to mean the laity, then we already have the source of a potentially very serious distortion of the real significance of *Lumen Gentium*.

In reality, the constitution begins, exactly as the Tractarian Newman began, with the Church as sacrament. Entitled "The Mystery of the Church," chapter I speaks of the Church as being "in the nature of sacrament" (art. 1). As with Newman, to speak of the Church is to speak first and foremost of the Holy Spirit: "The Spirit dwells in the Church and in the hearts of the faithful as in a temple," bestowing "upon her varied hierarchic and charismatic gifts" (art. 4). Hierarchy and charisms are thus linked together, both seen as proceeding from the Spirit. And again this is how hierarchical authority is seen: for among the "gifts" given by the Spirit to the Body of Christ, "the primary belongs to the grace of the apostles to whose authority the Spirit himself subjects even those who are endowed with charisms" (art. 7). This first chapter concludes by declaring that this visible, hierarchical Church which is also the mystical body of Christ "subsists in the Catholic Church, which is governed by the successor of Peter and by the bishops in communion with him" (art. 8). But the chapter is noteworthy for the absence of any specific reference either to clergy or laity.

In chapter II "The People of God" are those "who believe in

Christ" and who "are reborn ... from water and the Holy Spirit" in baptism. In this "messianic people" the Spirit "dwells as in a temple" (art. 9). The baptized constitute "a holy priesthood," although this "common priesthood of the faithful" differs "essentially and not only in degree" from "the ministerial or hierarchical priesthood" (art. 10). This "priestly community is brought into operation through the sacraments." First mentioned are naturally the sacraments of initiation - baptism, confirmation, and eucharist — which all the members of the people of God are expected to receive; then penance and anointing are mentioned, also sacraments which all the faithful would normally receive at some point or points in their lives; and then finally the two sacraments which not all the faithful do receive - holy orders and marriage. It is striking how the clergy and hierarchy are placed right among all the ordinary members of God's people who receive the sacraments of the Church, which is itself a kind of sacrament — "those among the faithful who have received Holy Orders ..." Article 11 ends by stressing that "all the faithful, whatever their condition or state ... are called" to perfection. Article 12 again stresses that the people of God are not just the laity, when, citing St Augustine, it speaks of "the whole people ... 'from the bishops to the last of the faithful'." And again the Holy Spirit is emphasised, who not only makes possible the sacraments but "distributes special graces among the faithful of every rank." Although these charisms have to be tested by those who have charge over the Church," this chapter studiously avoids talking in terms of clergy and laity.

But if the old Tridentine hierarchical model of the Church, which itself reflected the hierarchical nature of society, is rejected, there is no concession here to the secular influences of a popular democratic society which could all too easily interpret the people of God in terms of the electorate to which governments and politicians must answer. While in the political context it is merely an

academic point that ministers and members of the legislature are
themselves members of the same electorate — chapter II of
Lumen Gentium by no means treats the membership of the clergy
and hierarchy of the people of God as an academic irrelevance.

In chapter III, "The Church is Hierarchical," the Council was
concerned with unfinished business, the most important dogmatic
business it was to do. As Newman had clearly foreseen, there
would have to be another Council to place the definition of papal
infallibility within a larger ecclesiological context, here the whole
college of bishops of which the pope is a member as well as the
head. There is little about the clergy in the chapter which deals
with priests and deacons as "helpers" of the bishops (art. 20) in
the last two articles (28 and 29).

We now come to what most people presumably would think of as
perhaps the key chapter of *Lumen Gentium*, the charter for real
reform in the Church. But what is so remarkable about chapter IV,
"The Laity," is its singular lack of that *ressourcement* or retrieval of
the scriptural and patristic sources which is rightly thought of as
being at the heart of the Council's work. The chapter begins by saying that it intends to speak of "those Christians who are called the
laity" (art. 30), but no references are provided either in the text or
footnotes for this usage. And in the next article, it goes on to say that
"the term 'laity' is here understood to mean all the faithful except
those in Holy Orders and those who belong to a religious state
approved by the Church" (art. 31). But again no references are given
to support this statement. The references to the New Testament do
not refer to the "laity" as such because of course the word, not to
mention the concept, was unknown to the scriptural writers. There is
only one reference to the Fathers in the chapter, a quotation from a
sermon of Augustine: "To you I am the bishop, with you I am a
Christian" (art. 32). But this famous saying does not contain the
word "lay" and perfectly fits the ecclesiology of chapter II. The

authorities that in fact this chapter relies on are mainly modern papal allocutions and encyclicals. Unlike in the first two chapters, and indeed the third, we are no longer in the world of the early Church but in the modern clerical Church where the duties and rights of the so-called "laity" have to be stated.

A Church which is divided into clergy and laity has difficulties with those Christians whom canon law calls "religious" - at least with those religious who are not also priests. Chapter VI, "Religious," then, also, not surprisingly, leans heavily on modern papal pronouncements. It says that religious life is "not ... a kind of middle way between the clerical and lay conditions," but that rather it is "a form of life to which some Christians, both clerical and lay, are called" (art. 43). The Council seems to be groping for words which is not surprising if the Christian state has always to be defined in clerical-lay terms. Interestingly, this uncertainty is reflected in the code of canon law which is not obviously consistent in its treatment of religious. According to canon 588.1, "the state of consecrated life is neither clerical nor lay;" whereas canon 711 states that "consecration as a member of a secular institute does not change the member's canonical status among the people of God, be it lay or clerical." Canon 207.2 attempts to resolve the difficulty by changing the terms of reference, stating that religious who are "consecrated to God"are "drawn from both groups" (i.e., clergy and laity): "Their state, although it does not belong to the hierarchical structure of the Church, does pertain to its life and holiness." This last canon is repeated in The *Catechism of the Catholic Church* (art. 873). The recently promulgated code of canon law for the Eastern Churches, on the other hand, follows *Lumen Gentium* more closely when it says that the laity consists of all Christians except clergy *and religious* (canon 399).[21] To put it

[21] I owe this point to Fr. Clarence Gallagher, S.J.

bluntly, the Latin code is uncertain whether or not to call, say, Mother Theresa a laywoman, whereas the Eastern code is clear that she was not. The Latin code had to try and define so-called "secular institutes" and "societies of apostolic life" as well the traditional religious orders; but it now has to face the problem of how to define canonically the large numbers of men and women who belong to the new communities and movements, whom it seems odd to call merely lay people but who simply do not fit into the old categories.

3

These new groups, which are the most startling phenomenon of the late twentieth-century Church, are not the result of episcopal implementation of the decrees of the Second Vatican Council. Many regard them as a twentieth-century counterpart to the other great movements of the Spirit within the Church such as the desert monks of the early Church, the friars of the middle ages, and the Jesuits of the sixteenth century. If they are genuine manifestations of the Spirit, then we must say that they have arisen out of the charisms of baptized Christians - I deliberately avoid the term lay people because, although some at least of them are regularly called "lay movements," in actual fact some have been founded by priests, some by lay people. And within their ranks they contain clergy and religious as well as laity. Moreover, where the community or movement is empowered to ordain priests for its work, as is the case with some, then these priests have naturally to have already belonged as lay members. Could it be that these new groups are telling us something about the way the Church is to develop - and therefore also something about the real meaning of *Lumen Gentium*? After all, the Tridentine Church was not just created by the Council of Trent, or even bishops like St Charles Borromeo: without the charism in particular of St Ignatius Loyola and without the Society of Jesus Tridentine

Catholicism would be inconceivable.

Now these new communities, initiatives, movements - it is hard to find a term which can cover such very disparate groups as, say, Opus Dei and charismatic renewal - have two distinctive features in common which are important for the thesis of this paper. First, there are varying degrees of commitment, but the most committed members like the "numeraries" of Opus Dei or the covenanting members of a charismatic community may seem very close to so-called "religious" - perhaps even more religious than the average "religious" - but so far as canon law is concerned they are simply lay people. Second, within these groupings the conventional clerical-lay distinctions do not apply in the usual way they do in the Church at large: this is not because the distinction between the ministerial priesthood and the priesthood of all the baptized is in any way obscured - far from it as these groups would be called "conservative" by liberal Catholics anxious to enhance the power of the laity - but for two other reasons: first, because all the members of the group share in common the ethos or orientation of the community, which puts the clerical-lay distinction in a much less sharp perspective; second, because the lay members within the group may, like the so called "directors" in Opus Dei or the "catechists' of the Neo-Catechuminate movement, exercise considerable 'power', but a 'power' which is unlike the married diaconate or the eucharistic ministry in being completely separate from the ministerial priesthood.

I would like to conclude this paper by suggesting that just as Newman had a vision, like the first two chapters of *Lumen Gentium*, of a Church which was not simply divided into clergy and laity (with religious as an appendix), so there are signs that these new forms of Christian and apostolic life within the Church about which I have been speaking would not have come as a total surprise to him.

Newman's first contribution to the Oxford Movement in 1833 was to write not the first of the *Tracts for the Times* (although that was published first) but a paper which he intended to be "one of a series" for the *British Magazine*, "called the 'Church of the Fathers' ... on the principle of popularity as en element of Church power, as exemplified in the history of St Ambrose."[22] Far from being an established institution like the Church of England, Newman had a clear idea of the early Church as the people of God: as he vividly put it: "The early Church threw itself on the *people* ..."[23] In this first article about St Ambrose, he depicts not a clerical-lay Church, but a Church which allowed for prophets: "... a child's voice, as is reported, was heard in the midst of the crowd to say, 'Ambrose is bishop' ..."[24] Ambrose who was not even baptized, let alone in holy orders, was then unanimously elected bishop, not by the clergy, not by the laity, but by the whole people of God in Milan.

Those who belonged to the "Movement" which Newman now headed in the Church of England were called "Tractarians," and so far as Tractarianism was concerned it did not matter whether they ware clergy or laity. The Tracts were not exclusively written by the clergy: Newman was particularly pleased when his great friend John William Bowden wrote one, because he was a layman. Women, too, were actively involved: Newman wanted his friend Maria Giberne to try her hand at writing "some Apostolic stories" for children.[25] The novels of Charlotte M. Yonge were to prove as important as any sermons in propagating the Movement. Newman was struck by the fact that prominent precursors of the Movement like Alexander Knox, the Irish theologian, and Coleridge were

---

[22] LD, 4:18. See Ker, *Newman: A Biography*, 81.

[23] LD, 4:14.

[24] Newman, *Historical Sketches*, 1:343.

[25] LD, 5:387.

both "laymen and that is very remarkable," as was Dr Johnson, "another striking instance."[26] Leading members of the Tractarian Movement were laymen, often prominent in public life like Gladstone.

When the Roman Catholic hierarchy was restored to England in 1850, Newman's response to the violent anti-Popery campaign that erupted is very interesting. He thought it could be profitably exploited by making it an excuse for "getting up a great organization, going round the towns giving lectures, or making speeches ... starting a paper, a review etc."[27] He particularly felt that young Catholics should band together as the Tractarians had done. In other words, he seemed to have envisaged another "movement." Unfortunately, the English bishops had, he knew, "a terror of laymen, and I am sure they may be made in this day the strength of the Church."[28]

Newman himself embarked on a series of public lectures, intended to counteract anti-Catholic prejudice. They were published in book form as *Lectures on the Present Position of Catholics in England: Addressed to the Brothers of the Oratory.* These "Brothers of the Oratory" constituted the so-called "Little Oratory," which was the confraternity of laymen traditionally attached to an Oratory. It is remarkable that Newman considered that of all the Oratorian activities and works this was "more important than anything else."[29] But it is not so surprising when we consider the origins of the Oratory. After all, St Philip Neri had never intended the Oratory to become a religious order or even congregation, wanting, in Newman's words, to return "to primitive times."[30] The original nucleus was a group of laymen

---

[26] LD, 5:27.

[27] LD, 14:214.

[28] LD, 14:252.

[29] LD, 14:274.

[30] Placid Murray (ed.), *Newman the Oratorian: His Unpublished Oratorian Papers* (Dublin: Gill and Macmillan, 1969) 203.

who came together for discussion and prayer and study with
Philip. Community life came later when an inner or core group
began to live together, three of whose members came to be
ordained to the priesthood. In time, of course, the Oratory became
simply another congregation of priests, with the lay element
restricted to the lay brothers who did not have sufficient education
to become priests and who did the menial jobs in the community.
This had become the practice, but Newman knew what was correct at least in theory, writing in a letter: "The Brothers are our
equals ... The Father is above the Brother sacerdotally -- but in
the Oratory they are equal."[31] He even wanted women to be
involved and proposed to the Pope "the formation of a female
Oratory," that is, of course, "little" Oratory.[32] The original Oratory of Philip Neri reminds one of the kind of communities that
are now flourishing in the Church, unlike the traditional active
religious orders which are now rapidly declining.

To the Church in Corinth St. Paul wrote: "Now you together
are Christ's body; but each of you is a different part of it. In the
Church, God has given the first place to apostles, the second to
prophets, the third to teachers; after them, miracles, and after them
the gift of healing; helpers, good leaders, those with many languages" (1 Cor. 12:27-28) That is the kind of Church we read
about in the first two chapters of *Lumen Gentium* and that we can
find in Newman too. The three-fold order of bishop, priest, and
deacon Paul would have understood as a development and
enlargement of the apostolic ministry, that became necessary with
the death of the apostles and the growth of the Church. But would
he not have regarded the virtual reduction of all the other parts of
the Church to the "laity" as on the contrary a contraction and a
diminution of our idea of the Church?

[31] LD, 16:267.
[32] LD, 17:137.

I finish with two suggestions. The first is not original: namely, that the word "priest" should be replaced with the ancient word "presbyter," so that there should be no confusion between the ministerial priesthood and the common priesthood of the faithful. The second is that the word "laity," which implies a clerical Church, should be expunged from our vocabulary. Such suggestions are unlikely to find favour with either conservatives or liberals in the Church. But that would be a very Newmanian situation in which to find oneself.

NEWMAN ON JUSTIFICATION
AN EVANGELICAL ANGLICAN EVALUATION

Alister E. McGrath

In 1837, John Henry Newman delivered a series of lectures in the Adam de Brome chapel of the University Church of St Mary the Virgin, Oxford, on the theme of justification. The lectures are of significance in a number of respects. They belong to a cluster of writings, including *The Arians of the Fourth Century* (1833) and *Lectures on the Prophetical Office of the Church* (1837), in which historical analysis serves as a means of clarifying the distinctive position of the Church of England. Newman saw his *Lectures on Justification* as one of a series of works which was intended to illustrate "what has often been considered to be the charateristic position of the Anglican church, as lying in a supposed *Via Media*, admitting much and excluding much both of Roman and of Protestant teaching."[1] They offer us a means of assessing Newman, both as a scholar and a theologian, in terms of the quality and competence of his historical engagement.

In this paper, I have been offered the opportunity of setting out an evangelical Anglican assessment of Newman's position. By "evangelical Anglican" we are to understand the particular form of evangelicalism which has developed within the Church of England which places considerable emphasis upon the authority of Scripture and the need for personal conversion, while at the

---

[1] John Henry Newman, *Lectures on Justification*, 3rd ed. (London: Rivingtons, 1874) ix. These comments were added to the Third Edition. For the general background to these lectures, see Thomas L. Sheridan, *Newman on Justification* (Staten Island, NY: Alba, 1967).

same time valuing and wishing to honour the historic episcopacy and the place of tradition within Christian life and theology.[2] Although evangelicalism has grown substantially within the Church of England since the Second World War – more than 55% of those in full-time training for ministry in the Church of England would count themselves as evangelical – it was a significant presence within that church in earlier periods. Our interest here lies especially in the fact that Newman devotes the thirteenth and final "lecture on justification" to responding to the evangelical "mode of preaching and professing the gospel."[3] In this address, I propose to explore Newman's approach, and offer some reflections.

First, however, some introductory comments are in order. Every writer approaches a subject with an agenda, and I am no exception. The first major work of Newman's which I read was his *Parochial and Plain Sermons*, which I found to be a remarkably insightful presentation of some aspects of the Christian faith, rich in biblical citation, allusion and analysis. This was back in 1976, at a time when I was going through a period of theological questioning and movement which led me to move away from the evangelicalism which I had embraced in 1971 to a more catholic liturgical and liberal theological position. I was regularly to be found in the congregation of Pusey House on Sundays, although on occasion I would worship at the University Church itself. In 1976, I began the formal study of theology at Oxford, and formed the idea of undertaking a major theological project as a means of familiarising myself with the development of the Christian tradition. It was not entirely clear to me what I should study.

---

[2] For further comments, see James I. Packer, *The Evangelical Anglican Identity Problem* (Oxford: Latimer House, 1978); Alister McGrath, *Evangelicalism and the Future of Christianity* (London: Hodder & Stoughton, 1994).

[3] *Lectures on Justification*, xiv.

At this stage, I had not read Newman's *Lectures on Justification*, although I was aware both that Newman had engaged with this issue, and that hardly any Anglicans had thought it worth bothering to do so subsequently. On further examination, I discovered that no major work had been published on the historical development of the doctrine since 1870, the year in which Albrecht Benjamin Ritschl published his celebrated *Die christliche Lehre von der Rechtfertigung und Versöhnung*.[4] On 6 September 1978, I finally managed to buy my own copy of the third edition of Newman's *Lectures*. I put the work away safely, not wishing to read it until I was ready to do so.

From 1978 to 1980, I worked away at St John's College, Cambridge, on the development of the doctrine of justification in the medieval and Reformation periods, under the supervision of Professor Gordon Rupp, widely regarded as England's finest Luther scholar. It was an intellectually exhilarating time, in which I began to understand more of the enormously complex transitions which attended the emergence of the reforming theologies of both Luther and Calvin. By the middle of 1981, I had completed studying the development of the doctrine within Anglicanism to 1750, and finally felt able to pick up Newman's *Lectures*, and give them the attention which they deserved. By then, I was moving away from liberal catholicism, and was firmly on the road to a renewed engagement with and appreciation of evangelicalism.

As I read Newman, I found myself initially enjoying his English prose. It was not long, however, before I began to feel uneasy about Newman, both in terms of his scholarship and his general view on what Anglicanism ought to be. My unease centered primarily on the question of scholarly accuracy. Newman's account

---

[4] For the resulting publication, see Alister E. McGrath, *Iustitia Dei: A History of the Christian Doctrine of Justification*, 2 vols. (Cambridge: Cambridge University Press, 1986). Second edition in one volume, 1998.

of the doctrine of justification associated with Luther is seriously
inaccurate, and at one point appears to demonstrate a standard of
intellectual integrity which falls short of what one might have
hoped to encounter. Perhaps I felt a special irritation towards
Newman at this point because I had just spent a substantial period
of time wrestling with the nature and development of Luther's theology of justification, and took exception to the superficial
engagement with his ideas which I found in Newman. Or perhaps
it was because I had entertained a high view of Newman, and
found myself seriously embarrassed by what I read. At any rate,
here is Newman's summary of Luther's failings, which concludes
this course of lectures:[5]

> Luther found in the Church great moral corruptions countenanced
> by the highest authorities; he felt them; but instead of meeting them
> with divine weapons, he used one of his own. He adopted a doctrine
> original, specious, fascinating, persuasive, powerful against Rome,
> and wonderfully adapted, as if prophetically, to the genius of the
> times which were to follow. He found Christians in bondage to their
> works and observances; he released them by his doctrine of faith;
> and he left them in bondage to their feelings. He weaned them from
> seeking assurance of salvation in standing ordinances, at the cost of
> teaching them that a personal consciousness of it was promised to
> every one who believed. For outward signs he substituted inward;
> for reverence towards the church contemplation of self.

We have here a series of puzzling assertions concerning Luther,
of which I shall note a few, and indicate the responses which any
Oxford undergraduate studying Luther's works for the Final Honour School of Theology would be able to make.

1. "He found Christians in bondage to their works and obser-
   vances ... he left them in bondage to their feelings." This is

---

[5] *Lectures on Justification*, 339-340.

untenable. Luther's *theologia crucis* is aimed precisely at any form of reliance upon feelings. Luther has no doubt that theology must relate to experience, but the nature of that relationship is construed in terms of the primacy of theology over experience.[6]

2. "He weaned them from seeking assurance of salvation in standing ordinances, at the cost of teaching them that a personal consciousness of it was promised to every one who believed." Once more, Luther's "theology of the cross" flatly contradicts this point. For Luther, the grounds of Christian certainty most emphatically do *not* lie in any "personal consciousness of salvation", but only in the objective promises of God.[7] For Luther, security comes from looking outside of oneself, to the gracious promises of God delivered and secured in Christ, and made visible and tangible in the sacraments. Luther argues that the essence of sin is that humanity is *incurvatus in se*, "bent in on itself," in that it seeks both the grounds of salvation and reassurance in itself, rather than in Christ.

3. "For outward signs he substituted inward." I assume that this is to be interpreted as meaning that Luther puts personal consciousness of salvation above the sacraments. Precisely the opposite is true. Luther consistently declares that the sacraments are objective signs and reassurances of the promises of God, which are to be trusted and relied upon irrespective of the personal feelings and emotions of the believer.

---

[6] See the exhaustive analysis in Alister E. McGrath, *Luther's Theology of the Cross* (Oxford: Blackwell, 1985).

[7] See Randall C. Zachman, *The Assurance of Faith: Conscience in the Theology of Martin Luther and John Calvin* (Minneapolis: Fortress Press, 1993).

4. "... for reverence towards the church contemplation of self."
   Newman here seems to have bought into the Enlightenment
   view that Luther is a rugged and lonely individualist, who
   spurned the church in order to contemplate himself. We have
   already seen that the view that Luther bases security of faith on
   personal consciousness is the sort of thing we might find in the
   theological equivalent of *1066 and All That*. Yet we must add
   here that Luther's view of the church, like that of Calvin, is
   actually very high. The popular view of Luther's doctrine of
   justification is that it obviates the need for church, sacraments
   and ministry. Luther's view on this matter was rather different.

At this point, we must make several comments which may help
us view Newman's inept treatment of Luther in a more kindly
manner than might otherwise be the case.

1. The full scholarly edition of Luther's works was begun in
   1883, in celebration of the four hundredth anniversary of
   Luther's birth. Neither Newman (nor his contemporaries) could
   have hoped to have access to the full range of Luther's writings
   in their original language. In one sense, the modern study of
   Luther dates from after the First World War, when it became
   possible to engage with the primary sources in a detail which
   had hitherto been impossible.

2. A number of the English translations of Luther which would
   have been familiar to Newman were notoriously inaccurate.
   For example, the most widely used translation of Luther's 1535
   Commentary on Galatians (a work, it hardly needs to be added,
   which is of fundamental importance to the doctrine of justification) had its origins in 1575, and was reworked and reprinted
   until it achieved its final rescension in 1807 under "the Rev.

Erasmus Middleton, BD, Rector of Turvey, Bedfordshire." The
Middleton translation offers what I can only describe as a
somewhat free and imaginative rendering of Luther, adding
ideas which the translators clearly feel that Luther ought to
have included and omitting those which they felt were unhelp-
ful. To give you a idea of its general tone, we may look at its
translation of four words. At one point, Luther refers to *missis,
vigiliis, & c.*. The natural English translation of this phrase
would be "masses, vigils, and so on." Middleton, however,
offers a more imaginative translation: "masses, vigils, trentals,
and such trash."

3. It is entirely possible that Newman is viewing Luther through
   the lens of the evangelicalism that he knew within the Church
   of England during the 1830s. In other words, Newman is to be
   understood as critiquing the then prevailing evangelical image
   of Luther, rather than the views of Luther himself. Initially, this
   option is quite attractive. There is no doubt that the evangelicalism of the period was inclined to place considerable emphasis upon personal experience, and take a generally low view of
   the sacraments and church. It is a simple matter of fact that
   such evangelicals tended to adopt an iconic, rather than historically and theologically informed view of Luther. It would
   therefore be entirely proper to read the *Lectures on Justification* as a critique of contemporary evangelicalism – were it not
   for the fact that Newman explicitly identifies Luther himself,
   rather than any portrayal of Luther, as the object of his criticisms.

A further difficulty in understanding Newman's intentions
should be noted at this point. As we have seen, it is clear that
Luther himself is Newman's primary target in the *Lectures on Jus-*

tification. Yet it is generally conceded that evangelicalism within the Church of England at this time tended to draw upon Calvinist, rather than Lutheran, inspiration. The influence of Luther may have been considerable within the English church of the mid-sixteenth century; thereafter, it declined substantially.[8] The assumption that evangelicalism drew directly upon Luther for its views on justification is simply not historically warranted. Although many evangelicals of the period make positive reference to Luther, this often rests on little more than a perception that Luther set in motion a much-needed reform of the church. Where matters of theological substance are concerned, the evangelicalism that Newman knew tended to look to Reformed sources, more often indirectly than directly.

Yet Newman makes it clear that his primary concern is to engage with Luther and the "Lutheran" teachings on justification, on the basis of the assumption that evangelicals within the Church of England grounded their views upon his. At this point, I must confess that it is not entirely clear to me (and possibly was not to Newman either) whether he intends us to understand "Lutheran" to mean "the tradition proceeding from, and partly based upon, Luther;" or "the views of Luther himself." This point is important, in that Newman tends to interpret Luther from the perspective of later Lutheranism. This is particularly clear in relation to his treatment of the relationship between faith and Christ, which we may profitably explore.

Newman argues that Luther's fundamental belief is that the righteousness of Christ is imputed to believers through faith. This would suggest that Luther sees justification in abstract terms, expressed in terms of the impersonal imputation of qualities or

---

[8] See Basil Hall, "The Early Rise and Gradual Decline of Lutheranism in England (1500-1600)," in D. Baker (ed.), *Reform and Reformation: England and the Continent, c. 1500 – c. 1750* (Oxford: Blackwell, 1979) 103-131.

benefits of Christ to the believer rather than personal tranforma-
tion through the indwelling of Christ. While it is entirely proper to
suggest that some such criticism may be directed against Luther's
later followers, such as Philip Melanchthon, Luther cannot fairly
be critiqued at this juncture. In setting out this criticism, Newman
draws heavily (yet somewhat selectively) upon the 1535 Galatians
commentary. Yet that same commentary contains substantial sections dealing with the manner in which faith achieves a personal
and living relationship between the believer and Christ. "The
Christ who is grasped by faith and lives in the heart is the true
Christian righteousness, on account of which God counts us right-
eous, and grants us eternal life."[9] It is quite clear that Luther does
not understand faith as purely "fiduciary assent" or "trust",[10] but
as the means by which a real, personal and living relationship is
established between Christ and the believer. Luther's strongly personalist understanding of the relation of Christ and the believer is
particularly clearly set out in the 1520 work *The Freedom of a
Christian*.[11]

> Faith does not merely mean that the soul realizes that the divine
> word is full of all grace, free and holy; it also unites the soul with
> Christ, as a bride is united with her bridegroom. From such a mar-
> riage, as St Paul says (Ephesians 5:32-32), it follows that Christ and
> the soul become one body, so that they hold all things in common,
> whether for better or worse. This means that what Christ possesses
> belongs to the believing soul; and what the soul possesses, belongs
> to Christ. Thus Christ possesses all good things and holiness; these
> now belong to the soul. The soul possesses lots of vices and sin;
> these now belong to Christ. Here we have a happy exchange and
> struggle. Christ is God and a human being, who has never sinned
> and whose holiness is unconquerable, eternal and almighty. So he

[9] WA 40 I.229.28-29.

[10] *Lectures on Justification*, 256.

[11] *D. Martin Luthers Werke: Kritische Gesamtausgabe*, vol. 7 (Weimar:
Böhlaus, 1897) 25.26-26.9.

makes the sin of the believing soul his own through its wedding ring, which is faith, and acts as if he had done it [i.e., sin] himself, so that sin could be swallowed up in him. For his unconquerable righteousness is too strong for all sin, so that is made single and free from all its sins on account of its pledge, that is its faith, and can turn to the eternal righteousness of its bridegroom, Christ. Now is not this a happy business? Christ, the rich, noble, and holy bridegroom, takes in marriage this poor, contemptible and sinful little prostitute, takes away all her evil, and bestows all his goodness upon her! It is no longer possible for sin to overwhelm her, for she is now found in Christ and is swallowed up by him, so that she possesses a rich righteousness in her bridegroom.

I have set out this passage in full, as it clearly raises some difficulties for Newman's interpretation of Luther. Note in particular the unequivocal assertion that faith is more than cognitive assent or trust: "Faith does not merely mean that the soul realizes that the divine word is full of all grace, free and holy; it also unites the soul with Christ, as a bride is united with her bridegroom."

I also set this passage out in full for another reason. As I worked through Newman's presentation of Luther, I noted that he was prone to cite passages with ellipses indicating the omission of sections. For example, in the final lecture, he cites from Luther's Galatians commentary to make a point.[12] At two points in this citation, Newman indicates, through the use of an ellipsis (. . .) that material has been omitted. On consulting the original text to establish what has been omitted, one is left with the disconcerting discovery that the omitted material forces one to the conclusion that Luther has been less than fairly treated by Newman – assuming, of course, that Newman encountered the full version of Luther's text, and modified it for his own purposes.

[12] *Lectures on Justification*, 331-333. Compare this with the full text: WA 40 I.282.

The most serious case of such misrepresentation demands particular attention. Newman's view on justification is that faith and works both justify, although in different manners.[13]

> It seems, then, that whereas faith on our part fitly corresponds, or if the correlative, as it is called, to grace on God's part, sacraments are but the manifestation of grace, and good works are but the manifestation of faith; so that, whether we say we are justified by faith, or by works or sacraments, all these but mean this one doctrine, that we are justified by grace, which is given through sacraments, impetrated by faith, manifested in works.

This view is to be contrasted with Luther's view, which is that faith (understood as trust) alone justifies.

In a remarkable section, Newman then asserts that Luther corroborates this (that is, Newman's view), "not willingly ... but in consequence of the stress of texts urged against him." This frankly rather patronising statement is followed by a citation from Luther's 1535 Galatians commentary, as follows. In view of the seriousness of the charge which I am about to lay against Newman, I will cite the passage in full:[14]

> "It is usual with us," he says, "to view faith, sometimes apart from its work, sometimes with it. For as an artist speaks variously of his materials, and a gardner of a tree, as in bearing or not, so also the Holy Ghost speaks variously in Scripture concerning faith; at one time of what may be called abstract faith, faith as such: at another of concrete faith, faith in composition, or embodied. Faith, as such, or abstract, is meant, when Scripture speaks of justification, as such, or of the justified (Vid. Rom. and Gal.). But when it speaks of rewards and works, then it speaks of faith in composition, concrete or embodied. For instance: 'Faith which worketh by love'; 'This do, and thou shalt live'; 'If thou wilt enter into life, keep the commandments'; 'Whoso doeth these things, shall live in them'; 'Cease to do

---

[13] *Lectures on Justification*, 303.
[14] *Lectures on Justification*, 300-301.

evil, learn to do well'. In these and similar texts, which occur without number, in which mention is made of doing, believing doings
are always meant; as, when it says, 'This do, and thou shalt live', it
means, 'First see that thou art believing, that thy reason is right and
thy will good, that thou hast faith in Christ; that being secured,
work'." Then he proceeds: - "How is it wonderful, that to that
embodied faith, that is, faith working as was Abel's, in other words
to believing works, are annexed merits and rewards? Why should
not Scripture speak thus variously of faith, considering it so speaks
even of Christ, God and man; sometimes of his entire person, sometimes of one or other of his two natures, the divine or human? When
it speaks of one or other of these, it speaks of Christ in the abstract;
when of the divine made one with the human in one person, of
Christ as if in composition and incarnate. There is a well-known rule
in the Schools concerning the 'communicatio idiomatum', when the
attributes of his divinity are ascribed to his humanity, as is frequent
in Scripture; for instance, in Luke ii the angel calls the infant born
of the Virgin Mary 'the Saviour' of men, and 'the Lord' both of
angels and men, and in the preceding chapter, 'the Son of God'.
Hence I may say with literal truth, That infant who is lying in a
manger and in the Virgin's bosom, created heaven and earth, and is
the Lord of angels ... As it is truly said, Jesus the Son of Mary created all things, so is justification ascribed to faith incarnate or to
believing deeds."

This passage, as cited, clearly indicates that Luther concedes
that justification is to be ascribed to "believing deeds," an excellent summary of Newman's own position, as well as that of certain earlier Anglican divines, including George Bull. On the basis
of the biblical passages noted, Newman declares that Luther is
obliged – against his will, it would seem – to accept this inevitable
conclusion. Luther's doctrine of justification by faith alone is thus
to be set aside as irreconcilable with Scripture on the one hand,
and with Luther's own words on the other. The strategic location
of the citation within lecture 12 – it is the final and clinching argument – indicates that Newman is aware of its importance. Like a

conjurer producing an unexpected rabbit from a hat, Newman surprises his readers with the news that even Luther had to concede the case on this one.

But notice a curious feature of this passage. It has been cited extensively without any omissions. Yet suddenly, towards the end, we encounter an ellipsis, in the form of four periods. All of us who indulge in scholarship use this device, generally to save weary readers from having to wrestle with textual material which is not totally germane to the issue under discussion. Perhaps Newman has omitted part of a sentence, or maybe even a sentence or two, which is not relevant to the interpretation of the final dramatic sentence. Such, I imagine, would be the conclusion of many of his readers, although some would be puzzled as to the need for verbal economy at this stage, given the generous nature of the citation up to this point.

But to anyone familiar with Luther, the line of argumentation is suspicious. It is simply not what Luther consistently maintains throughout his extensive body of writings; nor would it be the kind of statement he would have made in such a significant work as the 1535 Galatians commentary. It is with sadness that I have to point out that the omitted portion is not a sentence but a section – and a section which so qualifies the meaning of the final sentence as to exclude Newman's interpretation of it. In what follows, we shall pick up Newman's citation at the penultimate sentence, and insert the omitted material, before proceeding to the final sentence. For the sake of clarity, the material which Newman included has been printed in italics:

> *Hence I may say with literal truth, That infant who is lying in a manger and in the Virgin's bosom, created heaven and earth, and is the Lord of angels.* I am indeed speaking about a man here. But "man" in this proposition is obviously a new term, and, as the sophists say, stands for the divinity; that is, this God who became

man created all things. Here creation is attributed to the divinity alone, since the humanity does not create. Nevertheless, it is correct to say that "the man created," because the divinity, which alone creates, is incarnate with the humanity, and therefore the humanity participates in the attributes of both predicates. [A list of biblical passages relating to this point follows]. Therefore the meaning of the passage "do this and you will live" is "you will live on account of this faithful doing; this doing will give you life solely on account of faith. Thus justification belongs to faith alone, just as creation belongs to the divinity. *As it is truly said, Jesus the Son of Mary created all things, so is justification ascribed to faith incarnate or to believing deeds."*

Throughout this analysis, we find Luther insisting that "faith alone justifies and does everything;" works are implicated only in a derivative manner. The significance of the passage which is omitted is that it unequivocally qualifies the final sentence so that its only meaning can be that of "faith alone justifies." Let me stress that I am not saying that Luther is right in what he wrote and meant; I am simply saying that this is want he wrote and meant. I deliberately used the phrase "the passage which is omitted." We must now confront a most difficult and vexing question: did Newman himself deliberately and knowingly omit the critical section of the passage, or did he encounter the passage in this mutilated form? My suspicion is that the latter option is much more probable, although I cannot prove this. None of us are infallible, and Newman may simply have copied the passage in this distorted version from another source. Evidence supportive of this suggestion can be found in the generally inaccurate citations which he provides from Luther, which suggest borrowing from secondary sources rather than an engagement with the original.

My criticisms of Newman's *Lectures on Justification* thus far are scholarly, rather than evangelical. Any unbiased scholar with expertise in the field would raise substantially the same questions. How-

ever, in what follows I wish to suggest that, both in this work and the
earlier *Arians of the Fourth Century*, Newman uses historical theology as little more than a thinly- veiled foil for his own theological
and ecclesiological agenda, which is firmly wedded to the realities of
the Church of England in the 1830s. In each case, Newman's enemy
is not so much the stated subject of his inquiry – whether Arians or
Luther – but Protestantism in general, and evangelicalism in particular. Equally, in each case the scholarship is flawed, even to the point
of involving what I must regrettably describe as deliberate distortion
for the somewhat petty purposes of scoring points. Rowan Williams,
in his excellent study of Arius, points out the severe limitations of
Newman's historical scholarship with regard to the heresiarch:[15]

> One must charitably say that Newman is not at his best here: a bril-
> liant argument, linking all sorts of diverse phenomena, is built up on
> a foundation of complacent bigotry and historical fantasy. However,
> setting aside for the moment the distasteful rhetoric of his exposi-
> tion, it should be possible to see something of what his polemical
> agenda really is. *The Arians of the Fourth Century* is, in large part,
> a tract in defence of what the early Oxford Movement thought of as
> spiritual religion and spiritual authority.

In both his *Arians of the Fourth Century* and *Lectures on Justification*, Newman's critique of evangelicalism is subtle and largely
indirect, tending to proceed by "eccentric, superficial and preju-
diced"[16] historical analysis of the past, on the basis of an assumed
linkage between disliked individuals of the past (Arius and Luther)
and the evangelicalism of the 1830s. As Williams correctly notes,
one obvious target of Newman's invective is the "stolid Evangelicalism" which rejects "mystical and symbolic readings of the world
in general and Scripture in particular."[17]

[15] Rowan Williams, *Arius: Heresy and Tradition* (London: DLT, 1987) 4-5.
[16] Williams, *Arius*, 6.
[17] Ibid., 5.

The same polemical agenda may be discerned within the pages of the *Lectures on Justification*. The Caroline Divines are clearly understood to have got things right, and forged a vision of the relation of faith and works in justification which even Luther had to admit was right, and which safeguarded Christians against an unhealthy reliance upon personal spiritual experience. From an evangelical perspective, Newman's arbitrary historical positivism, which leads him to regard the Caroline Divines as somehow defining the essence of Anglicanism, is quite unacceptable.[18] This has significant implications for his attempts to define the *via media*, which he generally takes to be a "middle way" between Protestantism and Catholicism. However, as Diarmaid MacCulloch as shown in his excellent recent study of Cranmer, the sixteenth-century archbishop's concern is actually better understood as an attempt to find a middle way between competing versions of Protestantism.[19]

I end this evaluation of Newman from an evangelical perspective by noting two points of importance. The first is that, as a matter of observable fact, modern evangelicalism within the Church of England pays relatively little attention to Newman. Perhaps they should pay more; but the fact is that, what Newman says that evangelicals find agreeable they find more agreeably stated elsewhere – for example, in the writings of H. P. Liddon, who many evangelicals regard as a pillar of theological orthodoxy, who may continue to act as a resource for today. The recognition of the importance of tradition on the part of evangelicals within the Church of England owes little that I can discern to Newman.[20]

The second point relates to Newman's influence on the shaping of

[18] McGrath, *Iustitia Dei*, 2:121-133.

[19] Diarmaid MacCulloch, *Thomas Cranmer: A Life* (New Haven: Yale University Press, 1996) 173-236.

[20] See James I. Packer, "The Comfort of Conservatism," in M. S. Horton (ed.), *Power Religion* (Chicago: Moody, 1990) 283-300. This important justifi-

English, and especially Anglican, theology. In his essay "An English Systematic Theology?," Professor Colin Gunton notes the tendency within many Anglican theologians "to find it extremely difficult to appropriate material from any tradition other than its own deriving from the period between the Middle Ages and the mid-nineteenth century."[21] One of the most regrettable aspects of the Oxford Movement is its dismissive attitude towards the Reformers. As our analysis of Newman indicates, this dismissal rests upon largely questionable grounds, rather than a serious and sustained engagement with the primary sources in the detail we have a right to expect. Perhaps it might be argued that such a style of engagement was characteristic of Newman's age, and need not therefore be counted against him. Perhaps there is merit in this point; nevertheless, its cumulative impact has been substantially less than beneficial to both the style and substance of English theology. As Stephen Sykes points out in a number of works (perhaps most forcefully in his *Integrity of Anglicanism*),[22] this reluctance to take the theology of the Reformation seriously has been a major reason for the theological impoverishment of Anglicanism.

This analysis of Newman from an evangelical Anglican perspective thus ends on a somewhat negative note, and may seem slightly out of place in the present volume. Perhaps sensing that Newman has little time for evangelicals, today's representatives of the movement have returned the compliment. As one who began with a very high estimation of Newman, I have to confess that I have ended up with a rather more critical view of him, both as a scholar and as religious statesman. I still sing his hymns; I am, however, a little more hesitant when it comes to singing his praises.

---

cation of the importance of tradition may well make points of which Newman would have approved; Newman, however, is clearly not their source.

[21] Colin Gunton, "An English Systematic Theology?," *Scottish Journal of Theology* 46 (1993) 479-496.

[22] Stephen Sykes, *The Integrity of Anglicanism* (London: Mowbrays, 1978).

NEWMAN, HUTTON AND UNITARIANISM

Sheridan GILLEY

For the Victorians, one of the principal issues of the intellectual life was the truth or falsehood of Christianity, which was shaped by what G. M. Young once described as the two main influences upon Victorian culture, the Utilitarian philosophy and Evangelical religion.[1] Both played a major part in Newman's intellectual development. His growth into High Churchmanship and then Roman Catholicism was an attempt to provide an adequate intellectual and institutional apologia and setting for his original Evangelical conversion. His polemic against Utilitarianism in *The Tamworth Reading Room* attacked a philosophy of a merely worldly usefulness which decked itself with the imaginative attractions of Catholicism. To these two influences, I would add a third, the insidious underlying allure of Unitarianism, the rejection of the Trinitarian idea of God as Father, Son and Spirit, and by implication of Christ's deity.

1. Unitarianism in England

Unitarianism was a religious position with affinities to Evangelicalism and Utilitarianism. It claimed to be Scriptural and useful, both Reformed and Catholic, and to be the outcome of the reasonable man's enquiry into religious truth.

---

[1] G. M. Young, *Victorian England: Portrait of an Age* (Oxford: Oxford University Press, 1939) 1.

Yet the number of Unitarians in Victorian England was small, and did not markedly increase with the century. When the only national religious census in English history was taken in March 1851, there were 229 Unitarian chapels and England and Wales, with about forty thousand morning and evening worshippers.[2] Their claim, however, was to a learned tradition. The term 'Unitarian', in Jonathan Clark's words, "was brought into general use from the late 1760s as a euphemism, applied by Arians and Socinians to themselves, and denoting their identity as a group."[3] Arianism, the denial of the full divinity of Christ, is the fourth-century heresy which was the subject of Newman's first book, and reduces Christ from very God of very God to an inferior deity. Socinianism derived its name from the Italian Sozzini family in the sixteenth century, and this anti-Trinitarianism, claiming to be based on Scripture, owed its origin less to northern Protestants than to the small number of Spanish and Italian Protestants like Servetus and Ochino.[4] Yet both Arianism and Socinianism gathered adherents in England from the 1680s.[5] In England, Unitarian chapels had mostly evolved from the Bible-bound former Presbyterian churches which in the later eighteenth century, rejected Evangelical Calvinism, though they also drew on the rationalism of Deism and of Anglican theologians like the neo-Socinian Samuel Clarke, and so attracted adherents from liberal Anglicanism, like their putative English founding-father, Theophilus Lindsey. This gave English Unitarianism an immediate double origin:

---

[2] Owen Chadwick, *The Victorian Church*, 2 vols. (London: Adam & Charles Black, 1971) 1:396.

[3] J. C. D. Clark, *English Society 1688-1832* (Cambridge: Cambridge University Press, 1988) xiii.

[4] E. M. Wilbur, *A History of Unitarianism: Socinianism and its Antecedents* (Cambridge, MS: Harvard University Press, 1947).

[5] Roland N. Stromberg, "Arians and Socinians," in *Religious Liberalism in Eighteenth- Century England* (Oxford: Oxford University Press, 1954) 34-51.

first, in an Enlightenment culture which rejected the doctrine of the Trinity as irrational, as a mystery above reason; and in the strict Biblical literalism which denied the Trinity because it was not taught in Scripture.

Unitarianism also had political implications. In the eighteenth century, it was illegal; the English State was explicitly founded on Trinitarian orthodoxy, and to attack Trinitarianism was to attack the State. Being anti-Trinitarian and not simply non-Trinitarian, Socinians and Arians were denied the freedom of public worship allowed under the Toleration Act of 1689 to the non-Trinitarian Jews and Quakers, and were condemned by the Blasphemy Act passed in 1697, the year in which a lad of eighteen, Thomas Aikenhead, was hanged between Edinburgh and Leith for denying the Trinity.[6] Thus the later Unitarians posed a threat which the Quakers and Jews did not, as the Achilles heel of orthodox Protestantism. One of the more spectacular events in the English reaction against the French Revolution was the sack in 1791 of the Unitarian Joseph Priestley's house in Birmingham by a Church and King mob. The Lake Poets, Wordsworth, Coleridge and Southey, became Unitarian in their youth in the 1790s, in embracing the principles of the Revolution. All three returned to the Church of England as they turned to Toryism, though Southey's private convictions remained Unitarian. It was only in 1813 that Unitarian worship was made lawful. Unitarians were anathema to Evangelicals, and in 1844, the State had to pass a law to prevent the Presbyterian Church in England from reclaiming formerly Presbyterian properties in Unitarian hands.

But if the Unitarians were a minor branch of English Dissent, they were a learned body, and made up in influence what they

[6] T. B. Macaulay, *The History of England from the Accession of James the Second*, 2 vols. (London: Longmans, Green, & Co, 1889) 2:620-621.

lacked in numbers.[7] Charles Dickens chose to worship in a Unitarian chapel. Mrs Gaskell was married to a Unitarian minister. The Unitarian-born Harriet Martineau was a leading light of political economy; her brother James reformed the Unitarian theology. Unitarians formed wealthy local dynasties, like the Chamberlains in Birmingham. In the aftermath of the reform of the municipal corporations in 1835, throwing them open to non-Anglicans, there were Unitarian mayors of Manchester and Liverpool. Some of their churches were of cathedral splendour, rivalling Anglicans.[8] Victorian England was like the modern United States, a place where even liberals wanted to be in the churches. The nearest that nineteenth-century America achieved to an intellectual aristocracy were the Boston Unitarians, and both in Britain and America in the nineteenth-century, Unitarians claimed to express the Zeitgeist as the very breath of God, to embody the spirit in the age. This accorded well with the high noonday of mid-Victorian optimism, as my own great-great grandfather's Unitarian creed summed this up: 'the Fatherhood of God, the Brotherhood of Man, the Leadership of Jesus, the Solemn Worth of Character, and the Progress of Man Onward and Upward for ever'.

2. Newman and Unitarianism

Modern Unitarians have abandoned almost all this creed, especially belief in God, but they remain numerous in name at least in the United States, which still maintains a faith in the Progress of

[7] See H. McLachlan, *The Unitarian Movement in the Religious Life of England. 1. Its Contribution to Thought and Learning, 1700-1900* (London: George Allen & Unwin, 1934); Barbara Smith (ed.), *Truth, Liberty, Religion: Essays Celebrating Two Hundred Years of Manchester College* (Manchester College, Oxford: 1986).

[8] See Ken Powell, *The Fall of Zion: Northern Chapel Architecture and its Future* (Save Britain's Heritage, 1980), in which a disproportionate number of the grander threatened or demolished church buildings seem to be Unitarian chapels.

Man (or to be politically, correct, of humankind), 'Onward and Upward for ever'. More traditional forms of Christianity, Catholic or Protestant, retain a suspicion of the implied perfectibility of humanity and the identification of moral and material progress. Nothing could be remoter from Newman's conviction, most sharply expressed in *The Tamworth Reading Room*, that increasing wealth could make sin more refined but no less sinful. Moreover Newman's whole development was a rejection not merely of rationalism and liberalism, but of both in their Unitarian form. Newman's Evangelical model, Thomas Scott of Aston Sandford, had been converted from Unitarianism to Evangelical Calvinism. Newman's brother Francis had gone in exactly the opposite direction, in part out of his discovery that if he were to believe in the Bible alone, then he would have to reject the doctrine of the Trinity because the Bible does not explicitly teach it. Francis Newman was too much the individualist to be called even a Unitarian; he preferred to call himself a theist.[9] Then there was the sad puzzle of the former Spanish Catholic priest Joseph Blanco White, who at Oriel College, taught Newman the use of the Roman Breviary. For many years a trophy of orthodox Protestantism, Blanco White disgraced his Protestant patrons, and especially Newman's sometime mentor Archbishop Whately, by leaving the Church of England for Unitarianism.

Moreover Unitarianism for Newman was only the end point of the Christological heresies with which he wrestled during his Anglican years, Arianism, Sabellianism, Nestorianism and Monophysitism. During Newman's brief flirtation with liberalism in 1827, he preached a 'subordinationist' sermon "On the Mediatorial Kingdom of Christ," which was criticised by his Oriel Noetic

---

[9] Ann Margaret Schellenberg, *Prize the Doubt: The Life and Work of Francis William Newman* (PhD Thesis, University of Durham, 1994).

friends and mentors, Hawkins, Blanco White and Whately, the last of whom suggested he was tending to Arianism.[10] Soon after the sermon, Newman recorded in a Memorandum that he as cordially disliked "all discussions concerning the *nature* of God, and speculations about the *mode* of His existence as Three and One, as the most strong opposer of Bishops Pearson and Beveridge - I do not even like the words Trinity, Person, Procession etc etc - indeed any systematic exposition of the doctrine but what is *relative to us and practical.*" In this practical sense, he remarked that "Arianism (in the main) is true - so is Sabellianism - so (in its first outline) Unitarianism - but none the *whole* Truth - Yet for *particular purposes*, according to particular occasions, it may be useful to represent the Catholic doctrine in this or that form."[11]

Newman wrote this before he entered on his study of the Fathers, and his statement is open to interpretation: from a Catholic viewpoint, Unitarians are right to stress the unity of God, and only wrong to deny the Trinity, and Newman was arguing that rhetorically, by what he later called an economy, a preacher might well expound the unity of God to his hearers. Again, by June 1828 Newman had turned to a much more obviously orthodox view, and he was later to reflect that his Oriel critics were "all then verging towards Sabellianism themselves:"[12] Sabellianism being the heresy which reduces the Trinity to facets or aspects of Deity. But Newman's deviant position in 1827 is significant of how easily a sensitive and brilliant young Anglican divine could stray into the enemy camp, in a Church which was vulnerable to the very sort of error from

[10] See Dom Placid Murray, OSB (ed.), Sermon 42, *John Henry Newman Sermons 1824-1843*, 5 vols (Oxford: Clarendon, 1991-) 1:329-343.

[11] Cited *ibid.*, p. 343; also Stephen Thomas, *Newman and Heresy: The Anglican Years* (Cambridge: Cambridge University Press, 1991) 18.

[12] *Ibid.*, 17.

which Newman would seek to save it. When Blanco White defected to the Unitarians, Newman seized on White's thesis that "Sabellianism is but Unitarianism in disguise,"[13] with a consequent false conception of Revelation itself as manifestation and not mystery, in which divine truth is reduced to a matter of human reason and human need, when it is greater than them and lies beyond them. This idea underlies Newman's polemic in *Tract 73* against such contemporary theologians as Thomas Erskine and Jacob Abbott whom he thought inclined to Sabellianism;[14] in his postscript to the tract on Friedrich Schleiermacher's treatise on Athanasian and Sabellian views of the Trinity;[15] and in his review of the 'Sabellian' Henry Hart Milman.[16] Erskine and Abbott, Schleiermacher and Milman, were Nicodemite or crypto-Unitarians, in reducing the character of God to what men can feel or understand. The young Newman was, therefore, no proto-Modernist, but as keen a detector, definer and dissector of heresies as Pope St. Pius X. As Cardinal Wiseman in Lent was said to have his lobster salad side, so one side of Newman was pure dogma.

Newman's argument was against the rationalist or liberal outliers of Unitarianism. But Unitarianism was also rooted in Protestant Biblicism, and was therefore the shadow on the wall when Newman argued against Protestantism the insufficiency of the Bible without the Church. As he put it to his Protestant critics in *Tract 85*, "If the words Altar, Absolution, or Succession,

---

[13] *Ibid.*, 81.

[14] Republished as "On the Introduction of Rationalistic Principles into Revealed Religion," *Essays Critical and Historical*, 2 vols. (London: Pickering, 1971) 1:30-99.

[15] *Ibid.*, 96-99.

[16] "Milman's View of Christianity," *Essays Critical and Historical*, 2:186-248.

are not in Scripture (supposing it), neither is the word Trinity."[17] Unitarianism was the *reductio ad absurdum* of orthodox Bible Protestantism, and the Tractarians cried *non placet* in 1843 as the University of Oxford conferred a degree on the American ambassador to Britain, Edward Everett, who was not only a Unitarian, but a former Boston Unitarian minister. It was an American and Bostonian, the former Unitarian Orestes Brownson, a convert in 1844 to Catholicism, who attacked the *Essay on the Development of Christian Doctrine,* in part because he thought that Newman had conceded too much to the Unitarian charge that the Trinity was not explicitly taught in Scripture.[18] While Brownson's personal relations with Newman changed from hostility to friendship,[19] there was a sense in which Newman granted his complaint, in seeing the fundamental doctrines of Biblical inspiration, the Holy Trinity, the Incarnation and grace as the products of developed tradition, "separate portions of which receive their perfect expression only gradually in the course of many centuries."[20]

3. Hutton and Unitarianism

Unitarianism was, however, deeply divided about whether to abandon one of its starting points, Scriptural literalism, under the influence of the Unitarian Charles Hennell's *Inquiry Concerning the Origin of Christianity* (1838) and of German Biblical criticism,

---

[17] "Holy Scripture in its Relation to the Catholic Creed," *Tract 85* (1838), in *Discussions and Arguments on Various Subjects* (London: Longmans, Green, and Co, 1911) 123.

[18] Owen Chadwick, *From Bossuet to Newman,* 2nd ed. (Cambridge: Cambridge University Press, 1987) 170-173.

[19] Vincent Ferrer Blehl, SJ, "John Henry Newman and Orestes A. Brownson as Educational Philosophers," *Recusant History* 23 (1997) 408-417.

[20] J. Derek Holmes (ed), *The Theological Papers of John Henry Newman on Biblical Inspiration and on Infallibility* (Oxford: Clarendon, 1979) 43.

popularised in England by Hennell's friend, George Eliot, through her translation of D. F. Strauss's *Life of Jesus* (1846).[21] This debate was the setting of the young Richard Holt Hutton,[22] whose father and grandfather were both Unitarian ministers. Born in 1826, Hut- 1826-1897 ton did his first degree at the 'Godless' University College in Gower Street, where he met his closest friend, Walter Bagehot, at a time when Unitarianism was being transformed by James Martineau, a sometime junior colleague in Dublin of Hutton's grandfather. Martineau was the apostle of the new Unitarian school, setting out to bring Unitarianism up to date with German scholarship and German idealist philosophy. Hutton also sought a new basis for his Unitarian faith in the latest German scholarship at the Universities of Bonn and Heidelberg, where he was tutor to Martineau's son Russell. He returned to England to prepare for the Unitarian ministry at Manchester New College, where he missed by a year the teaching of Newman's brother Francis. Hutton was considered too dangerous a radical for the Unitarian ministry, and his first occupation was in 1850 as Assistant Principal to Arthur Hugh Clough at University Hall in Gordon Square, founded by Unitarians as a residence for students at the 'Godless' University College. Hutton went to the West Indies to recover from an infected lung, but his young wife died there of yellow fever. On returning to England he worked for Unitarian publications, the weekly *Inquirer* and the quarterly *Prospective Review* and was, with Walter Bagehot, a founding editor of the *National Review*, which achieved a wider readership than Unitarians.

---

[21] Basil Willey, *Nineteenth Century Studies: Coleridge to Matthew Arnold* (London: Chatto & Windus, 1955) 204-226: McLachlan, pp. 52-53.

[22] The main modern work on Hutton is Malcolm Woodfield's *R.H. Hutton: Critic and Theologian* (Oxford: Clarendon, 1986) which has a chapter on Hutton and Newman (43-79). This especially identifies Hutton's major writings on Newman in *The Spectator* (202-204). Robert H. Tener and Woodfield have edited *A*

Hutton was, however, increasingly uncomfortable as a Unitarian, and under the influence of the Broad Church Anglican Frederick Denison Maurice, he came to a belief in the Incarnation. Maurice's father had also been a Unitarian minister who had seen his wife and daughters embrace Evangelical Calvinism, and Maurice's own turning to the Church of England was something of an epoch in the history of Liberal Anglicanism, difficult to appreciate for those of us like Newman, who "ever thought him hazy,'"[23] or more pejoratively, as a fluffy-minded Prayer Book fundamentalist.

Hutton's discovery of orthodoxy through Maurice is significant of that wider early Victorian recovery of Christianity of which Newman was a major prophet. Hutton's defence of his conversion in his pamphlet, *The Incarnation and Principles of Evidence* of 1862, tried to show his Unitarian friends how the free heart and intellect could, without either an infallible Church or Bible, enter into a full belief in the Incarnation, which carried its own evidence for its truth. It is difficult to reduce this eloquent document to the bare bones of argument, from the magnificent rhetoric in which it is expressed. Hutton declared that there are two elements in faith in Christ: first, reliable human testimony to his historical existence, and to his claims about himself; and second, reliable proof intrinsic to itself of the claim that Christ was God incarnate: for "this alone, answers the cry of the ages and of our own consciences for divine light and help, [and] the two coalesce into an historical faith, which is something far

Victorian Spectator: Uncollected Writings of R.H. Hutton (Bristol: The Bristol Press, 1989) which reprints Hutton's review of the *Parochial and Plain Sermons* (151-156). See also James Drummond & C.B. Upton, *The Life and Letters of James Martineau*, 2 vols. (London: James Nisbet & Co., 1902), for the intellectual background from which he sprang. An article on Hutton and Newman with a different emphasis to my own has appeared since the writing of this paper:

more than assent to historical testimony ..."[24] Conscience and heart and reason can see that Christ affords the deepest knowledge of a God who in Christ bears witness to Himself.

And if the Incarnation is true it implies the Trinity, by telling us "something of God's absolute and essential nature, something which does not merely describe what He is *to us*, but what He is in himself. If Christ is the Eternal Son of God, God is indeed and in essence a Father; the social nature, the spring of love is of the very essence of the Eternal being; the communication of his life, the reciprocation of his affection dates from beyond time - belongs, in other words, to the very being of God ... I can answer for myself," wrote Hutton, "that the Unitarian conviction that God is - *as* God and in his eternal essence - a single and, so to say, solitary personality, influenced my imagination and the whole colour of my faith most profoundly. Such a conviction, thoroughly realised, renders it impossible to identify any of the social attributes with his real *essence* - renders it difficult not to regard power as the true root of all other divine life. If we are to believe that *the Father* was from all time, we must believe that He was *as* a Father - that is, that love was actual in Him as well as potential, that the communication of life and thought and fullness of joy was of the inmost nature of God, and never began to be, if God never began to be ... If ... we pray to One who has revealed his own eternity through the Eternal Son - if in the spirit of the liturgies, Catholic and Protestant, we alternate our prayers to the eternal originating love, and to that filial love in which it has been eternally mirrored,

Edward J. Enright, O.S.A., "Between the Devil and the Blue Sea: John Henry Newman and Richard Holt Hutton," *Recusant History* 24 (1998) 507-522.

[23] Newman to Lord Lyttelton, 26 July 1864, in C. S. Dessain and Edward E. Kelly, SJ (eds.), *The Letters and Diaries of John Henry Newman* (London: Nelson,1971) 21: 504. (Henceforth cited as *L&D*).

[24] R. H. Hutton, "The Incarnation and Principles of Evidence," in *Essays Theological and Literary*, 2 vols. (London: Daldy, Isbister, & Co, 1877) 1:229.

turning from the 'Father of heaven' to the 'Son, Redeemer of the world', and back again to Him in whom that Son for ever rests - then we keep a God essentially *social* before our hearts and minds, and fill our imagination with no solitary grandeur." "He was essentially the Father, essentially Love, essentially something infinitely more than Knowledge or Power, essentially communicating and receiving a living affection, essentially all that the heart can desire."[25] For Hutton, the Unitarian God did not love man enough to become one.

This proof, if proof it is, is both moral and metaphysical, commending itself to both conscience and reason in the light which it sheds on the human condition and the power of renewal which it brings to human lives. Hutton refers to two of Newman's authorities, Athanasius and Bishop Butler; but the very clarity of his vision removed the need for an infallible Church or Scripture. The evidence to heart, mind and conscience of Incarnation and Trinity was sufficient in itself. This arguably deprives the doctrines of Trinity and Incarnation of the very dimension of mystery which Newman thought must attach to them, if the human spirit can so wholly grasp them: Newman's objection to Unitarianism in the first place. Nor does it deal with the problem of the enlightened heart and intellect which does not see its way to Hutton's conclusion. Hutton's Trinitarian idea of the society or community of the Godhead never passed into ecclesiology, of the Trinitarian society of the Church: in his stubborn individualism, he remained a liberal Protestant, hostile to Newman's view that liberalism might go over into libertinism or atheism; indeed, as he was to put it in his review of Newman's sermons, Newman's was "a false creed, - false chiefly by its misinterpretation of and comparative contempt

---

[25] *Ibid.*, 231-235.

[26] "Dr. Newman's Oxford Sermons," *The Spectator*, 5 December 1868, p. 1436; cited in Tener and Woodfield, *A Victorian Spectator*, 151.

for the new intellectual forces of our own day ..."[26] Because Hutton believed that the purpose of Revelation was to convey directly without ecclesial intermediaries the Trinitarian character of God, he held a low opinion of the institutional aspect of religion, and outside the formulations of Trinity and Incarnation, a low view of most intellectual doctrine, where Newman's view of both was a high one. On the other hand, Hutton's understanding of the role of conscience and of the spiritual life in relation to belief was rather like Newman's, and in this he recognised in Newman one of the great authentic religious voices of the age.

Yet Hutton was dissatisfied with his own position, for while his critical study of Scripture left him no time for Biblical literalism, he had strong yearnings for an infallible Church to put its seal on religious truth. His Unitarian upbringing left him with little of the old Protestant horror of Rome, and he even envied Romanists for enjoying a calm self-confidence in the truth which he thought was an aid to spiritual growth.[27] But though Hutton shared with Newman a belief that religious truth must be personal, practical and moral, he deduced from this the very opposite of the Roman position, believing that an infallible Church, to be a convincing teacher, would also have to be an impeccable one. This was to be in part why he was to worry Newman with the questions about wicked popes which had never really worried Newman. Hutton equally rejected Anglo-Catholicism as a half-hearted step in the Roman direction, even if its inerrant Church authority lay firmly in the past, in the long departed authority of the Early Church.

From 1861 until just before his death in 1897, Hutton was joint editor and part-owner of the weekly *Spectator*. He extended its circulation and wrote for it about several thousand essays and reviews, on every aspect of literature, politics, theology, and a

---

[27] "Preface to the Second Edition," *Essays Theological and Literary*, 1:vii–xi.

good many other disciplines beside these. He thereby became for a large part of the Victorian reading public the leading critic of nineteenth-century literature, which he interpreted according to his own criteria of its enlargement of the inner life. Hutton's particular interest in literature was distinctly religious, in discerning and defining the 'implicit Christianity' in the literary output of his day, not always as the product of a direct commitment, but of the power to perceive and re-create an imaginative reality which was ultimately God-given, and to reassert the presence of spiritual values in a secularising world. In this, Hutton expounded an oddly mingled liberalism and traditionalism, in which his own orthodoxy was increasingly exposed. In the Preface he wrote in 1876 for the second edition of his theological and literary essays published in 1877, he recognised that the English intellectual current was now running in the opposite direction from his youth, towards agnosticism and atheism, even while the Roman Catholic Church was ever more strongly reasserting her infallible authority, and Anglo-Catholicism renewed the dogmatic school in that weathervane to the world, the Church of England. This deepened Hutton's private uneasiness and left him feeling high and dry between infidelity and infallibilism, with his belief in the sufficiency of the individual reason and conscience for faith shot to pieces by snipers from either side.

In his monograph on Hutton, Malcolm Woodfield points out that Hutton's self-confidence in public was in contrast to the unease of his private utterances;[28] an agony aunt must be confident in herself, and Hutton's doubts were not in harmony with his role as a Marjorie Proops to the anxious intellectual classes of his day. His function can be put more positively. "Perhaps it has never before happened," wrote Newman's biographer Wilfrid Ward of Hutton, "that

---

[28] See, for example, his letters to Newman. See Woodfield, *R.H. Hutton*, 21.

Catholics, Anglicans, and inquiring Agnostics have repaired, on occasion, to an editor's office in the Strand with feelings somewhat akin to those with which the Savoyard went to St. Francis de Sales, for advice in perplexity or a stimulus to do his duty."[29] Hutton's own favourite writers were Newman, Arnold, Wordsworth, Tennyson, Jane Austen and George Eliot. This is a conventional assemblage of nineteenth-century sages, collectively comprising the nineteenth-century literary Church, which for Arnold himself became a substitute for Christianity. Newman is the obvious anomaly in this list, for none of the others articulated Newman's orthodoxy, and there was nothing 'implicit' about Newman's Christianity, whatever one says about the others. This suggests an ambiguity about Hutton. His early work was for denominational publications, though they were Unitarian ones. His main work afterwards was a sort of self-secularisation, for the non-denominational *Spectator*, which spanned the gulf between the literary set, with its babel of self-contradictory religious opinions, and conventional Christianity.

There is, therefore, a paradox about Hutton, that as his own theological convictions became more orthodox, the world and the function that he served became less so. As an interpreter of Newman, his role was also paradoxical, the presentation of a Newman for non-Roman Catholics, of a Newman who had about him a spiritual and intellectual greatness which any one of any opinions could revere.

4. Hutton and Newman

Hutton dated his original fascination with Newman from the age of eighteen,[30] as he later wrote to Newman, speaking of "the passage in which Willis describes the mass in 'Loss and Gain'

---

[29] Wilfrid Ward, *Ten Personal Studies* (London: Longmans, Green, & Co., 1908) 67.

[30] Woodfield points out that Hutton was twenty-two when *Loss and Gain* was published. See Woodfield, *R.H. Hutton*, 51.

[which] very nearly made a Willis of me, - a man I mean who
dives experimentally into the Church in the hope of faith rather
than one who goes into it because he sees it to be true."[31] Hutton
demanded proof of the Church's credentials before entering it. Yet
Willis's speech haunted him for reasons he could not analyse, with
its distinction between Catholic and Protestant worship as belonging to different religions, and the vision of the Mass as the descent
of God upon the altars: as Willis says, not as just a form of words,
but as "a great action, the greatest action that can be on earth ...
not the invocation merely, but ... the evocation of the Eternal ...
before whom angels bow and devils tremble."[32]

The first of Hutton's identified thirty-six articles on Newman,
in 1850,[33] was a review of Newman's *Discourses Addressed to
Mixed Congregations*. In the same year he was present at the
delivery of Newman's *Lectures on Certain Difficulties Felt by
Anglicans*, which he was to describe as "the first book of Newman's generally read amongst Protestants, in which the measure
of his literary power could be adequately taken;" "which adds but
little to our insight into his [Newman's] mind, though it adds
much to our estimate of his powers."[34] This and the *Lectures on
the Present Position of Catholics in England* were the works in
which Hutton felt that Newman had first shown most delightfully
his gift for sarcasm: which fascinated Hutton, as we shall see.

Hutton's actual relationship with Newman began in 1864 when
he was less than three years into his editorship of *The Spectator*,
and intervened decisively in the debate over the *Apologia* to award

---

[31] Hutton to Newman, 15 June 1864, *L&D*, 21:120.

[32] *Loss and Gain: The Story of a Convert* (London: Longmans, Green & Co,
1848). We refer to the edition of 1891, chapter 20, 328.

[33] Woodfield, *R.H. Hutton*, 202-204.

[34] Richard Holt Hutton, *Cardinal Newman* (London: Methuen & Co, 1891).
We refer to the edition of 1905. See 207. (Henceforth cited *Newman*).

the palm of victory to Newman over Kingsley. We are here in a
realm of intense allegiances: Kingsley was even more F.D. Maurice's disciple than Hutton was, and in theological conviction, as a
Broad Church Anglican, Hutton was a great deal nearer to Kingsley than he was to Newman. Hutton's two-part review of Newman's initial reply to Kingsley, entitled "Father Newman's Sarcasm," backhandedly complimented Kingsley for affording "a
genuine literary pleasure to all who can find intellectual pleasure
in the play of great powers of sarcasm, by bringing Father Newman from his retirement, and showing not only one of the greatest
of English writers, but, perhaps, the very greatest master of delicate and polished sarcasm in the English language ... Mr. Kingsley is a choice though, perhaps, too helpless a victim for the full
exercise of Father Newman's powers ... the title of one of his
books, 'Loose Thoughts for Loose Thinkers', represents too
closely the character of his rough but manly intellect, so that a
more opportune Protestant ram for Father Newman's sacrificial
knife could scarcely have been found."[35] This comparison was not
wholly in Newman's favour: Hutton declared "that one of the
greatest secrets of Dr. Newman's wonderful power is an intellectual basis for his mind of that peculiar hardness tending to cruelty
which most easily allies itself with a keen intellectual sense of the
supernatural ..." This is connected with another of Newman's
qualities, "a sort of pitiful tenderness, under which there runs a
current of hidden triumph in the power of the Catholic faith and
dogma to override all human ties, and dissolve all human joys and
griefs by the power of its mightier affinities."[36]

This seizes precisely on two of the moods of the *Apologia*, and
in Newman's works, as in Pascal's: a terrifying irony about this
world, and a concomitant overwhelming sense of the superior

[35] *The Spectator*, 20 February 1864: cited in *L&D*, 21:61.
[36] *Ibid.*

reality of another, which is rooted in that even more terrifying combination of savage irony with pity in the blinding light of the eternal in the character of Our Lord in the Gospels. The passage also expresses Hutton's reserve, deriving from F. D. Maurice, who regarded Revelation as personal rather than propositional, about anything as systematic as Roman Catholicism. Newman was grateful to Hutton, not only for the essay, but for defending him against the insinuation of the High Church *Saturday Review* that his morality was one of political expediency and slyness.[37] On the other hand, there is Hutton's own insinuation that to be a dogmatist is to be cruel. In apologising to Newman for his use of "cruel," Hutton compared him with the only other theologian who had impressed him deeply, the very antisystematic and volcanic F.D. Maurice. Newman thought, Hutton declared, out of "a deep attachment to a dogmatic and systematic theological view of the universe:"[38] the whole of this self-coherent faith was implicit in everything he wrote.

This oversystematises Newman's own view of Revelation, which he had insisted against the clarity of liberal schemes like the Unitarian, "is not a revealed *system*, but consists of a number of detatched and incomplete truths belonging to a vast system unrevealed, of doctrines and injunctions mysteriously connected together; that is, connected by unknown media, and bearing upon unknown portions of the system;"[39] as "a doctrine *lying hid* in language,"[40] in the very language which reveals it, to be compared with a landscape seen by twilight, when there is both light and darkness. In any case, Hutton preferred Maurice's less subtle com-

---

[37] *The Saturday Review*, 27 February 1864: cited in *L&D*, 21:63-64.

[38] Hutton to Newman, 28 February 1864. See *L&D*, 21:68.

[39] "On the Introduction of Rationalistic Principles into Revealed Religion," (*Tract 73*), 42.

[40] *Ibid.*, p. 41.

bination of occasional blinding insight with lack of system. In this as in other things he differed from Newman, as a liberal who thought that the free soul like his own could willingly enter into faith: and that nothing essential was to be gained or added to that faith by the authority of an infallible Church.

On the other hand, Hutton considered Kingsley's imputation of cunning to Newman unfair, and in *The Spectator*, roundly denounced Kingsley's reply in *What, then, does Dr Newman mean?* for "scattering far and wide aspersions on the craft and subtlety of the Roman Catholic communion in general, and Dr. Newman in particular ... Mr Kingsley ... aggravates the original injustice a hundredfold ... He raises, in fact, as large a cloud of dust as he can round his opponent, appeals to every Protestant pre-possession against him, ... and retires without vindicating his assertion in the least ... He permits himself a perfect licence of insinuation, so long as these insinuations are suggested by the vague sort of animal scent by which he chooses to judge of other men's drift and meaning."[41]

"I can't tell," Newman wrote to Hutton in gratitude, "till I read the article again carefully how far I follow you in everything you say of me ... you have uttered on the whole what I should say of myself ... but ... you have done me a great service in doing so, as bearing external testimony."[42] This was before Newman got down to composing the *Apologia* proper, and as a friendly and influential voice from the Protestant world, Hutton had a part in stimulating Newman to write it. Hutton subsequently congratulated Newman on his "triumphant vindication" of himself, but used the occasion to ask Newman for a fuller answer to his own difficulties in believing in an infallible

---

[41] "Roman Catholic Casuistry and Protestant Prejudice," *The Spectator*, 26 March 1864. See *L&D*, 21:89.

[42] Newman to Hutton, 27 March 1864. See *L&D*, 21:90.

Church. While conceding "the Roman theology fuller of self-revealing truth than almost any other of the coherent *systems*," Hutton insisted that his own faith and divine revelation in general came not through the Church but direct from God: "The Church seems to me the expression of a faith once attained," wrote Hutton to Newman, "not the means of giving it."[43] Yet it was in this letter that Hutton confessed to his fascination with the passage about Willis and the Mass in *Loss and Gain* already cited; it was as if he were hungry for the very Church which his demand for proof of her would always deny.

Newman argued in his reply that the Church was necessary to give a public definition to the faith held in common; there must be an objective character to Revelation in the faith of the Church, beyond the subjective conviction of the individual. Yet he denied that he taught "that 'authority' is the 'only road to truth in theology'," and granted that truth could come through a medium other than the Church. Hutton could have "a real, (or what Catholics call a divine) faith, coming of supernatural grace, in the Incarnation, even though you gained it from the Scriptures." But the Church is "the ordinary, normal Oracle" of Revelation, though an individual might find faith through "a Greek poem or philosophical treatise ... nay even the Koran." All true religion had its source in God, wherever the believer might encounter it.[44] Newman entered as far into Hutton's views as he dared to go. He declined to embark on a detailed discussion of Hutton's essay, "The Incarnation and Principles of Evidence," and Hutton strongly dissented from Newman's hostile critique of a liberalism resembling his own.

Newman called on Hutton in 1866, the only occasion that they

---

[43] Hutton to Newman, 15 June 1864. See *L&D*, 21:120.
[44] Newman to Hutton, 18 June 1864. See *L&D*, 21:121-2.

met,[45] but it was Newman who took up Hutton's work again with its author, the day after he finished the *Grammar of Assent*. "I can't help thinking that the end of my own performance will please you," he wrote to Hutton, "and agrees with your own doctrine,"in spite of other great differences between them.[46] The point of their correspondence remained the same, Hutton's wish to believe in the Church, and his inability to do so, because of the Church's past teaching on burning heretics and the eternal torment of the damned, even the inclusion of the book of Tobit in the Bible, given that a single counter-instance of fallible teaching, in Hutton's view of it, would disprove the doctrine of ecclesial infallibility. Newman's response was what he elsewhere was to call "a wise and gentle *minimism*,"[47] stressing how little had been defined about Biblical inspiration and hell-fire. Hutton's own review of the *Grammar of Assent* in *The Spectator* evoked Newman's "great pleasure to me to find how exactly you have translated me, in some places with a happiness of statement which I feel I had not hit myself,"[48] while disputing Hutton's hostility to Tobit and his understanding of the character of assent, which Hutton had thought admitted of degrees. On Hutton's side of the correspondence, however, was the continuing quest for a fuller faith, with a sense that the world of faith was slipping away: "I sometimes almost despair of gaining in this life the light I crave."[49] "The tendency of the religion of the day to dissipate itself in the vaguest sentiment and smoke oppresses me more and more, and often makes me turn to your Church with a vague passionate yearning

---

[45] On 27 June. See *L&D*, 22:254.

[46] Newman to Hutton, 13 February 1870. See *L&D*, 25:29.

[47] *A Letter addressed to His Grace the Duke of Norfolk* (London: Pickering, 1875) 125.

[48] Newman to Hutton, 27 and 28 April 1870. See *L&D*, 25:111.

[49] Hutton to Newman, 21 March 1871. See *L&D*, 25:303.

that I feel to be dangerous and even distrustful of God ... I feel as if the tendencies of the day were all witnessing against the only truth I can firmly grasp ... But when I look more narrowly at your Church I see nothing but what daunts me still more on the other side -...": principally in its dogmatic attachment to the Creeds, which were formulated on unsatisfactory evidence. He preferred like the young Newman "to see England bigoted, superstitious, gloomy, almost cruel, to seeing her without faith in the supernatural,"[50] but in the end the Catholic Church failed to come up to the objective standard of proper public proof and disproof.

Nothing, then, that Newman could say could shake Hutton's disbelief in the Church: neither side would convert the other. Each recognised in the other a sympathy and a hunger for religious truth. Newman's personal feelings about Hutton were summed up in a hyperbolic letter of 1867, when he presented Hutton with the collected volume of his poetry which Hutton had asked him to republish, with another copy for Hutton's colleague Walter Bagehot, who had written on the poetic qualities of Newman's prose: "literally speaking," wrote Newman to Hutton, "you were the first who ever said a good word to me about any of the things I had written. None of my friends have ever done so ... "[51] Newman declined Hutton's efforts to attract him to the Metaphysical Society, but even more extravagantly in 1872, Newman wrote to him as "one of those to whom the angels on Christmas night sent greeting as 'hominibus bonae voluntatis' ... what you write perplexes me often - but when a man is really and truly seeking the Pearl of great price, how can one help joining oneself in heart and spirit with him?"[52] They ceased to correspond between 1873 and 1883. In his last great service to Newman during the Cardinal's

---

[50] Hutton to Newman, 20 February 1872. See *L&D*, 26:38-39.
[51] Newman to Hutton, 18 December 1867. See *L&D*, 23:384.
[52] Newman to Hutton, 29 December 1872. See *L&D*, 26:224.

lifetime, Hutton replied in *The Contemporary Review* to the Congregationalist Principal Fairbairn's attack on Newman as a sceptic: "to treat your *mind* as sceptical because you follow so clearly the windings of the sceptical reasoning seems to me a most singular perversion of the truth."[53]

The refutation of Thomas Huxley's very similar argument that Newman was a sceptic is one theme of Hutton's book about Newman, written in 1890, the year of the Cardinal's death, and published in 1891. Fr Dessain described it as "one of the first and one of the best short biographies of Newman,"[54] and it is by way of tribute to what Hutton regarded as a great religious mind of the Victorian age. Yet it is a critical work, especially in its rejection of aspects of Newman's thought on the intellectual and institutional dimensions of religion, while being the sort of criticism which does justice to its subject and makes it clearer. Some of Hutton's own views remain opaque. His judgement on Newman's first book, *The Arians of the Fourth Century*, acknowledges that in defending orthodox dogma, Newman "was defending what is at once essential to the very life and essence of the story of Christ's sacrifice for man in which Divine revelation culminates, and yet that in thus defending it, there is a very great danger of losing sight of the core of the revelation,"[55] among those for whom the letter kills. Hutton wrote that Newman "thought of dogma a little too much as the essence, instead of as the mere protective covering, of revelation. The substance of revelation is the character of God, and dogma is only necessary to those whose minds cannot enter into this marvellous revelation ..."[56] Hutton complained in Newman of that attachment to dogma which makes Newman other

---

[53] Hutton to Newman, 11 March 1886. See *L&D*, 31:125.
[54] *L&D*, 21:549.
[55] Hutton, *Newman*, 29.
[56] *Ibid.*, 30.

than a proto-Modernist. On the other hand, Hutton seems to recognise that "for the predominantly intellectual, dogmatic theology is a noble study," and that there is a greater danger for believers "who, while clinging to the gospel of Christ, try to get rid of all the subtleties and distinctions of theological science."[57] It is simply not clear where his conclusion lies, with Newman's insistence on the need for dogma or against it.

On the institutional side of Anglo-Catholicism, Hutton showed a polite scepticism of the whole attempt to define the Anglican *Via Media*, yet he also displayed an acute sensitivity about Newman's own sense of its tentative and ambiguous character, about the many twists and turnings in Newman's attempt to define it, and in his gradual departure from it. It is significant of Hutton's own background in Unitarianism rather than Protestantism that he found the Lutheran doctrine of justification by faith alone, the doctrine on which Lutherans thought that the Church stands or fall, "incredible, intolerable to piety" and "horrible."[58] There is also his sometime Unitarian sympathy with Newman's demonstration in *Tract 85* that orthodox Christianity could not rest solely on Scripture. All in all, however, Hutton saw the continuity of Newman's mental and spiritual development, so that the submission of the sometime Evangelical to Rome was not fundamentally the reversal of his earlier convictions, but their completion.

The point is connected with another of great value. While Hutton only devoted one chapter to the greater part of Newman's Catholic life, he wanted to show, against Protestant criticism, that Newman's career as a Roman Catholic had been more fertile and productive than his Anglican one, as the fulfilment of the writer and the man. It was an advantage as well as a drawback that Hut-

---

[57] *Ibid.*, pp. 30-31.
[58] *Ibid.*, p. 84.

ton wrote before the nearly full public revelation of Newman's difficulties with other Roman Catholics, which began with Purcell's *Life of Cardinal Manning* in 1895, so that Hutton could concentrate on Newman's Catholic writings: Hutton wrote:

> From the moment when Newman became a Roman Catholic, the freest and happiest, though not perhaps the most fascinating, epoch of his life may be said to have commenced. I do not know that he ever again displayed quite the same intensity of restrained and subdued passion as found expression in many of his Oxford sermons. But in irony, in humour, in eloquence, in imaginative force, the writings of the later and, as we may call it, the emancipated portion of his career far surpass the writings of his theological apprenticeship.[59]

Against the general Anglican view that Newman had wasted his genius on Rome, this is a striking image of the Roman Catholic Newman, coming from a practising liberal Anglican, as a man "emancipated" by his conversion to Roman Catholicism. Newman's Roman Catholic works, wrote Hutton, include "the most effective book he ever wrote, and certainly the most remarkable of his controversial writings."[60] Hutton dealt with *Loss and Gain* and *Callista*, which he called "the most completely characteristic of Newman's books ... none, unless it be *The Dream of Gerontius*, expresses as this does the depth of his spiritual passion, the singular wholeness, unity, and steady concentration of purpose connecting all his thoughts, words, and deeds."[61] Hutton devoted considerable space to the *Discourses Addressed to Mixed Congregations.* He was especially appreciative of the irony of Newman's *Lectures on Certain Difficulties Felt by Anglicans* and of the *Lectures on the Present Position of Catholics in England*, as the books in

---

[59] *Ibid.*, 190.
[60] *Ibid.*
[61] *Ibid.*, 225.

which Newman, breaking from the restraint of the Anglican doctrine of reserve, found his mature literary voice.

Ian Ker has suggested a corrective to Hutton's allied view that Newman's satirical gifts, so manifest in these Roman Catholic works, "was not present, and powerfully present, in his Anglican period," even if this gift "blossomed and flowered" after his submission to Rome. Ker also, however, describes Hutton as "the first critic to write seriously about Newman as a writer," declaring, in very similar words to Fr Dessain's, the judgement that Hutton's *Newman* was "one of the first and best biographical studies of Newman after his death."[62] Hutton's book has excurses on *The Idea of a University*, the *Apologia* and the *Grammar of Assent*. *The Letter to the Duke of Norfolk* is briefly mentioned. In short, Hutton's summary gave the reader the first valuable summary and overview of Newman's writings as a Roman Catholic. The final chapter, on *The Dream of Gerontius*, concludes with Hutton's reflections on the unity of Newman's life:

> a life that has fed itself from beginning to end on the substance of Divine revelation, and that has measured the whole length and breadth and depth of human doubt without fascination and without dread - a life at once both severe and tender, both passionate and self-controlled, with more in it perhaps of an ascetic love of suffering than of actual suffering, more of mortification than of unhappiness, more of sensibility and sensitiveness than of actual anguish, but still a lonely and severe and saintly life. No life known to me in the last century of our national history can for a moment compare with it, so far as we can judge of such deep matters, in unity of meaning and constancy of purpose. It has been carved, as it were, out of one solid block of spiritual substance, and though there may be weak and wavering lines here and there in the carving, it is not easy to detect any flaw in the material upon which the long indefatigable labour has been spent.[63]

[62] Ian Ker, "Newman the Satirist," in Ian Ker and Alan G. Hill (eds.), *Newman after a Hundred Years* (Oxford: Clarendon, 1990) 5.

[63] Hutton, *Newman*, 249-250.

This touches on hagiography, yet Hutton's conception of the personal and spiritual unity of Newman's life and thought is a profound one, which has continued to influence biographers of Newman to the present; even if Newman 's personal life as a Roman Catholic, as distinct from his spiritual one, was sometimes unhappier than Hutton supposed. And it also suggests Hutton's importance as a commentator on Newman. First, Hutton was the guide and mentor of a literary public who were the more prepared to recognise Newman's greatness because Hutton so eloquently expounded it. Second, Hutton knew his own mind, but usually appreciated Newman's position on the very points with which he disagreed with him. And that I think we owe in part to a Unitarian tradition which was without a Protestant prejudice against Roman Catholicism, even if its standpoint was sometimes a prejudice of its own.

Hutton remained a champion of Newman's posthumous reputation, meeting head-on the onslaught on Newman by Edwin Abbott, a controversy to which Abbott devoted three fat volumes.[64] Hutton rejected Abbott's attack on Newman's essay on ecclesiastical miracles as a "theological caning,"[65] and Hutton's main influence upon Newman's studies in the next generation was through his patronage of the young Wilfrid Ward, whom Hutton encouraged to defend Newman against Abbott,[66] a controversy in which *The Spectator* took a leading part.[67] Hutton had guided

---

[64] Edwin A. Abbott, *Philomythus: An Antidote against Credulity* (London: Macmillan, 1891); *The Anglican Career of Cardinal Newman*, 2 vols. (London: Macmillan, 1891). See the reviews of Abbott listed in Woodfield, *R.H. Hutton*, 203.

[65] "Dr Abbott's Attack on Cardinal Newman," *The Spectator*, 18 April 1891, p. 538.

[66] "Philalethes: Some Words on a Misconception of Cardinal Newman," *The Contemporary Review* 60 (July, 1891) 32-51.

[67] There are a number of exchanges between Ward and Abbott in *The Spectator* in April and May, 1891.

Ward in writing his first philosophical works, and then his Roman Catholic biographies. Ward's *Life of Newman* was to give Newman studies a fixed point for more than a generation, and behind Ward stood the figure of Hutton, who as he had defended Newman before England in 1864, still guarded his memory. During the last decade of his life, Hutton went to Mass on Sundays, giving rise to a rumour of his conversion, and there is a touch of pathos about this, as if he still hoped to find in the mystery of the altar the truth which he had once glimpsed in *Loss and Gain.*

And that, I think, makes Hutton more than a purveyor of essence of Newman heavily diluted by copious draughts of F.D. Maurician rosewater. I sometimes feel that a liberalism like Hutton's was significant of the decay of religion and of the dissolution of dogma, an eddy in the receding sea of faith. Yet Roman Catholicism found it easier to make its way in a world in which agnosticism and atheism attracted only minorities, and which was still in Hutton's sense Christian. The Catholic Church presents quite a different character to a society which is pagan and no longer believes in God. Yet there is much to be said for Newman's method with converts, of beginning from convictions already held, and for his tenderness to those like Hutton who are fellow-travellers in a faith to which they cannot quite commit themselves. Newman did not bring Hutton to that fullness of truth which Roman Catholics believe lies in Roman Catholicism, but he helped confirm him in the faith he held. The older Newman took his friends wherever he found him. We would do well to consider his example.

NEWMAN AND THE NEOPLATONIC TRADITION IN ENGLAND

Louis Dupré

The topic for this paper was inspired by a short article Louis Bouyer published in the first issue of *Monastic Studies* (Pentecost 1963), "Newman and English Platonism." Subsequent years have confirmed the strong impression the essay made on me when it first appeared. Of course, Platonism of one sort or another has since the fourth century been a constant companion of Christian theology. But after the Reformation it reentered Anglican piety in a new and surprising way. What attracted the Calvinist theologians of Cambridge's Emmanuel College to it was, on the one hand, a spiritual empiricism that assumed, as already Calvin in the *Institutes* had done, that there must be an *experience* of God and, on the other hand, against Puritan fideism, the desire to restore reason to its rightful place in the theory and practice of faith. If faith was to present any truth claims at all, it had to do so within an inclusive order of human knowledge. Earlier efforts toward that end had shown, however, how difficult it was to avoid a subordination of faith to reason. Socinianism and antinominianism had started to rear their heads also in England where Deism was rapidly becoming Christianity's principal enemy.

Nathaniel Culverwell's *Elegant and Learned Discourse of the Light of Nature* (1652) may count as an early attempt to find a *via media* between fideism and rationalism. The fellow of Emmanuel College set himself as goal "to vindicate the use of reason in matters of religion" and at the same time "to chastise the sauciness of

Socinus and his followers who dare set Hagar above her mistress, and make faith wait at the elbow of corrupt and distorted reason." Culverwell, instead, intends "to take off the head of that uncircumcised Philistine with his own sword, but better sharpened; and then to lay it up behind the Ephod in the sanctuary."[1] Culverwell's successor posthumously dedicated the book to the master of Emmanuel College, Anthony Tuckney, who himself had supported the rational quality of dogmatic principles of theology. Culverwell's own position stood half-way between Hooker's Thomist theory of natural law and the Platonism of his fellow Emannuelian, Benjamin Whichcote. All through his work he repeated the verse taken from *Proverbs* 20:27: "The spirit of man is the candle of the Lord," interpreted by Bacon's famous principle: "Give unto reason the things that are reason's and unto *faith* the things that are *faith*." Yet, contrary to Bacon, Culverwell assumed a perfect harmony between nature and grace whereby grace illuminates (rather than restricts) the mind's natural capacity. Culverwell's theory of reason as participating of the divine light may have been influenced by the slightly older Benjamin Whichcote, though Whichcote himself was more Aristotelian than Platonist.[2]

The metaphor of natural reason being illuminated by divine light inspired the thought of three younger Emmanuel theologians, Cudworth, Smith, and More. Among them the mystically inclined John Smith initiated a tradition of spiritual empiricism that eventually led to Newman.[3] For him, all knowledge begins with an intellectual touch, a sensation of the soul. All modes of knowing

[1] Nathaniel Culverwell, *An Elegant and Learned Discourse on the Light of Nature* (1652), (eds.) Robert A. Greene & Hugh MacCallum (Toronto: University of Toronto Press, 1971). See "To the Reader," p. 6.

[2] Such is the interpretation of Greene & MacCallum (eds.), in "Introduction," *The Light of Nature*, xlvii-xlviii.

[3] On the mystical character of Smith's theory, see John K. Ryan, "John Smith: Platonist and Mystic," in *The New Scholasticism* 20 (1946) 1ff. But Basil

require the mind to withdraw from bodily things and need the assistance of the divine light.[4] Nor does the highest exercise of reason consist in rational discourse but in a contemplative openness to the divine illumination. This essential passivity -- *Deum pati* -- distinguishes Christian Platonism from its ancient variety. It is not the only difference, as we shall see, but it may well be the most significant one. The divine light "carries the soul to the mount of transfiguration for a prospect of the promised land."[5] Smith grounds the belief in the soul's immortality on what he calls the "naked intuition of eternal truth," as Plotinus and Proclus had done, criticizing "that flat and dull philosophy which these later ages have brought forth."[6] The soul possesses a natural sense of God that renders so-called arguments for God's existence superfluous. God's *nature*, however, remains entirely beyond our knowledge.

The ascent to God is no purely intellectual matter, but as for Newman, it is stimulated by what Plato had described as the soul's appetite for the supreme good.[7] "Not the nimbleness and agility of our own reason stirs up these eager affections within us - but some more potent nature which has planted a restless motion within us that might carry us to itself."[8] The idea that affection motivates knowledge of God and that all knowledge participates in God's nature anticipated two basic principles that Newman was to develop. So did, in a different way, Smith's emphasis on the religious significance of ethics. He combines this mystical attraction

Willey in *Christianity Past and Present* (1952) considers him a forerunner of rationalist deism.

[4] John Smith, "The True Way and Method of Attaining Divine Knowledge," in *Select Discourses* (1660). Republished by Garland Press, Hamden, 1978.

[5] John Smith, "True Religion," in *Select Discourses*, 417.

[6] John Smith, *The Immortality of the Soul*, 103.

[7] Smith, *Select Discourses*, 135.

[8] Ibid., 136.

with a powerful ethical drive. To partake in God's nature requires that we follow the law of nature, the divine seal "embosomed in the souls." Hence, striving to resemble God means to live according to God's law.[9]

Other prefigurations of Newman's thought appear in Ralph Cudworth's *True Intellectual System of the Universe* (1678), which argues that all ancient civilizations were implicitly acquainted with monotheism, though it was mostly veiled in the form of one god reigning supreme over all others. Polytheism - which even Socrates and Plato did not overcome - referred to intellectual forces whom humans ought to honor, not to gods in the Christian sense of that term. Plotinus and Proclus explicitly affirmed that one God stood at the origin of the many divine forces. If God is present in all things, He must certainly be present in all human minds. Cudworth anticipates Newman's idea of God's presence in conscience, the basis of a phenomenology of religion such as Rudolf Otto was to elaborate later.[10] Nor did the Cambridge Platonist reduce the divine presence to one of efficient causality - a position already refuted by Anaxagoras - but described as a more intimate, formal one. Newman's interpretation of divine causality never ceased to reflect a similar Neoplatonic union between God and the soul.

The Cambridge theologians created an intellectual and mystical current that increasingly came to influence Anglican theology, particularly after it merged with the native empiricist philosophy. Christian Platonism had always entailed an empirical attitude, insofar as it assumed the mind to be essentially passive with regard to divine illumination. One of the major figures in empiricist philosophy achieved partly under the influence of the

[9] Ibid., 157.

[10] See Cyril O'Regan, "Newman and von Balthasar: The Christological Contexting of the Numinous," in *Eglise et Théologie* 26 (1995) 165-202.

Cambridge theologians a full intellectual synthesis with Platonism. Bishop George Berkeley all too often appears in the history of philosophy as a transitional figure between Locke's empiricist realism and Hume's skepticism. He does, indeed, subscribe to the empiricist thesis that all mental activity begins with sense perception. Yet, for Berkeley, perceptions function not as *causes* of ideas, but merely as occasions. Reality *itself* is ideal - not the material object of subjective sensations. Even the name "*subjective* idealism" commonly attached to Berkeley's theory misrepresents him, for it fails to account for his conviction that objects continue to exist even when no human eye perceives them. To claim that God perceives them, as he does, is inconsistent only with a sensationalist interpretation of *esse est percipi*. In fact, the divine "perception," for Berkeley, functions as the source of our ideas. One may quibble with the appropriateness of the term "perception," but the objective, theological nature of Berkeley's idealism leaves no doubt. Christian thinkers, especially the Platonizing ones, had consistently maintained that all reality exists ideally in God. Berkeley drew the more radical conclusion that this ideal inexistence was its one and only reality.[11]

His response, then, that God still perceives objects that no human mind can observe reveals the overriding theological concern that motivated his philosophical endeavors. *To be* means first and foremost to exist as idea in God. Through ideas God grants the human mind access to this intradivine existence. Nor does any part of the real leave this ideal in-existence, as Malebranche had maintained, for if it did, God's self-expression in creation would become detached from its Creator. The fact that the mind actively reflects on its ideas, develops rules for articulating the regularity of nature, and conceives philosophical notions about God, the self,

[11] Nicholas Everitt, "Quasi-Berkeleyan Idealism as Perspicuous Theism," in *Faith and Philosophy* 14 (1997) 353-377.

and the ultimate nature of the real, does not contradict its fundamental passivity with regard to the ideas. It merely indicates that
God has created beings capable of arranging and rearranging
them.

Berkeley forestalls the charge of pantheism by stressing that the
omnipresence of the divine which he, even as Cudworth, found in
ancient Egyptian, Pythagorean, and Neoplatonic thought, is by no
means "atheistic."[12] His target is naturalism, which he considered
inevitable once the dependence of the creature on God becomes
reduced to the extrinsic link of efficient causality. With Cudworth
(to whom he repeatedly refers), he argues that all things exist in
God. Philosophical idealism serves to justify theological principles. But he regarded that idealism as built on solid philosophical
ground. The nature of all knowledge presupposes the ideal quality
of the real - a principle on which the German idealists of the early
nineteenth century were to base their position. How could the
ideal act of knowledge know its object other than in an ideal way?
The charge that idealism is based upon the fallacy of egocentric
predicament holds only if the nature of the real is entirely defined
by the ideal quality of *human* perception. Far from asserting that
thesis, however, Berkeley claims that objects of cognition derive
their ideality from their existence in God. Human cognition does
no more than imperfectly partake of that divine ideality.

Nature provides no more than signs - indications - of God's
presence. It does not reveal the nature of that presence. "God
speaks to men by the intervention and use of arbitrary, outward,
sensible signs, having no resemblance or necessary connection
with the things they stand for and suggest."[13] *Ideas* transform the
phenomena of sense perception into *signs*, endowing them with a

---

[12] George Berkeley, *Siris* # 300, 326, 352, in A.A. Luce & T.E. Jessup (eds.),
The Works of George Berkeley (London: Thomas Nelson, 1950) 5:139, 149, 158.

[13] *Alciphron* IV, 7 in *Works*, 3:149.

meaning that of themselves they do not possess. Only ideas render
sense perceptions intelligible, predictable, and coherent, as they
convert successions of phenomena into fixed rules and thereby lay
the foundation for science. In his much underestimated work,
Siris, Berkeley shows how our ideas of this world assume a new
function when serving as *signs* of a divine reality that lies beyond
all ideas. "Sense and experience acquaint us with the course and
analogy of appearances or natural effects. Thought, reason, intellect introduces us into the knowledge of their cause."[14] Here
Berkeley uses the term *cause* in the only way he considers legiti-
mate, namely, as referring to the metaphysical origin of reality.
The discussion of the nature of our knowledge of God discloses
the true source of Berkeley's theory and the direction of his
thought. He refers to Proclus who compares the succession of
mental stages to a religious initiation. At first, the initiate meets
many gods, but once fully initiated he receives a divine illumination and comes to participate in the one divine nature. "In like
manner, Berkeley concludes, if the soul look abroad, she beholds
the shadows and images of things, but returning into herself she
unravels and beholds her own essence."[15]

The major significance of Berkeley's work for a discussion of
Newman's intellectual sources lies in his theory of signs. Religious signs reveal the *presence* of God, but not God's nature.
Newman as well as Berkeley remains within the Platonic-mystical
tradition of negative theology. A theory of signs or symbols supports such a theology far more adequately than a theory of analogy. It would be hard to prove that Newman underwent any direct
impact of Berkeley's philosophy. Far more likely did the theory of
signs reach him via bishop Joseph Butler's *Analogy of Religion
Natural and Revealed* (1736), of which the *Apologia* admits that it

[14] *Siris* # 264 in *Works*, 5:124.
[15] *Ibid.*, # 333, 152.

seriously influenced him. The term "analogy" in the title of Butler's work is intriguing, since the author denies that we possess
any ability of speaking directly of God, while the traditional theory of analogy assumes that we have some positive knowledge of
God. Since no road leads directly from the created world to its
transcendent foundation, Butler, like other negative theologians, is
forced to speak of "symbols," "conjectures," and vague "corre-
spondences." Contrary to analogous concepts religious symbols
raise questions of ultimacy without implying a *direct* relation to
the transcendent principle. They function as *signs* of a divine presence, but never present "proofs" for that presence nor do they
provide direct images for it. The concept of analogy rests on the
assumption of a resemblance between an effect and its divine
cause. In its modern version, that causality is reduced to one of
extrinsic efficacy. In Butler's sacramental vision creatures are
signs of God's presence; they are not images resembling an original prototype.

In the second part of the *Analogy* Butler interprets biblical
typology by the same rule: the sign bears no direct resemblance to
the signified. Christians have always read the Bible as a prefigura-
tion of the Gospel. One of the oldest texts of the New Testament -
Peter's Pentecostal speech as reported in the *Acts of the Apostles* -
stresses the bond of meaning that links the new faith with the
older one. Through the centuries, however, what began as a religious typology came to be interpreted as a prediction of every
move of Christ. This contrived literalism had, however indirectly,
its source in the critical studies of the biblical text that began in
the early Renaissance and was embraced by reformed exegetes.
The nature of symbolic typology eludes, to some extent, Butler
himself who, feeling bound by the notion of scriptural inerrancy,
presents Christ's life as "the completion of prophecy" whereby
prophecy is defined as the history of events before they came to

pass (II, 7, 30). Thus he claims that a long series of prophecies applicable to later events presents proof that "it was intended of them" (II, 7, 23). Still Butler understands well that the meaning of a text may be extended beyond its author's intention - a principle we accept for the reading of all significant literary works. "To say that the scriptures and the things contained in them can have no other or further meaning than those persons thought or had, who first recited or wrote them, is evidently saying that those persons were original, proper, and sole authors of those books, i.e., that they are not inspired, which is absurd ..." (II, 7, 25). Even the historical fulfillment of a prophecy in the Old Testament (such as the one in Daniel 7:8 refers to the person of Antiochus Epiphanes) does not prevent it from having a later, more comprehensive fulfillment in Christian times (II, 7, 27). Understanding the full meaning of a prophecy requires a deeper sense for grasping what is invisible and future, as spiritual persons possess, "who not only see but base a general practical feeling that what is to come will be present and that things are not less real for their not being the objects of sense" (II, 6, 13).

Newman also emphatically defends the *spiritual sense* of Scripture. He considers a typological reading of the Old Testament not only admissible, but required for a full understanding of the Gospel message. In his *Essay on the Development of Christian Doctrine* he singles out the exclusive attachment to the letter of Scripture as the main source of heresy, as the Antioch School's literalism proves: "The history of that School is summed up in the broad characteristic fact, on the one hand that it devoted itself to the literal and critical interpretation of Scripture, and on the other that it gave rise first to the Arian and then to the Nestorian heresy."[16] Only a spiritual interpretation of Scripture allows a

---

[16] John Henry Newman, *An Essay on the Development of Christian Doctrine*, Ch. VI, Sect. 3, § 2 (Garden City: Doubleday, 1960) 276.

development of doctrine. Later in the same text he claims that it may almost be laid down as an historical fact that "the mystical interpretation and orthodoxy will stand or fall together."[17]

In the *Apologia* Newman acknowledges his debt to Butler on two accounts. One is the Platonic "analogy" between the celestial and the terrestrial realms, whereby "the less important one is economically and sacramentally connected with the more momentous system."[18] The concept of a dual reality appealed to Newman who, already as a child, had experienced a "distrust of the reality of material phenomena," a distrust which he later interpreted as "the mystical or sacramental principle of the real."[19] We may recall Newman's mysterious sermon on the invisible world. "The things which are seen are but a part, and but a secondary part of the beings about us, were it only on this ground, that Almighty God, the Being of beings, is not in their number, but among 'the things which are not seen'."[20] That invisible realm also includes the angels and the dead. "We are then in a world of spirits, as well as in a world of sense, and we hold communion with it, and take part of it, though we are not conscious of doing so."[21]

The other Butlerian principle that influenced him, the sufficiency of probable reasons for a justification of faith, may appear to result from a nominalist fideism far removed from Platonic thought. Such it would undoubtedly be, if the *experience* of faith did not provide a foundation of certainty to it. Probability alone stands opposed to absolute certainty, Newman concedes, and

---

[17] *Ibid.*, Ch. VII, Sect. 4, § 5, p. 327.

[18] John Henry Newman, *Apologia pro vita sua* (London: Longmans, Green, 1879) 10.

[19] Ibid.

[20] John Henry Newman, *Parochial and Plain Sermons*, Bk. IV, 13 (San Francisco: Ignatius Press, 1997) 861.

[21] Ibid., 863.

would "resolve truth into an opinion."[22] But an experience of matters divine conveyed through faith may transform, at least for the believer, probability into certainty. But since such an experience is strictly personal, one cannot argue that a mere probability of arguments would suffice to render the act of faith universally *rational*. Newman attempts to strengthen the weight of the probable by requiring an "assemblage of concurring and converging probabilities."[23] Still, in his early sermons, the weight rested mainly on trust. His sermon "Religious Faith Rational" sounds quite pessimistic about the powers of human knowledge. "Indeed, when we come to examine the subject, it will be found that, strictly speaking, we know little more than that we exist, and that there is an unseen Power whom we are bound to obey. Beyond this we must *trust* our senses, memory, and reasoning powers; then other authorities: - so that, in fact, almost all we do, every day of our lives, is on trust, *i.e., faith*."[24] He considered such an act of trust "quite a rational procedure," though as a general epistemic principle, it would rate no higher than fideism. But, again, in that sermon Newman is not formulating a philosophical principle: he is speaking about religious faith and faith, he claims, presents a direct experience: "We obey God primarily because we actually *feel his presence* in our consciences bidding us obey Him."[25] In an 1839 university sermon he calls the objective evidence offered by Paul in support of the Christian message "slight," but strengthened by the *probabilities Paul "stirred" in his audience.*[26]

---

[22] Newman, *Apologia*, 19.

[23] Ibid., 20.

[24] John Henry Newman, "Religious Faith Rational," in *Parochial and Plain Sermons*, Bk. I, 15, p. 127.

[25] Ibid., 129.

[26] John Henry Newman, "The Nature of Faith in Relation to Reason" (1839), # 2, *University Sermons* (London: SPCK, 1970) 203.

Here, as often in his early writings, Newman wavered between an empiricist theory of knowledge and a "visionary" concept of faith. Only the senses are granted us for "direct and immediate acquaintance with things external to us." Even the senses provide no certainty about the external world unless their experience is supplemented by reason, which proceeds from things that are perceived to things that are not (*Ibid.*, # 7). But the powers of reason are weak and require the active cooperation of the will to attain certainty. Once we know a person, we can predict which position he/she will take in a dispute on almost any subject. "It often happens that in apparently indifferent practices or usages or sentiments, or in questions of science, or politics, or literature, we can almost prophecy beforehand from their religious or moral views where certain persons will stand" (*Ibid.*, # 15).

Though in his later years Newman abandoned the skepticism of his youth, in the *Grammar of Assent* he still reasserts the need for a deliberate act of the will in any theoretical assent. Even if the conclusions of a preceding ratiocinative process are obvious, Newman thinks: "I could have withheld my assent."[27] But if I consider the conclusion inescapable, how could I withhold assent? Does certain evidence not compel assent?[28] Taken as a general theory of knowledge Newman's position hardly differs from Hume's. But, of course, that is not what Newman intends. He is thinking primarily of the particular case of moral and religious assent. In existential concerns it never occurs that first I possess full evidence to which I then grant assent. In such matters assent surpasses the strictly cognitive order and a voluntary decision is needed to bridge the gap between evidence, in this case always

---

[27] John Henry Newman, *An Essay in Aid of a Grammar of Assent* (New York: Doubleday, 1955) 187.

[28] See Bernard Mayo, "Belief and Constraint," in Phillip Griffiths (ed.), *Knowledge and Beliefs*, (Oxford: Oxford University Press, 1967) 147-161.

incomplete, and its practical acceptance. Nor does this decision render the act of faith irrational. Indeed, Newman considers it irrational *not* to believe when evidence, though incomplete, moves the mind toward a morally desirable object. Nor does he regard the moral inducement a merely subjective motive. The undeniable awareness of a transcendent presence in conscience transforms what otherwise might still have remained a mere empiricism of feelings into an objective fact.

The idea of a divine *presence*, already formulated by the Cappadocian Fathers and by Augustine introduces a mystical, Platonic view of experience that has little in common with the subjective one of British empiricism. According to the Cambridge Platonist John Smith, the spiritual intuition recognizes its object as directly as an act of perception does. "The soul has its sense, as well as the body."[29] The mind directly intuits moral right and wrong without having to reason about it, and it does so in the light of an unmediated awareness of obligation to a transcendent authority. That authority is experienced as *present*, even though its nature remains wholly unknown. For Newman as for Smith, the transcendent presence is primarily experienced in the moral consciousness. Newman did not consider the imperative of conscience a "proof" for the existence of God. In fact, he admitted that he had never been able to develop a conclusive proof for God's existence. But he regarded the experience of a transcendent presence so indissolubly united to the moral experience as to render that presence "luminously self-evident." The question remains, however, whether the real apprehension of a private experience can be formulated as a universal, notional principle. Newman simply assumes that all humans experience the moral obligation as transcendent. This seems dubious. Yet the issue may not be decisive,

---

[29] John Smith, "Of the True Way and Method of Attaining to Divine Knowledge," in *Select Discourses* (Hamden, CT: Garland Press, 1978).

since Newman assumes only the awareness of a transcendent obligation that *may be* interpreted as deriving from a religious source, but *must* not necessarily be so. Indeed, his sense of moral obligation reminds us of Kant's. But it clearly goes well beyond the merely subjective "moral sense" presented by Shaftesbury and Hume. His theory may be called empiricist only in the sense of a "radical" empiricism, that is, in William James's sense of a theory, that includes the spiritual experience.[30] As such, it is more Augustinian than empiricist.

But Newman's moral sense of presence is paralleled by an equally strong and pervasive feeling of God's absence in the world. Presence and absence had, of course, been simultaneously characteristic of the Platonic mystical negative theology. What distinguishes Newman's version of it, however, is the fact that he mostly attributes this negative quality to the particular condition of a secular culture. Modern culture has lowered our ability to perceive the transcendent presence and heightened our difficulty in interpreting it religiously. Even God's presence to the soul can be felt only by the soul that has not dulled its moral sensitivity. It requires a religious sensitivity to sense the moral obligation as the stern command or the kind invitation of *someone* who accepts or reprehends me. In the world, allegedly God's dwelling place, we experience mainly God's absence. We know the passage in *A Grammar of Assent*:

> What strikes the mind so forcibly and so painfully, is His absence (if I may so speak) from His own world. It is a silence that speaks. It is as if others had got possession of His work. Why does not He, our Maker and Ruler, give us some immediate knowledge of Himself?[31]

---

[30] J.H. Walgrave, "Newman's 'Groeien naar het Licht'," in *Collationes* 9 (1979) 29. On the transcendent quality of the moral sense, see Walgrave, *Newman the Theologian*, trans. A.V. Littledale (New York: Sheed and Ward, 1960) 201-234.

In the moving sermon "Waiting for Christ" the religious alienation is emphasized even more strongly.

> When he came in the flesh "He was in the world, and the world was made by Him, and the world knew Him not." Nor did He strive nor cry, nor lift up His voice in the streets. So it is now. He still is here; He still whispers to us, He still makes signs to us. But His voice is too low, and the world's din is so loud, and His signs are so covert, and the world is so restless, that it is difficult to determine when He addresses us, and what He says. Religious men cannot but feel, in various ways, that His providence is guiding them and blessing them personally on the whole; yet when they attempt to put their finger upon the times and places, the traces of His presence disappear ...[32]

The same hiddenness of God is expressed in the Advent sermon that opens Book VI of the *Parochial Sermons*: "A thick black veil is spread between this world and the next. We mortal men range up and down it, to and fro, and see nothing. There is no access through it into the next world. In the Gospel this veil is not removed; it remains but now and then marvelous disclosures are made to us of what is behind it. At times we seem to catch a glimpse of a Form which we shall see hereafter face to face ..."[33] Nor are the signs of conscience totally unambiguous. They also are only "phenomena," that is, "pictures that gives us no exact measure or character of the unknown things beyond them."[34] They are "true as far as it goes but not adequate." Newman doubts whether the image of God thus conveyed would ever be elicited without the assistance of revelation.

Of course, the idea of God's hiddenness results not merely from the secular state of our culture - it forms an integral part of Chris-

[31] Ibid., 39.
[32] Newman, *Parochial Sermons* VI, p. 248.
[33] Ibid., VI, 1, pp. 964-65.
[34] Newman, *Grammar of Assent*, Ch. V, § 1, p. 100.

tian theology of all time and particularly of negative theology. Newman refers to the hiddenness of God: "And so when God walks the earth, He gives us means of knowing that He does so, though He is a hidden God, and does not display His glory openly."[35] But as negative theology denies the likeness between God and creation, it stresses all the more the creature's *symbolic* significance. The world may be no more than a trace, a *vestigium* (Bonaventure) rather than an image of God. But it is nevertheless the bearer of God's *presence*, however little we *feel* it. All of the creature's being is God's being, and without this being it would literally be nothing at all. Any creature, however lowly, incarnates God's presence and, to the spiritual mind, functions as a symbol, not through an analogy that starts from the creature, but through an inverse analogy that originates in the Creator.[36] Newman, steeped in Alexandrian, Platonic theology, keenly perceived this symbolic quality of the world. To him, the world appeared thoroughly sacramental without being "similar" to the hidden God. Both the total presence of God and the absence of similarity are indicated (though not formalized) in the quoted text, as in many others. The visible world presents no similarity to the invisible one; nevertheless it renders us "sensible of something more than earthly."[37] It even allows an occasional glimpse of that invisible kingdom. Newman refers to such a glimpse when witnessing the rebirth of spring: the world shows forth in secret powers and the hidden source reveals its presence without itself becoming manifest. "What we see is the outward shell of an eternal kingdom and on that kingdom we fix the eyes of our faith."[38]

[35] In his sermon on "The Omnipotence of God the Reason for Faith and Hope."

[36] C.F. Kelley, *Meister Eckhart on Divine Knowledge* (New Haven: Yale University Press, 1977).

[37] Ibid., 965.

[38] Newman, *Parochial Sermons* IV, 13, p. 866.

Perhaps most Platonic in Newman's spirituality is the role he attributes to memory in religious life. It appears in that strangely appealing Easter sermon, "Christ Manifested in Remembrance," a meditation on the Emmaus disciples who recognized Christ only after He had disappeared. Newman broadens the significance of this epiphany in memory to a universal law of divine manifestation, on the basis of John 12:16: "These things understood not His disciples at the first, but when Jesus was glorified, then remembered they that these things were written of Him." No sooner did the travelers to Emmaus begin to recognize Him or He vanished out of their sight. "Such is God's rule in Scripture, to dispense His blessings silently and secretly; so that we do not discern them at the time, except by faith, afterwards only."[39]

Still, much as Newman was influenced by the Alexandrian Fathers and Augustine, he was not a "Platonist." For him, the remembrance of the past gives no direct access to divine truth, as Plato's *anamnesis* did. It merely makes the past event shine with a *new light*, transforming it into a *symbol* of the invisible. "What is dark while it is meeting us, reflects the Sun of Righteousness when it is past."[40] But this world never amounts to *more* than a symbol. It "reflects" the light, it does not become light; intrinsically united to God, it nevertheless remains totally dissimilar. "There is nothing of heaven in the face of society, in the news of the day there is nothing of heaven; in the faces of the many, or of the great or of the rich, or of the busy, there is nothing of heaven; in the words of the eloquent, or the deeds of the powerful, or the counsels of the wise, or the resolves of the lordly, or the pomp of the wealthy, there is nothing of heaven. And yet the Everblessed Spirit of God is here."[41] In this sermon the unique meaning of the

---

[39] Ibid., IV, 17, p. 898.
[40] *Ibid.*, p. 902.
[41] Ibid.

light symbolism that pervades Newman's thought, early and late, stands most clearly revealed. What we know is God's light, not God, but in that light all things come to shine with a divine glow: *In lumine tuo videbimus lumen.* The metaphor discloses the deeper meaning of Newman's words at the most critical period of his life. When laid up in Palermo, at the brink of death, he exclaimed repeatedly in delirium: "I have not sinned against the light." A few weeks later, when a calm at sea kept his ship in the Strait of Bonifacio he wrote the poem: "Lead, kindly Light."

'IN AN ISOLATED AND, PHILOSOPHICALLY, UNINFLUENTIAL WAY' NEWMAN AND OXFORD PHILOSOPHY

Fergus KERR

Anthony Kenny, not having space to describe Newman's "general contribution to philosophy," limits himself to describing and discussing his contribution to the philosophy of religion, and even there only to what he has to say about the nature and justification of religious belief.[1] Thus, one distinguished Oxford philosopher regards Newman's contribution to philosophy as quite extensive, certainly worth discussing, and going well beyond the bounds of religion. While "in recent decades professional philosophers in the analytic tradition have become interested in the topics that concerned him," however, they display little interest in Newman's own contribution. Kenny points to Wittgenstein's much-discussed *On Certainty*, notes that begin with an explicit reference to Newman, and deal with many of the same topics as the *Grammar*, and to the work of Alvin Plantinga — "the most influential philosopher of religion in the analytic tradition at the present time."[2]

The reason for this absence of interest on the part of professional philosophers in the analytic tradition is, Kenny suggests, that Newman's "philosophical background is one that now seems alien to many." Basically, Newman "was a philosopher in the

---

[1] Anthony Kenny, "Newman as a Philosopher of Religion," in David Brown (ed.), *Newman: A Man for Our Time* (London: SPCK, 1990) 98-122.

[2] Kenny, "Newman as a Philosopher of Religion," 100.

British empiricist tradition." He was "nominalistic in tempera-
ment;" his theory of meaning was "strongly imagist." "When he
argues he argues with Locke and Hume." In effect, Kenny
implies, Newman's philosophical work is unread by philosophers
in the analytic tradition, and so in Oxford, because they have
moved beyond empiricism. They no longer argue with Locke and
Hume.

"Among twentieth-century professional philosophers," Kenny
says, "the only one until recently to place Newman in the top rank
was H.H. Price"[3] — "until recently": a phrase that suggests
change is in the air. "Until comparatively recently, and even
today," Cyril Barrett writes, "it may be considered eccentric to
regard Newman as a philosopher."[4]

That H.H. Price should think so highly of Newman's philosophical work would only confirm Kenny's hunch that philosophers in the analytic tradition nowadays ignore it because of its
background in British empiricism. Price, who held the chair of
logic in Oxford from 1935 to 1959, when he was succeeded by
A.J. Ayer, was "regarded by many of his colleagues as a reincar-
nation of old-fashioned empiricism."[5] In *Belief* , the major work
of his old age, published in 1969, he discusses Newman's criticism of Locke's ethics of belief, and, separately, the distinction
between notional and real assent. But the book did not make much
mark among professional philosophers, let alone bring Newman's
ideas into mainstream discussions of epistemology. *Perception*,
his principal work, came out in 1932; it belongs to the dossier of
sense-data epistemologies which were discredited, finally, as far

---

[3] Ibid.

[4] Cyril Barrett, "Newman and Wittgenstein on the Rationality of Religious
Belief," in Ian Ker (ed.), *Newman and Conversion* (Edinburgh: T&T Clark,
1997) 89-99.

[5] Kenny, "Newman as a Philosopher of Religion,"100.

as philosophers in Oxford are concerned, by J.L. Austin's lectures in the late 1950s. Thus, if Newman's philosophy of religion depends on such theories of perception, no post-empiricist philosopher, at Oxford or anywhere else, could take it seriously. That is, roughly, Anthony Kenny's story.

Cyril Barrett tells a rather different story. He is not surprised that "it has taken so long to recognize Newman as a philosopher"[6] — which he clearly considers him to be, and thinks is now happening. Philosophers have not been interested because Newman's interest in philosophy was so limited, preoccupied as he was by theology, apologetics and "matters spiritual and pastoral." Secondly, his knowledge of philosophy was very limited — "apart from Locke, a little of Hume and Mill's *Logic*, he knew hardly any modern philosophy, and seems to have been totally ignorant of German or other Continental philosophy."

No doubt, a philosopher with an interest in the theological implications of certain epistemological issues would not be treated sympathetically in the pervasively secular environment of analytic philosophy. It is less clear that a philosopher's ignorance of the history of philosophy, and of Continental philosophy in particular, would make his work uninteresting to colleagues in the analytic school. As we shall see (Section IV), Newman's knowledge of modern philosophy was, anyway, rather less limited than Barrett seems to assume.

Thirdly, as Barrett reminds us, alluding to Sermon XI, Newman regarded metaphysical proof as "rare, immaterial and difficult to embrace" — again, however, surely an unlikely reason for analytic philosophers to ignore his work. Fourthly, as Barrett says, Newman would have nothing to do with the scientific model of

---

[6] Barrett, "Newman and Wittgenstein on the Rationality of Religious Belief," 89.

the acquisition of truth as a model for explaining religious belief
— a reason, certainly, that would prevent philosophers of a logi-
cal-positivist cast of mind from finding him congenial, but that
should, in principle, have made him a precursor of the many
Oxford philosophers (not to mention Wittgenstein, John Wisdom
and others elsewhere) who were resistant, precisely, to such veri-
ficationist scientism. On the other hand, since he believed that a
rational — though not a scientific — account could be given of
religious belief, he would not be found congenial, Barrett says, by
"Kantians such as Schleiermacher who regarded religious belief
as the product of feeling and intuition, rather than of thought and
reasoning."[7]

None of these reasons for ignoring Newman as a philosopher
seems indisputably obvious. Fashions come and go, in analytic
philosophy as elsewhere, often in ways that are hard to explain:
perhaps that is as much as can be said. It should be noted, however, that two distinguished philosophers, both living in Oxford,
see signs of Newman's being taken seriously — at last — as a
philosopher. [8]

II

There is no entry devoted to John Henry Newman in *The
Oxford Companion to Philosophy*, a beautiful book of over a thousand pages: "the most authoritative and engaging philosophical
reference book in English," according to the blurb. "It gives clear
and reliable guidance to all areas of philosophy and to the ideas of

[7] Barrett, "Newman and Wittgenstein on the Rationality of Religious
Belief," 90.

[8] Anthony Kenny, formerly Master of Balliol College, has been a major
figure in philosophy in Oxford since his book *Action, Emotion and Will*
appeared in 1963; Cyril Barrett, S.J., editor of Wittgenstein's *Lectures and
Conversations on Aesthetics, Psychology & Religious Belief*, 1966, taught at
Warwick University for many years but now resides in Oxford.

all notable philosophers from antiquity to the present day."[9]

Should Newman have had his own entry? It won't do to object that, since he was a theologian, he could have no place in a philosophical reference book: Karl Barth is mentioned in the entry on the history of the philosophy of religion, Bultmann in the article on existentialism, and each gets an entry under his own name, Barth's quite lengthy. Newman, one might argue, is perhaps a fairly minor figure in the history of Western thought, from Thales to Derek Parfit. Perhaps; but Orestes Brownson gets his own entry, twenty lines, "New England social critic, political advocate, religious controversialist, philosopher, and journalist." His conversion to Roman Catholicism in 1844 "caused dismay among his former transcendentalist compatriots; as a Catholic Brownson was as creative, outspoken, and controversial as he had been as a transcendentalist." It is difficult to understand how the editors, admitting Brownson, did not remember Newman or decided to leave him out. Goethe gets an entry, as German poet and thinker, explicitly not a philosopher ("For philosophy in the strict sense I had no organ"), but one who "had a lively appreciation of the works of Kant and other philosophers."

One can always pick holes in a reference book. But Newman is not mentioned even in either of the lengthy entries on the history of the philosophy of religion (by Mark D. Jordan, of the University of Notre Dame) and on problems of the philosophy of religion (Richard G. Swinburne). Interestingly, however, he figures in the entry on Oxford philosophy, as we shall see (Section III).

A Companion to Philosophy of Religion, recently published in Oxford, and running to 650 pages, shows no interest in Newman either, except in the article on "Tradition," as we shall see (Section VII). [10]

---

[9] Ted Honderich (ed.), *The Oxford Companion to Philosophy* (Oxford and New York: Oxford University Press, 1995).

[10] Philip L. Quinn & Charles Taliaferro (eds.), *A Companion to Philosophy of Religion* (Oxford: Blackwell Publishers, 1997).

Neither of these very good and no doubt skilfully market-researched companions to philosophy, which will shape the interests of a generation of philosophy students all over the English-speaking world, will introduce them to Newman. What is it about Newman as a philosopher, or about philosophy as exhibited in these Oxford handbooks, that makes it so easy to ignore the greatest thinker Oxford produced in the nineteenth century? [11]

III

The entry on "Oxford philosophy" in *The Oxford Companion to Philosophy* is by Anthony Quinton: "British philosopher, based in Oxford and a member of the House of Lords," as we read in the entry devoted to him — *The Nature of Things*, his "lengthiest work," exploring the concept of substance, results in "a form of materialism."

Philosophy began in Oxford, Quinton records, in the early thirteenth century, with Robert Grosseteste, flourished in the fourteenth with Duns Scotus and William of Ockham, but, after the Black Death, the heresies of Wyclif and the imposition of ecclesiastical control, Oxford lay "for the most part, philosophically infertile" for some 500 years — thus, until the "anglicized Hegelianism" of the late nineteenth century (T. H. Green, F.H. Bradley). Hobbes and Locke studied in Oxford, true enough, but found the place uncongenial, and "neither became a philosopher until a considerable time after they had left it."

There were, however, two other philosophers, during these barren centuries, whom Quinton recalls as follows: "Two distin-

---

[11] Candidates in the honour school of theology at Oxford may choose "John Henry Newman and the Oxford Movement" from nine options in the optional additional paper "Further Studies in History and Doctrine;" the texts prescribed are *Via Media, Development* chapters 1-5; and *University Sermons* IV, X, XI, XIII and XV. There would be no need to study Newman for the Philosophy of Religion paper.

guished philosophers taught in Oxford around the middle of the nineteenth century in an isolated and, philosophically, uninfluential way: J.H. Newman, drawing on Aristotle, the British Empiricists, and Bishop Butler, and H.L. Mansel, chief disciple of the last important Scottish philosopher, Sir William Hamilton." Quinton even gestures towards a certain continuity in the college precincts across the barren centuries: "Newman's theory of belief and Mansel's theory of the limits of religious thought remotely echo the resistance of Scotus and Ockham to the pretensions of reason in the domain of religious belief."

Mansel (1820-1871), the first Waynflete professor of moral and metaphysical philosophy at Oxford, provoked much hostile criticism, notably from F.D. Maurice and John Stuart Mill, especially because of his Bampton Lectures, *The Limits of Religious Thought* (1858), in which he argued that the truths of religion are not speculative but regulative: like Newman, he does not receive an entry to himself in *The Oxford Companion to Philosophy*.

Though it lingered on in R.G. Collingwood, Hegelian metaphysical idealism was driven out of Oxford, Quinton goes on, partly by J. Cook Wilson and H.A. Prichard, but mainly by the new Cambridge ideas of Russell and Moore "imported with style, rigour and authority by H.H. Price," and in due course "given a more radical turn by Gilbert Ryle." This gave rise to "Oxford philosophy," "linguistic analysis," "logical empiricism," etc., which held sway in the 1950s. But, so Quinton contends, with J.L. Austin's death in 1960, A.J. Ayer's return in 1959, and a focusing of interest on the work of W.V. Quine and other American philosophers, "the ordinary-language school disintegrated and nothing specifically Oxonian has replaced it." In effect, Austin's death ended the hegemony of linguistic analysis; Ayer brought back classical empiricism; and the Americans rehabilitated systematic and speculative metaphysics, in a range of positions from

Quine's naturalized epistemology to Nelson Goodman's irrealism. For almost forty years now, whatever the perception in the wider world, philosophy in Oxford has been marked by great diversity. What is striking about philosophy in Oxford today, Quinton suggests, is that there is now no such thing as "Oxford philosophy."

This would be easily confirmed by a cursory glance at the diversity of courses offered in the very large philosophy faculty in Oxford. While it is impossible to avoid Frege and philosophical logic,[12] it is possible to study (and sit examinations!) in all the great ancient and modern philosophers (though scarcely the medievals), including Hegel, and even Nietzsche and Heidegger, as well as the fashionable Anglophone agenda, ranging from cognitive science to constructing theories of meaning for natural language. The kaleidoscope of philosophical options on offer in Oxford at present, and in traditionally analytic philosophy departments throughout the English-speaking world, is such, then, that no single explanation for ignoring Newman is viable.

Newman is important enough as a philosopher to figure in Quinton's short history of philosophy in Oxford, even if, paradoxically, nowhere else in *The Oxford Companion*. Quinton does not quite say, of course, that Newman *taught philosophy*. As a tutor, Newman certainly *taught* — but what he taught was both more and less than what we now understand by professional philosophy. It is a little odd, however, to speak of his teaching in Oxford "around the middle of the nineteenth century": he had withdrawn from college teaching by 1841; he published the *University Sermons*, his most influential philosophical work, in 1843; and in 1845 he left Oxford for good. It is arguable that his work as a philosopher was even more significant after he left Oxford. If we bring in the notes which, of course, he never intended to publish,

---

[12] A compulsory paper in the joint philosophy/theology honour school.

we find him, in the privacy of his room in Birmingham, thinking more adventurously about philosophical topics than he ever seems to have done in his Oxford days. Perhaps we might say that Newman was not so much a philosopher who taught in Oxford, as a philosopher who was decisively shaped by being taught, and by teaching, in Oxford, but who, from the beginning, in Quinton's phrase, taught "in an isolated and, philosophically, uninfluential way" — at least until now.[13]

IV

Newman's background in British empiricism has not always disqualified him from being respected as an interesting philosopher by Oxford-trained philosophers. On the contrary, that was precisely what made his philosophical work congenial to such philosophers as J.M. Cameron and D.M. MacKinnon.[14] But they reached their appreciation without reading Newman in the light of Edward Sillem's map of Newman's philosophical development[15] — which raises one or two problems.

Sillem's story goes as follows. In the first place, as an undergraduate, Newman was introduced to the work of Aristotle, and in particular to the *Rhetoric, Poetics* and *Nicomachean Ethics*, the

[13] For Anthony Quinton's great respect for Newman see his "The Idea of a University: Newman's and others"," in *From Wodehouse to Wittgenstein: Essays* (London: Carcanet, 1998) 131-153.

[14] For Cameron see, *inter alia* , "Newman and Empiricism," in *Victorian Studies* 4 (1960) 99-117; and "Newman and the Empiricist Tradition," in John Coulson & A.M. Allchin (eds.), *The Rediscovery of Newman: An Oxford Symposium* (London and Melbourne: Sheed and Ward, 1967) 76-96. For MacKinnon see *Newman's University Sermons* with introductory essays by D.M. MacKinnon and J.D. Holmes (London: SPCK, 1970) 9-23, at the end of which MacKinnon expresses his "deep indebtedness" to Cameron.

[15] Edward Sillem (ed.), *The Philosophical Notebook of John Henry Newman*, vol. 1: *General Introduction to the Study of Newman's Philosophy* (Louvain: Nauwelaerts, 1969) 149-240.

set books. This should have made Newman congenial in the hey-
day of "Oxford philosophy." One cannot read Gilbert Ryle and
J.L. Austin and fail to see their debt to Aristotle. Even if Aristotle's *Rhetoric* was not a set text in their undergraduate days, they
were clearly much closer in spirit to the *Ethics* than the *Metaphysics.*

(2) Secondly, Newman was exposed in the Oriel common room to
Whately and the Noetics — his own colleagues and elders who
were continuing Paley's evidentialist apologetics and who held, in
Whately's key formulation, that "all Reasoning, on whatever subject, is one and the same process, which may be clearly exhibited
in the form of Syllogisms."[16] In effect, that is the lesson of *Language, Truth and Logic*, the manifesto of logical positivism that
A.J. Ayer published in Oxford in 1936.

(3) Third, Sillem lists the decisive impact on the young Newman of
Bishop Butler's *Analogy of Religion*, "an era in [his] religious
opinions," as Newman himself noted.[17] According to MacKinnon,
Newman's *University Sermons* are "a very valuable commentary
on Butler's views," specifically in connection with the idea of
morality as "something self-evident, luminous, categorically
imperative" — "we recognize its authority upon us without being
compelled to wait for the solution of this or that cosmological or
theological riddle."[18] On Sillem's reading, on the other hand, Butler did not so much confront Newman with "the categorical
imperative of conscience," as MacKinnon claims, but "saved him
from the attractions of rationalism and opened his mind to a dif-

---

[16] Sillem, *Philosophical Notebook*, 164, citing Richard Whately, *Elements of Logic* (1826), p. 207, a standard textbook in Oxford for decades to come.

[17] Ibid., p. 170, citing *Apologia* (Oxford: Oxford University Press, 1931) 113.

[18] D.M. MacKinnon, *A Study in Ethical Theory* (London: Adam & Charles Black, 1957) 184.

ferent form of thinking theocentrically about mysteries both in religion and in nature, and impressed upon him the fact that one and the same God is at work in the Church and in the whole order of nature."[19] In effect, for Sillem, Butler's *Analogy* brought Newman close to the Christian Platonism that would become more and more important, as he read the Fathers, whereas for MacKinnon, it "was another manifestation of that same subtle empiricist temper which he found so congenial."[20]

The fourth element in Newman's intellectual formation was, (4) then, so Sillem maintains, his reading in the Alexandrian Fathers, Clement and Origen — the "broad philosophy" that "carried me away," "the philosophy, not the theological doctrine," "music to my inward ear," "as if the response to ideas, which, with little external to encourage them, I had cherished so long" — as he said, in famous phrases.[21]

While these four are by far the most important "sources" of Newman's philosophy, Sillem holds, he lists four more, less decisive yet helping to shape his mind as a philosopher.

The first of these is Newman's familiarity with the natural (5) philosophies of Isaac Newton and Francis Bacon and the advances made in mathematics — something that saved him from the hostility to science that characterised so many contemporary divines.[22]

Next, and only now, Sillem lists Newman's debt to British (6) empiricism.[23] Without making a to-do about it, Sillem expresses considerable scepticism about the claims made by Martin D'Arcy and James Collins that Newman owed so much to Locke that he

---

[19] Sillem, *Philosophical Notebook*, 181.
[20] MacKinnon, "Introduction," *Newman's University Sermons*, 14.
[21] Sillem, *Philosophical Notebook*, 181, citing *Apologia*, 127-128.
[22] Ibid., 183-191.
[23] Ibid., 191-203.

was in effect himself simply a British empiricist.[24] He also doubts
J.M. Cameron's claims about the influence of Hume.[25] Though
Newman possessed Hume's *Essays and Treatises* (1770 edition),
"as far as I can see," Sillem says, "we have no evidence that he
ever read anything by Hume from the day he went up to Oxford
save the *Essay on Miracles*." As for Locke, though the *Essay concerning Human Understanding* was probably the first work of philosophy he ever read, and though he possessed the attractive three-
volume 1751 edition of Locke's works, "there are very few of
Newman's pencil markings and marginal remarks" in these volumes. "What there are," according to Sillem, "come only in the
fourth book," and, judging by the handwriting, these look as
though they were made much later than his Oxford days, probably
when he was writing the *Grammar*.

Sillem's case, then, is that, on the evidence that we have, <u>Newman
never read Hume and only studied Locke</u> so late in his life, that it is
inappropriate to read him as indebted to the empiricist tradition to
any serious degree. We return to this below (Section VI).

(7)   The third of these less significant influences on Newman's
philosophical ideas, Sillem argues, was <u>Abraham Tucker</u>.[26] Newman possessed the two-volume edition of 1842, edited by
Tucker's grandson St John Mildmay, and, according to Sillem, he
made a few pencil markings in the first volume, about Tucker's
theory of the acquisition of knowledge in experience. Sillem is out
to persuade us, from internal textual evidence, that the *University
Sermons* exhibit a "kind of thinking" that has its "natural roots,"
not in the empiricism of Locke but in the philosophical psychology of Tucker.[27] While readers as different as Paley and Hazlitt

[24] Ibid., 192.
[25] Ibid., 203.
[26] Ibid., 203-220.
[27] Ibid., 220.

produced abbreviated editions, and the complete version was reprinted, it may be doubted if Newman, or many others, ever read Tucker's work *in extenso*.

Finally, Edward Sillem catalogues what he regards as *very* minor influences. Newman had read rather more Berkeley than the remark in the *Apologia* suggests, but no more than to see that he was not a Berkeleian.[28] He was interested in the Scottish Common Sense school. His volume of Reid is "extensively marked and a large number of notes are pencilled around the text" — including the following note, early in the book: "Reid is certainly shallow — i.e. not subtle, he mistakes others."[29] In 1857 he started to read John Stuart Mill's *System of Logic*, when he was hoping to return to England, no doubt, as Sillem plausibly suggests,[30] to find out what was happening intellectually. He must have been confirmed in his opposition to the desire to conduct the moral sciences like natural sciences and mathematics: Whately's principle all over again.

Sillem's list of Newman's sources as a philosopher concludes with his disappointment that there was no one in Rome in the 1840s who was capable of interesting him in Thomas Aquinas.[31] He had possessed the complete works since 1818 but, though there are plenty of pencil markings to prove that he quite often consulted Thomas's works, we may agree with Sillem that Newman's mind was never seriously influenced philosophically by Aquinas.

V

Sillem's minor sources include the "great interest"[32] which Newman took in Chalybaeus's *Historical Development of Speculative Philosophy from Kant to Hegel*. While Newman could not

---

[28] Ibid., 220-221.
[29] Ibid., 223.
[30] Ibid., 224.
[31] Ibid., 234-238.

read German, and his copy of the Meiklejohn translation of Kant's
Critique of Pure Reason has half the pages uncut, his notes in the
Chalybaeus book, fragmentary and gnomic as they are, yet "of
extraordinary interest," as Cameron says,[33] are a fascinating
glimpse into Newman's mind and a testimony to his considerable
insight as a philosopher.

Consider the following three remarks:

> N.B. In treating the subject of metaphysics, one should begin with
> remarks about the *assumption* of supposing that we must refer
> everything to *one* principle.[34]

> Another remark to be made is (agst all *my* life long convictions,
> their obstinate assumption that all things must be reduced to *one*
> principle.[35]

> Observe how the Ionian, Italic etc philosophers were always aiming
> at *one* cause. The idea is deeply fixed in human nature, & therefore
> cannot be lightly spoken of in these Germans. Besides, what do
> Theists aim at but *one* first cause? [36]

Then, as now, courses in metaphysics, whether following Aristotle, Suarez or Wolff, usually plunge straight into the standard
topics: first principles and causes, being as being, the actual and
the possible, etc. As Sillem rightly maintains, Newman's reading

[32] Ibid., 227. Chalybaeus's book, translated into English by Alfred
Edersheim, was published, with an introduction by Sir William Hamilton
(Edinburgh: T&T Clark, 1854).

[33] J.M.Cameron, "John Henry Newman and the Tractarian Movement," in
Ninian Smart et al. (eds.), *Nineteenth Century Religious Thought in the West*,
(Cambridge: Cambridge University Press, 1985) 2:69-109. See p. 108.

[34] Sillem, *Philosophical Notebook*, 232.

[35] Ibid., 228.

[36] Ibid., 233.

of Chalybaeus only confirmed him in his life long conviction that a purely *a priori* metaphysics was purely illusory. The whole cast of his mind was "towards reflection on the concrete realities we know in experience." He expected reflection on experience to be unified in theology; but he objected to the way that the German idealists were, as it seemed, "trying to begin where a system of metaphysics ought to end," as Sillem puts it.

Sillem's discussion is very acute. In the light of more recent developments, however, Newman's remarks seem even more perceptive and radical. Wittgenstein once thought of starting his book with a note on metaphysics as magic, as trying to keep something sublime spellbound in one's words.[37] Derrida, and many other labourers in his wake, seek to uncover as *the* metaphysical exigency the compulsively repeated choice of an origin held to be simple, intact, normative, self-identical, etc., so as *then* to think in terms of complexity, diversity, etc.[38] Here, in 1859, as he read Chalybaeus' expositions of one German philosophical system after another, the thought came to Newman that no one should enter into the technicalities of any particular system without questioning the very assumption motivating the whole enterprise: German idealism, *Identitätsphilosophie*, monism. Why *must* we refer everything to one principle? And why to *one* principle? Prior to getting to grips with texts or problems in metaphysics, Newman suggests, we need to consider the assumption — the presupposition, even the prejudice — that everything "must" be referred to one single principle at all.

Suspicion of every "must" in philosophical discourse is a very characteristic Wittgensteinian move. Learning to be suspicious of

[37] "Remarks on Frazer's *Golden Bough* ," in James C. Klagge & Alfred Nordmann (eds.), *Philosophical Occasions 1912-1951* (Indianapolis and Cambridge: Hackett, 1993) 116.

[38] See, for example, Jacques Derrida, *Limited Inc* (Evanston, IL.: Northwestern University Press, 1988) 93.

the drive to unify, the overwhelming will to homogenize, to reduce multiplicity and difference to unity, the many to some *one* — whether the pure and enduring self-identity of what is as such, whether substance, subject, will, law, or whatever — has become a standard strategy in post-Nietzschean philosophical work. Philosophers like Richard Rorty — "modern philosophy amounts to an attempt by human beings to wrest power from God"[39] — contend that the tradition from the Enlightenment onwards that has supposedly renounced theology continues, compulsively, to operate crypto-theologically. The longing to find the one single unique cause is deeply rooted in human nature, Newman sees: it needs more serious investigation, at the threshold of metaphysics, than Newman suspects "these Germans" of allowing and achieving.

"Newman disliked metaphysics of the German kind," Kenny says, quoting the familiar passage about how "rare and immaterial (if I may use the words) is metaphysical proof."[40] But Newman goes on to speak of how difficult it is to cope with metaphysics "even when presented to us by philosophers in whose clearness of mind and good sense we fully confide." He is surely not thinking of German idealists; it is much more likely he means Locke. Newman may well have "disliked" the German philosophers about whom he read in Chalybaeus. But his questioning was not at the level of their attempts at proof, however rarefied and sophisticated, but rather at the preliminary "archaic" level, so to speak, where he wanted to lay bare the unconsidered and even unconscious motivation of idealist metaphysics, which he suspected of residing in a predetermined insistence on explicating all diversity in terms of a preconception of totalizing unity.

[39] *Truth and Progress: Philosophical Papers* (Cambridge: Cambridge University Press, 1998) 3:143.

[40] Kenny, "Newman as a Philosopher of Religion," 100; Sermon XI.

Chalybaeus' exposition of German philosophy was not a "source" of Newman's philosophy in any sense, however minor. Rather, his notes on what he read in Chalybaeus display the mature Newman's near-Derridean skill at locating the repressed other, so to speak, in the mainstream metaphysical tradition. He did not work out the implications of these insights; but they testify to his philosophical originality and acumen.

VI

On the other hand, for all Sillem's insistence on how little evidence we have that he read them, surely the British empiricists were far more important in Newman's intellectual formation than Sillem allows.

In his introduction to the 1970 paperback edition of *University Sermons*, written of course without knowing Sillem's work or Newman's *Philosophical Notebook*, Donald MacKinnon hails them as "one of the achieved English masterpieces on the crucial theological issue of the relations of faith and reason," insisting that "no one who is seriously concerned with the epistemology of Christian belief can neglect them." He concentrates on "bringing out something of the pedigree, the subtlety, the complexity, and the profoundly interrogative character of Newman's explorations in these sermons."[41] At once he refers to "the great British empiricists," contending that "it is one element in the importance of these Sermons that they convey their author's serious engagement with certain aspects of the British empiricist tradition, in its first great crystallization in the work of Locke, Berkeley, and Hume." While detecting little influence of Berkeley on Newman's thought, and recalling that the *Grammar* engages explicitly with Locke, MacKinnon maintains that Newman's "study of Hume is perva-

---

[41] MacKinnon, "Introduction," *Newman's University Sermons*, 9.

sive in the Sermons." Clearly, as one who respected Hume as a great philosopher, MacKinnon finds the evidence of Newman's familiarity with Hume on the page as he reads — while, of course, never making any attempt to demonstrate, biographically or textually, that Newman was acquainted with any particular passage in Hume's writings. Newman "sought to argue with the empiricists on their own ground," rather than (like some of his contemporaries) "taking refuge in the declaration of an alternative metaphysical evaluation of the human mind" (German idealism, presumably). Newman "recognised that the empiricist tradition was an inherently complex one, and that the work of an unquestioned philosophical genius such as David Hume was not likely to yield all its secrets to men who sought to convey its essence in two or three easily assimilable formulae." In support of all these claims, presumably MacKinnon would simply have referred anyone who doubted them to re-read Newman.

Furthermore, "Newman's own informality and untidiness, interrupted by passages of sharp and rigorous argument, recalls the complex and in places self-contradictory character of Locke's *Essay*." Indeed, "for all the differences of their form," MacKinnon suggests, "there is a certain spiritual kinship between Newman's *University Sermons* and Locke's *Essay*." "Spiritual" may seem an odd epithet: what MacKinnon means, as he goes on to say, is that we become aware of this kinship as soon as we try "to identify Newman's views concerning the relation between faith and reason" — "nothing but the work as a whole is enough to show the reader what those views were."

The problem is not easy to resolve. On the one hand, with his careful study of the books in Newman's library, the pencil markings, etc., Edward Sillem concludes that, on the evidence available, we have to say that Newman read little by Locke and almost nothing by Hume. On the other hand, on the evidence of Newman's writings, MacKinnon takes it for granted that they are per-vaded by knowledge of Hume and Locke.

But how much of a book need Newman have read before begin-ning to appropriate ideas (as perhaps with Tucker) or to repudiate them (as with his reading of a history of German idealism)? Wittgenstein, for example, read far more than once was said but we know too that his fairly wide reading in philosophy and in other subjects, was often little more than riffling through the pages or concentrating on a few pages with pencil in hand — his "Remarks on Frazer's *Golden Bough*," the most interesting set of notes in the *Nachlass* on the nature of religion, comes to mind.[42] Reading it with a friend, Wittgenstein interrupted so often with cries of horror at Frazer's rationalistic explanations of primitive religious customs that they never got further than a little way into the first of the thirteen volumes. Perhaps, like Wittgenstein in this as in other respects, Newman absorbed a great deal without read-ing every single word of the books in his possession. Perhaps he read all the Locke he needed to. In any case, he must have spent many hours in college libraries perusing books in editions which he never himself owned — books, too, which he never even wanted to possess.

Sillem, in any case, has a fairly strict definition of empiricist philosophy in mind. MacKinnon, however, distinguishes three levels of empiricism.[43] First, we might mean the doctrine that "all material concepts must be cashable in terms of sensory and/or introspective experience" (sense data theories, phenomenalism, Mill's "objects are the permanent possibilities of sensation," etc.). Secondly, "more sophisticatedly," we might deny that there are any synthetic *a priori* truths (logical positivism, perhaps Quine's

---

[42] See Ray Monk, *Ludwig Wittgenstein: The Duty of Genius* (London: Jonathan Cape, 1990) 310.

[43] MacKinnon, "Introduction," *Newman's University Sermons*, 11.

insistence on philosophy as a branch of science, etc.). But we may conceive empiricism "more loosely as a temper of mind that acknowledges the authority of a vast number of very different sorts of intellectual procedure, of methods of moving from premises to conclusion, as appropriate in one field as they are inappropriate in another."

True, as MacKinnon says, Newman no doubt learnt from Aristotle's *Ethics* that an inquiry can only achieve the precision (*akribeia*) that its subject-matter permits. But "the Humean influence is strong." Newman "reveals the depth of his debt to Hume," MacKinnon maintains, in the way that he plays the claims of an informal over against a strictly formalized logic. Without denying the role of syllogistic, he pointed to the ways in which knowledge is actually acquired and truth discovered. This is the Newman who had the "implicit conviction that the empiricist tradition, understood as conveying counsels of flexibility and subtlety in assessing the rationality of intellectual procedures, provides the surest context within which to attack the question of the relation of faith and reason."[44]

We are a "long way from the self-confident empiricism that we associate with the logical positivism of the thirties," MacKinnon concludes, "but we are still very close to other emphases equally characteristic of the empiricist tradition." He specifies as follows: "There is the steadfast refusal to over-simplify; there is the insistence that the kind of arguments we offer in any field must be appropriate to the field about which we are arguing; there is the admission of the areas of which we must plead agnosticism." Above all, "throughout these Sermons we are repeatedly invited to break the cake of custom, to refuse to be bound in the fetters of our prejudices, to recognize that in the dominant philosophical tra-

---

[44] Ibid., 16.

dition of the age emphasis is laid on the hazard, the element of openness and risk implicit in inductive procedure, in contradistinction from the security enjoyed by the man who will only argue *e praecognitis et praeconcessis.*[45] Indeed, for Newman, "such an openness as the empiricist temper counsels is something in which men could discern a parable of the sort of openness of mind that faith demanded."[46] Now, paradoxically, the spirit of empiricism turns out to be, not the ruthless scientism of the young Ayer but, on the contrary, what MacKinnon characterizes elsewhere, in connection with Butler and Locke, as "an implicit hostility to rationalistic self-confidence, a sceptical unwillingness to delimit *a priori.*"[47] What was "profoundly inimical to the empiricist temper as [Newman] had received it," MacKinnon concludes, was when men "imprisoned themselves in the doubtless comforting womb of their own established assurance that the secrets of the world were known to them, at least in principle, the methods required for their perfect study at their finger-tips."[48]

Ieuan Williams, quite independently of MacKinnon, finds a somewhat similar complexity in Hume.[49] On the one hand, there is the Hume admired by A.J Ayer and others, who seeks "to explain the principles of human nature," to produce a scientific account of human nature consistent with Newtonian physics, very much the kind of scientism, positivism, physicalism, etc., that Newman encountered in Whately, and which is very common in philosophy today (though much more in American universities than in Oxford). There is the other side to Hume, however, who insists

[45] Ibid., 19-20.

[46] Ibid., 21.

[47] MacKinnon, *A Study of Ethical Theory*, 198-199.

[48] MacKinnon, "Introduction," *Newman's University Sermons*, 21.

[49] Ieuan Williams, "Faith and Scepticism: Newman and the Naturalist Tradition," *Philosophical Investigations* 15 (1992) 51-66.

that "Nature by an absolute and uncontrollable necessity has determined us to judge as well as to breathe and feel," and who declares that "all reasonings concerning causes and effects are derived from nothing but custom; and that belief is more properly an act of the sensitive, than of the cogitative part of our nature." Along this line, Williams maintains, Newman emphasizes a human being's nature as active and operating instinctively, rather than rational and primarily contemplative being. In this he would be following out the naturalistic conception of human life high-lighted in Hume by Norman Kemp Smith,[50] rather than the more familiar "unmitigated scepticism." Williams argues, very instructively, that, though Newman's struggle against scepticism may not completely succeed, his efforts are well worth retrieving, since the *Grammar* "occupies an interesting and important place in that tradition which began with Hume and certainly did not come to an end with Newman." Here, in fact, according to Ieuan Williams, the *Grammar* leads straight into Wittgenstein's *On Certainty*, which places Newman's work at the centre of at least one current debate.

VII

The notion of custom brings us, finally, to Basil Mitchell's remarks about Newman in the entry on tradition in the Blackwell *Companion to Philosophy of Religion.*

In his essay in *Newman after a hundred years,*[51] Mitchell notes that Newman's importance as a philosopher "is only now beginning to be acknowledged." The reason that he offers for the long neglect

---

[50] Originally in "The Naturalism of David Hume," a series of articles in *Mind* (1905).

[51] Basil Mitchell, "Newman as a Philosopher," in Ian Ker & Alan G. Hill (eds.), *Newman After a Hundred Years* (Oxford: Clarendon Press, 1990) 223-246.

differs from those suggested by Kenny and Barrett (Section I). Newman was "firmly rooted in the empiricist tradition of Locke and
Hume," and far removed from idealist metaphysics, facts which
should have made him congenial to philosophers for much of the last
century, except that they have been "predominantly hostile or indifferent to religious belief." Newman was, of course, deeply unhappy
with Locke's claim that the existence of God is a truth provable by a
combination of the cosmological and teleological arguments — the
position — "very much more thoroughly worked out" — that
Mitchell finds in Richard Swinburne's book *The Existence of God*.[52]

Be that as it may, he outlines, in the entry on tradition,[53] the
familiar story: modern philosophy, in Descartes, Locke, Hume,
Kant, and the others, rests on repudiation of ecclesiastical authority and rejection of tradition as a bearer of knowledge. We have to
rely on reason and experience alone; the individual alone bears
responsibility for his or her beliefs, "the typical modern hero is
free, independent, and lonely," etc. However, now that philosophers (in the analytic tradition[54]) begin to understand that everyone, and not just the religious believer, is influenced by antecedent
assumptions which are carried by some tradition of thought or
practice, Newman's objections to Locke's failure to recognize this
brings the *University Sermons* and the *Grammar* into a current
debate. Indeed, Mitchell lists them in his short bibliography. He
goes on to raise serious problems with Newman's vindication of
tradition, but that only shows that Newman is being treated as a
worthwhile interlocutor in the conversation.

The only philosopher Mitchell actually names is Alasdair Mac-
Intyre, who, though he taught there for a few years, would hardly

---

[52] Ibid., 241

[53] See *A Companion to Philosophy of Religion*, 591-597.

[54] Interestingly, half a dozen books about the origins of analytic philosophy
have recently been published by philosophers trained in that tradition.

be everyone's idea of an Oxford philosopher. In the book that grew from his Carlyle Lectures in Oxford in 1982, MacIntyre acknowledged a "massive debt" to Newman, describing him as "a far more important theorist of tradition" (than Edmund Burke), generally ignored, however, because he worked primarily as a theologian.[55] MacIntyre directs his readers to *The Arians of the Fourth Century* and *An Essay on the Development of Christian Doctrine* for Newman's account of tradition: perhaps a direction not very likely to be followed in a sustained way by many philosophers, however much they may wish to learn from a precursor in this debate.

The last paragraph of a lecture recently delivered in Oxford goes as follows:

> The feature of language that really matters is rather this: that a natural language, the sort of language into which human beings are first initiated, serves as a repository of tradition, a storehouse of historically accumulated wisdom about what is a reason for what. The tradition is subject to reflective modification by each generation that inherits it. Indeed, a standing obligation to engage in critical reflection is itself part of the inheritance ... But if an individual human being is to realize her potential of taking her place in that succession, which is the same thing as acquiring a mind, the capacity to think and act intentionally, at all, the first thing that needs to happen is for her to be initiated into a tradition as its stands.[56]

A footnote directs us to the work of Hans Georg Gadamer, the onetime student of Heidegger and a major figure in what is increasingly known as hermeneutical (over against analytic) philosophy. This retrieval of the concept of tradition, paradoxically in the John Locke Lectures given in Oxford in 1991 by John

---

[55] Alasdair MacIntyre, *Whose Justice? Which Rationality?* (London: Duckworth, 1988) 353-354.

[56] John McDowell, *Mind and World* (Cambridge, MA: Harvard University Press, 1994) 126.

McDowell, very much an Oxford philosopher (though now at Pittsburgh), clearly moves philosophy in Oxford on to the post-modern agenda. McDowell never mentions Newman, and the theological amalgam of his thinking may prove too much for most philosophers to swallow. Yet, with the empiricist cast of his mind as defined by Donald MacKinnon, and his labour on the role of tradition, Newman need not be the isolated figure, in philosophy, that he was in his liftetime.

'WHAT DO YOU WANT'?
NEWMAN'S OCEAN OF
INTERMINABLE SCEPTICISM

WILLIAM MYERS

1. *The Economical Principle:* The Philosophical Notebook

The purpose of this paper is to explain why Newman's economical principle is both a dangerous and an excellent idea.

"The principle of the Economy," according to *Apologia Pro Vita Sua*, "comes under the head of Prudence" and relates primarily to "religious conduct or statement."[1] But Newman also refers us to his argument in *The Arians of the Fourth Century* (1833) that human consciousness can only entertain "shadowy representations of realities," and that *everything* we feel, think and say is modified and limited by how we feel, think and say it. When the mind first masters this idea, he admits, it seems "to have cut all the ties which bind it to the universe, and to be floated off upon the ocean of interminable scepticism." God, of course, "cannot deceive," so the information supplied by the senses "must be practically certain." Nevertheless *all* our thinking remains "philosophically inaccurate."[2]

This idea re-emerges in the last University Sermon. The same mathematical fact, Newman points out, can be *represented* in both a curve and an algebraic equation. Different mathematical mediums can thus express the "same necessary truths," but we have no

---

[1] John Henry Newman, *Apologia Pro Vita Sua*, edited with an Introduction and Notes, by William Oddie, Everyman's Library (London: J. M. Dent, 1993) 354.

[2] John Henry Cardinal Newman, *The Arians of the Fourth Century*, 5th ed. (London: Pickering and Co., 1883) 75-76.

idea what those truths are "except in the terms of such economical representations."[3] Gottlob Frege would later make precisely
this point about mathematical functions.[4] However it is only in
The Philosophical Notebook - begun in 1859 and continued inter-
mittently until the end of Newman's life - that the implications of
these ideas are finally clarified.

The passage quoted from *The Arians of the Fourth Century* is
copied back into the *Notebook*.[5] The *Notebook* also returns to the
problems of mathematical truth. Temporal and spatial data, Newman notes, can be *represented* in both differentials and fluxions.
But while fluxions are minutely related to the idea of motion, differentials are wholly independent of space and time. From which
it would appear that space and time are themselves economies.[6]

This thinking is based on a remarkably modern understanding
of *representational systems*. Let us take, therefore, a modern
example. The sound track on an old film translates temporal relations between sounds into spatial relations between shapes: in
effect, it eliminates the temporal dimension, while *exactly* pre-
serving what may be called the *form* of the sound- waves. The
Notebook applies this principle to space as well as time. The entire
phenomenal universe, Newman suggests, may be like the sound
track on a film - the *formal representation* of a reality which in
itself is otherwise unthinkable, as sound in itself is unseeable. A

---

[3] John Henry Newman, *Newman's University Sermons: Fifteen Sermons
Preached before the University of Oxford 1826-43*, with Introductory Essays by
D. M. MacKinnon and J. D. Holmes, 2nd impression (London: SPCK, 1979) 345.

[4] Gottlob Frege, "Function and Concept," in Brian McGuiness (ed.), *Collected Papers on Mathematics, Logic, and Philosophy* (Oxford: Basil Blackwell,
1984) 40.

[5] John Henry Newman, *The Philosophical Notebook*, Edward Sillem (ed.), 2
vols. (Louvain: Nauwelaerts Publishing House, 1970) 2:65, 67.

[6] Ibid., 2:110-119. Newman's extended efforts in these pages to relate this
basic insight to the vagaries of the binomial theorem are intensely interesting but
outside the scope of this paper.

recent theorist, Slavoj Žižek, has argued that "the relativity of time and space" could not be formulated "prior to our age."[7] But in July 1860, we find Newman wondering whether there is "any where absolute size? or absolute distance? Need space universal be more than a point?"[8] Six years later he suggests that, as "space has three dimensions, perhaps also has time. Succession is length ... Perhaps there is a way of looking at time, such, that myriads of millions of centuries may be the millionth part of a second, or a point."[9] This is not exactly Einstein, but it is emphatically not Newton either, nor even Kant. Elsewhere in the *Notebook* Newman writes, "I don't believe in the existence of space as a reality ... I don't believe in time."[10]

But the principle of economies surely has its limits, if not at the level of material reality, at least at the human level. Music can be represented in digital blips, but isn't an actual performance what is really there? Perhaps; but no single performance of a piece of music *is* that music, if only because every performance works on memories or anticipations of other performances and other pieces. Nor is the score the music *in itself*, the music *as such* - a further reading might yield new insights even to the composer. Thus what Newman says of the content of mathematical expressions applies also to music - it cannot be accessed *as such*. Is this true of all experience?

The suggestion seems counter-intuitive. The *Notebook*, accordingly, shows Newman trying to identify something that *can* be accessed immediately, the "raw or pure effect of the senses," as against the mind's "power of creation or origination ...[or] combi-

[7] Slavoj Žižek, *The Metastases of Enjoyment: Six Essays on Woman and Causality* (London, New York: Verso, 1994) 200.

[8] Newman, *Philosophical Notebook*, 2:125.

[9] Ibid., 2:165.

[10] Ibid., 2:39.

nation."[11] Initially, he is "quite certain" that simple introspection will confirm the distinction and establish the mind's indpendent powers. He cites the case of the man who "laughed the second time he was racked: He said the pain could not be repeated." He himself had "the nerve of a tooth cauterised." He "never had such pain in [his] life." A subsequent, more protracted operation was much less horrible. "I recollect at the time," he notes, "attributing the difference ... to the novelty and want of novelty," the former being raw or pure, the latter felt in relation. It would seem, he concludes, that the "objects ... presented by the senses are unmeaning, till they are interpreted by mind; & the mind interprets out of its own resources."[12]

But characteristically he gives a hearing to "the other side"[13] as well, and comes to the (for him) startling, and very Positivist conclusion that it is at least arguable that accumulating sense experience on its own might account, first, for knowledge of the self, second, for knowledge of another like the self, and, third, for knowledge of "the idea of person. I am one person - he another ... here," Newman observes, "a vast deal ... is gained from sense without any origination of the mind - except so far as faculties & operations have been brought into use."[14] Mill could not have put it more strongly. Elsewhere Newman suggests that as the mind interprets "the senses by its own ideas, so ... that the information supplied by experience thro' the senses interprets the experience of the mind." From this, he argues, it follows that even conscience is indescribable "except from the example & analogy of sensible experiences."[15]

[11] Ibid., 2:93.
[12] Ibid., 2:95.
[13] Ibid., 2:97.
[14] Ibid., 2:99.
[15] Ibid., 2:96.

He accordingly changes the original assertion that he was "quite certain" introspection would disclose the distinctiveness of the mind's native powers from the "raw or pure effect of the senses;" he now recognises that this is the case only "at first sight;"[16] and six months after his initial speculations on the subject, he returns to the example of the man about to be racked a second time, and now concludes that the second racking would make recall of the first impossible, because the victim would now be able to compare the first experience with the second. "So, when a man has once committed a crime, henceforth he cannot view it with the same eyes as before he had committed it. Thus," he concludes "it is plain, we cannot ascertain what our nature witnesses [relative] to this or that"[17] - in the case of conscience and in the case of acute pain. Subsequent observations in the Notebook reinforce this conclusion. Newman recalls, for example, seeing "something as if on the floor near [him] and [saying] 'What dirty piece of carpet is that?' It turned out to be the sleeve of [his] cotta, which was clean from the wash."[18] Another time, he found his tea "unpleasant" until he realised it was coffee - "and very good coffee." But he now accepts that none of these examples register the "raw or pure effect of the senses." They are all experiences of difference from established "combinations." But if all experience "may depend on relation,"[19] there is no escape from economies.

This was not an insight original to Newman. Already in 1830, Sir William Hamilton was arguing that, since all phenomena depend on "difference," and even "mind and matter ... are known only in correlation and contrast ... [every] conception of self nec-

16 Ibid., 2:93.
17 Ibid., 2:88.
18 Ibid., 2:123.
19 Ibid., 2:110.

essarily involves a conception of not-self."[20] But if I am always dimly aware of something else when I focus on self, no account of "me" can be more than an economy, a story conditioned by the split between what is variously felt as not-me, and whatever it is that does the feeling.

Newman knew Hamilton's work well, and we find a similar argument in the Notebook. The soul, he asserts, must be roused by "some external stimulus" if it is to reflect upon itself, and thereby gain "the notion of unity ... individuality ... and ... independent existence."[21] "'Sentio, ergo sum' ['I feel, therefore I am'] ... from what I have experience of I argue the certainty of that of which I have not experience, viz. my existence, my existence being a fact external to consciousness."[22] Self cannot be known immediately (it has to be inferred from a primordial sensation). This argument takes him to the threshold of Ludwig Wittgenstein's case against solipsism and private languages. He would agree, in effect, with the Wittgensteinian view that it is impossible for anyone to "make a discriminating reference to himself in complete detachment from his body."[23]

Anyone familiar with psychoanalytic and literary theory as it has developed in the last forty years or so will also have encountered ideas like these, if in a rather different intellectual context. Newman's analysis of the "raw or pure effect of the senses" is precisely how Jacques Lacan analyses "the Real." As the neo-Lacanian Žižek puts it, "the Real, qua trauma, is not the ultimate 'unspeakable' truth ... but that which makes every articulated

---

[20] [Sir William Hamilton], "Philosophy of Perception," *The Edinburgh Review* 50 (Edinburgh: Ballantyne & Co., 1830)165.

[21] Newman, *Philosophical Notebook*, 2:23.

[22] Ibid., 2:78.

[23] David Pears, *The False Prison: A Study of the Development of Wittgenstein's Philosophy, 2 vols.* (Oxford: The Clarendon Press, 1988) 2:240.

symbolic truth for ever 'not all' ... [and] makes it impossible to 'tell everything'"[24] - it is the horror that the twice-racked man feels when he realises that the second racking makes it impossible for him to describe the "raw or pure" effect of the first. Moreover, the idea that the self is known only in conjunction with a primitive sensation corresponds with Lacan's famous "l'objet petit a," the little "something else" always present in self-awareness.[25] For Lacan, self-awareness "is bound up with that which determines it - namely, a privileged object, which has emerged from some primal separation."[26] This structural gap in self-awareness takes us to the epicentre of the economical principle.

Newman would not have been at all surprised to find he had thus anticipated later thinkers like Wittgenstein and Lacan. On the day he clarified his "sentio, ergo sum," he wrote in the Notebook, "if there is any thing at once new & good" in a writer's thinking about subjects of this kind, "years must elapse, the writer must be long dead, before it is acknowledged and received."[27] He was convinced that the individual mind has idiosyncratic ways of "abstracting" from the data of experience, which are independent of the "logical evolutions of science."[28] These, once again in proto-Wittgensteinian fashion, he was inclined to regard as "a rule of the game, not in the nature of things." Logic, Wittgenstein writes, "takes its rise ... from an urge to understand the basis, or essence, of everything empirical ... However ... it is of the essence

---

[24] Slavoj Žižek, *The Plague of Fantasies* (London, New York: Verso, 1997) 216.

[25] See Jacques Lacan, *Ecrits: A Selection*, trans. Alan Sheridan (London: Routledge, 1993) xi

[26] Jacques Lacan, *The Four Fundamental Concepts of Psycho-analysis*, Jacques-Alain Miller (ed.), Alan Sheridan (trans.) (London: Penguin Books, 1994) 83.

[27] Newman, *Philosophical Notebook*, 2:86.

[28] Ibid., 2:132.

of our investigation that we do not seek to learn anything new by
it. We want to understand something that is already in plain
view."[29]

Sir Isaac Newton exemplifies this principle for Newman. In
1865, a proof was at last discovered for "Newton's rule for
ascertaining the imaginary roots of equations." What pleased
Newman about this discovery was that the proof had been so
long in coming, and that Sir Isaac himself had not needed it,
because he had seen it "by his genius. In like manner," Newman
suggests, "common sense may anticipate evidence in the matter
or religion, and the certainty of the Catholic may be justified by
the philosopher ages hence."[30] One of his own obiter dicta, illustrates this very point. "As sound goes higher & lower than a
given ear," he asks, "why not sight than a given eye?"[31] Characteristically he suggests that this striking anticipation of radia-
tion theory would explain how Balaam's ass saw the angel, and
Balaam did not.

But Newman would not have been surprised either to find that
these same ideas are currently regarded with considerable suspicion by the Magisterium. The last entry in the Notebook, dated
"september 24. 1888," reads, "What I write, I do not state dog-
matically, but categorically that is, in investigation, nor have I
confidence enough in what I have advanced to warrant publication."[32] Nearly thirty years earlier he had written that he only
aimed "at what is only probable,"[33] and in 1866 that specific
statements might not "approve themselves ... fully to theolo-

[29] Ludwig Wittgenstein, *Philosophical Investigations*, 42e ed., trans. G.E.M.
Anscombe (Oxford: Basil Blackwell, 1986).

[30] Ibid., 2:130.

[31] Ibid., 2:137.

[32] Ibid., 2:6.

[33] Ibid., 2:87.

gians."[34] He was conscious, at one point, that his ideas might be thought to compromise the doctrine that "our Lord took His flesh from Mary,"[35] and though he was confident they did not do so, he wrote under correction.

He was right to be cautious. To suggest that there is *no* secure point to which the mind can anchor itself; that time and space are illusory; that "the raw or pure effect of the senses" is known only negatively, as different from other experience; that self-knowledge is unstable insofar as it is bound up with a variable non-self; and that there is a core of incompleteness in all experience, even experience of the self and experience of conscience - this is to cast oneself adrift on an ocean of scepticism that indeed threatens to be interminable.

2. *Constitutions and symptoms*: Who's to Blame?

The worrying implications of the economical principle, moreover, do not stop there. They extend also into the collective life of society at large. I propose to illustrate some of these difficulties through *Who's to Blame?*, the series of short articles ostensibly about the Crimean War which Newman published pseudonymously in 1854, using reductive journalistic categories ("the British Lion," "the Muscovite,"[36] "human nature"[37]), and a simplistic political fable in which a Man (representing Government) promises a Horse (representing the citizenry) victory over its enemy, the Stag (representing external and internal enemies), "if he would let him mount him."[38]

---

[34] Ibid., 2:86.

[35] Ibid., 2:116.

[36] John Henry Newman, *Who's to Blame? (Addressed to the Editor of* The Catholic Standard. *By* Catholicus.) in John Henry Cardinal Newman, *Discussions and Arguments on Various Subjects* (London: Longmans, Green, and Co., 1899) 309.

[37] Ibid., 318.

[38] Ibid., 314.

More subtly, however, *Who's to Blame?* distinguishes
between "state," "Nation" and "Constitution." The *State* consists
of the forces of control and defence. The *Nation* is the communal
activity of a people, its business, culture, social life. Uniting them
is the *Constitution*, which is not just a body of law, but also of
ideas, "trivial ... [and] superstitious," or "great and beautiful," but
functioning as "eternal truths, whether they be such or not," as
"first principles ... natural ties, a cause to fight for."[39] This considerably strengthens the idea of political, and particularly Protestant, Tradition on which Newman had written so trenchantly in his
Lectures on the Present Position of Catholics in England (1851).
A remarkably similar idea has recently been proposed by Žižek:
in all societies, he writes, "there is a kind of 'trans-ideological'
kernel ... (notions and sentiments of solidarity, justice, belonging
to a community etc.)" which the governing ideology "*has* to bat-
ten on and manipulate."[40] The rider has *always* to adjust to the
temper of the horse. *Who's to Blame?* is primarily about the
British Constitution in this sense.

Newman's approach to it is forbearing and ambivalent. Take
his description of the Army and the Church:

> In England, sensitively suspicious of combination and system, three
> precautions have been taken in dealing with the soldier and the par-
> son, - (I hope I may be familiar without offence), - precautions taken
> from the necessary treatment of wild animals, - (1) to tie him up, (2)
> to pare his claws, and (3) to keep him low; then he will be both safe
> and useful; - the result is a National Church, and a Constitutional
> Army.[41]

This is Newman at his satirical best. With precision and economy, he makes a telling political judgment - that the deep-seated

---

[39] Ibid., 315.

[40] Žižek, *The Plague of Fantasies*, 21.

[41] Newman, *Who's to Blame?*, 357.

preference of the English Nation for the gentleman-amateur derives, not from any high valuation of gentlemanliness, but rather from a covert fear of being accountable. But there is more in this passage than acute political insight: there is also a Swiftian savagery and relish in the way Newman ties up, pares down and keeps low the animals in his metaphor; yet this note of anger is mingled with an aloof, amused acceptance, which, I shall argue, discloses a way of viewing the world of incalculable philosophical and moral significance.

The note of anger first appears in a discussion of Juries, introduced with the bland observation, that the "end of the Judicature is justice." Though Jurymen are untrained, and are "chosen ... as representatives of a class," they are, Newman assures us, "under the direction of a properly educated and experienced dignitary, called by courtesy the Judge." The irony is sharp but momentary, and the discussion continues with the proposition that Juries are *politically* beneficial in associating those liable to serve in them "with the established order of things," and that they stop the Courts acting in ways unacceptable to the Nation. It is right, Newman declares, striking a suspicious note of bland common sense, "that Public Opinion should give the law to Law" and decide matters "of national concern." Juries ensure that "the good of the country" takes "the lead of private interest; for better far is it" - and here he pounces - "that injustice should be done to a pack of individuals, than that the maxims of the Nation" should be set at naught by "it own paid officials."[42]

The obvious explanation for this cutting, Caiphas-inspired judgment is the Achilli affair, Newman's unjust and disgraceful conviction in 1852 for criminal libeling the renegade Italian priest,

---

[42] Ibid., 348-350.

Giacinto Achilli, in *Present Position of Catholics*. Nevertheless, *Who's to Blame?* remains wonderfully detached from the situation it depicts. By describing the victims of miscarriages of justice as a "pack," Newman conceals the fact that he is one of them. The corruptions in the British Constitution are left in place, almost, indeed, sanctioned. "It is not a high system," we are told, "but no human system is such;" the Russian knout and the American tar-barrel "are less pleasant;" under the British system the individual is at least generally consulted. "Injustice is the exception; a free and easy mode of living is the rule. It is a venal *régime; que voulez-vous?*."[43]

Social processes like these, as Žižek explains, exemplify what he calls the sadistic superego that comes into play when the "Law ... is compelled to search for support in an *illegal* enjoyment."[44] Public law, Zizek argues, is always founded on an illegal seizure of power which it can never admit to, but which demands covert acknowledgment - the Henrician Reformation and the Revolution of 1688 are obvious examples. There is, in effect, a moral gap at the heart of every legal system, which is structurally comparable with the gap at the heart of self-consciousness. Just as, psychologically and culturally, "the Real" is encountered as "that which makes every articulated truth for ever 'not all', [and] makes it impossible to 'tell everything'," so, in political and legal terms, it appears as the crime which no legal code can ever address or redress, i.e., the crime of its own primordial illegality. But whereas the discontinuity of self-awareness is a private anxiety, the extra-legal basis of law generates a sense of communal guilt. In Newman's words, "Men call themselves the *nation* when they

---

[43] Ibid., 352.
[44] Žižek, *The Metastases of Enjoyment*, 54.

sin in a body, and think that the nation, being a name, has nothing
to answer for, and may do what it will."[45] The "primordial lie that
founds a community," Žižek writes, "... is ultimately always
based upon some shared guilt or, more precisely, upon the *fetishistic disavowal of this guilt.*"[46] So it was that what Newman calls
"the anti-Catholic virulence of the present race of Englishmen"[47]
could represent the "spirit of community"[48] for his fellow-countrymen. By violating "the explicit rules of community life,"[49]
anti-Catholic virulence enabled the Lord Chief Justice and Sir
John Taylor Coleridge to run in spirit alongside the patriotic Birmingham street urchins who pursued Newman before his trial with
the gleeful cry "six months in quod!"[50]

All Newman will say of these practices, however, is *"Que
voulez-vous?."* Lacan would have approved. He regarded the
symptoms of a mental disorder as "absolutely particular" to the
life of the person under analysis,[51] and made no attempt to elimi-
nate them by uncovering their hidden "causes." When the
analysand asks the Lacanian analyst, therefore, "As the expert
here, what do *you* want me to want?," the only appropriate reply,
Lacan writes, is "'Che vuoi?', 'What do you want?'" - this alone
leads the analysand "to the path of his own desire."[52] "The
analysand" in *Who's to Blame?* is the reader, me, eager to know

---

[45] John Henry Newman, *Parochial and Plain Sermons*, 8 vols. (London,
Oxford, and Cambridge: Rivingtons, 1869) 4:97.

[46] Žižek, *The Metastases of Enjoyment*, 57.

[47] Newman, *Who's to Blame?*, 322.

[48] Žižek, *The Metastases of Enjoyment*, 55.

[49] Ibid., 54.

[50] Ian Ker, *John Henry Newman: A Biography* (Oxford, New York: Oxford
University Press, 1990) 374.

[51] Lacan, *Ecrits*, 81.

[52] Ibid., 312.

what Newman wants, as diagnostician in this case. But the only answer I get is his Lacanian question - *"Que voulez- vous?,"* *"Che vuoi?"*

This is why Newman is so disturbing. He not only confronts us with the problem of the gaps and fissures at the heart of all our thinking, all our feeling, all our relationships, political as well as personal, but he refuses to fill them in for us. He leaves *us* to decide what we want, to make our *own* choices about the fissures in our minds, in society, in the world - all symbolised, perhaps, by the locked Jury room in which, on 24 June 1852, twelve of his fellow-countrymen dishonestly gave the law to Law, and convicted Newman of criminally libeling Giacinto Achilli, false, fleeting, perjured Giacinto.

3. *"What do you want?"*: Callista

We can now make some preliminary judgments about the economical principle in the light of Lacanian categories. Lacan identifies two levels of mental life, two modes of economy, the Imaginary, arising out of sense-experience, especially seeing, and the Symbolic, constituted in language and other cultural economies - he calls these "the Big Other." Both unite in an endlessly fruitful combination of economies: think of opera, of liturgy, of sport, of a Roman Triumph. But, as we have observed, we are all somewhat anxiously aware of the incompleteness inherent in both, an incompleteness that is inevitable if the significance of what we see and of what we symbolise is wholly constituted by differences between the elements composing them. Systems so constituted are forever precluded from direct engagement with the Real. Denied immediate access to the raw or pure effect the senses, our mental lives are none the less predicated and dependent on the assumption that at least in principle reality and language might be brought into *complete* correlation So too, the Law is predicated on an assertion of its own omni-competence in the fields of crime and punishment, which ignores the history of its own foundation.

At the personal level, then, neither the Imaginary nor the Symbolic can give complete answers to the question "What do you want?;" nor can either answer the two subordinate questions arising from it - "What is to be desired?," and "What or who does the desiring?" I shall now briefly consider the dilemmas arising from this incompleteness by examining the desires of the heroine of Newman's historical novel, *Callista* (1855), and those of her brother, Aristo.

The ego, Lacan maintains, is "formed of a verbal nucleus,"[53] and the unconscious likewise has "the structure of language,"[54] specifically, of metaphor and metonymy. The parables in Matthew 13 illustrate what this means. As parables, they are all metaphors, but equally they are not *just* parables; each is a little story in its own right, and to call them parables is to identify the whole by a part, a part common to them all. The relation between them is therefore metonymic; they form a metonymic chain. However there is a gappiness in metaphor and metonymy, just as there is in consciousness, and the law: what mustard seed, leaven and buried treasure have in common can only be amplified in another image, say of a pearl. So, as well as giving us *something* to think about, metaphor and metonymy give us *nothing* to think about. They too are haunted by the Real, that which falls outside their "power of combination" and "makes it impossible to "tell everything"," but which is also at their heart.

[53] Ibid., 89.
[54] Ibid., 298.

Now the Real is something most of us would rather avoid. In analysis, for example, the ego, according to Lacan, "represents the centre of all the *resistances* to ... treatment."[55] Rather than face *everything* that desire entails, including the unassimilable Real, the analysand clings like a limpet to the mere signifiers of desire, and so to the systems of understanding that exclude the Real. For, though each of these partial objects finally disappoints, we can always move to the next, from a pearl that has lost its lustre to a net bulging with still-glittering fish: we would rather choose another, comfortably knowable signifier than enter the unknowable kingdom. "What sort of subject," Lacan asks, "can we conceive" for desire thus compulsively on the move?[56] His answer is impeccably Augustinian - one whose instincts are "eternally stretching forth towards the *desire for something else*." [57]

But, as well as being linguistic in its form, desire, Lacan suggests, is socially determined in its content. It is *always* "*qua* Other"[58] - in Christian terms, *qua* the world - that we decide what we desire. This is certainly how Aristo's mind is constituted. An accommodating conformist, his desire becomes "lost in a will that is the will of the other."[59] He wants to know what the world expects young men like him to want so that he can want it too. His goal is what Lacan derides as the "American" project of "obtaining 'success' ... [and] demanding 'happiness'"[60] - happiness as society defines it - and he thinks Callista mad because hers isn't. So he finally takes his restless heart into the post-modern disorders of Carthage, leaving her to her terrible fate.

[55] Ibid., 23.
[56] Ibid., 298.
[57] Ibid., 167.
[58] Ibid., 312.
[59] Ibid.,105.
[60] Ibid., 127.

His flight is from the Real, that which both the individual consciousness and society are structurally incapable of assimilating,
but of which both are reminders, as a candle is a reminder of the
dark. The Real makes its first appearance in *Callista* in that great
tour de force of descriptive prose, the account of the swarm of
locusts. In this virtuoso revisiting of one of the great Biblical
themes, exact and concrete images create opportunities for astonishingly rich scriptural and theological allusion. But to stop there
would be to miss the explicit recognition in the narrative that it is
only at the point where understanding and signification fail that
the terrible power of the Real, "that which makes every articulated
truth for ever 'not all'," can at last be felt:

> The hideous swarms lay dead in the moist steaming underwoods, in
> the green swamps, in the sheltered valleys, in the ditches and fur-
> rows of the fields, amid the monuments of their own prowess, the
> ruined crops and the dishonoured vineyards. A poisonous element,
> issuing from their remains, mingled with the atmosphere, and cor-
> rupted it. The dismayed peasant found that a pestilence had begun;
> a new visitation, not confined to the territory which the enemy had
> made its own, but extending far and wide, as the atmosphere
> extends, in all directions.[61]

The ultimate horror is only reached when the concrete - the
corpses of the locusts in ditches and furrows - yields to the
unspecifiable - a "poisonous element;" when the knowable but
concealed is replaced by a visitation as omnipresent and intangible
as the atmosphere itself; in short, when it is no longer possible to
"tell everything."

This intrusion of the undeniable and inexpressible into the
social economy of Sicca continues when "the pestilence ... at last

---

[61] John Henry Cardinal Newman, *Callista: A Tale of the Third Century* (London and New York: Longmans, Green, and Co., 1893) 176-177.

appears in alleys, and in the cellars,"[62] of the town.Where else
could the Real manifest itself? Locusts and disease speak of the
unspeakable only to those who have ears to hear with: without
human beings they would be mere facts of nature - no more and
no less unspeakable than anything else. It is therefore the Real, as
elicited by locusts and plague in the human economies of mind
and heart, which sets the mob on to the Christians, and so leads to
Callista's martyrdom, and a further encounter with the Real, when
she is thrust into "the public cesspool,"[63] "the loathsome
Barathrum, lacus or pit, called Tullianum," named after "the original prison at Rome" - outside the City yet, like the well in
Jerusalem into which the Prophet Jeremiah was thrust, at its heart
- an enclosed space, more unspeakable than an English Jury-room,
but, like the latter, a dark and secret place round which a great
empire revolves, without which, indeed, it could not function.
Finally Callista is put on the rack, to feel a pain so raw and pure
that it can only be felt once, and never thereafter remembered.
Faced with this nightmare, and asked "What do you want?,"
Aristo can only cry, "Not *that*!" - and who can blame him?

But what does Callista herself want in this unimaginable con-
frontation with the Real? What is the nature of a desire which
leads to such an appalling outcome? Like Aristo, she at first tries
to base her desire on the desire of others, specifically that of the
young Christian, Agellius. But he wants her; and this undermines,
she thinks, the seriousness of his belief in a spiritual world.

> ... All things again are vanity; I had hoped there was something
> somewhere more than I could see; but there is nothing. Here am I a
> living, breathing woman, with an over-flowing heart, with keen
> affections, with a yearning after some object which may possess me

[62] Ibid., 177.
[63] Ibid., 365.

... I cannot fall back upon that drear, folorn state, which philosophers call wisdom, and moralists call virtue ...[64]

What is the still-pagan Callista repudiating here, and what
does this tell us about her desire?

First, she is repudiating sex - she finds "noble Grecian forms"
and "manly" voices attractive (much more attractive than poor
Agellius), but they cannot give her what she is looking for. However, in repudiating the world's so-called wisdom and virtue, she
is also rejecting her own role in the Big Other, as Lacanians
understand it.

Symbols, Lacan writes, "envelop" human life,[65] and the foundational symbol is a name - "Father." Motherhood is not a pure
signifier in the same way - it is a physically-given fact. But "no
one would ever know" about fatherhood "without a signifier."[66]
Yet on this arbitrary sign, kinship systems, laws against incest,
"the never-failing cycle" of "wives and goods," and therefore
civilization itself are precariously founded.[67] Callista's chastity is
not, therefore, a private matter. It challenges the patriarchal Big
Other - Sicca, Rome, "the movement of the 'Great Debt'."[68]

This is why she *must* sacrifice to the gods of the city. Such
sacrifices, of course, are mere formalities, but that is their point.
Human beings need wholeness, and have to pretend that the Big
Other supplies it, even though the Big Other is based on illegality,
in Rome's case the imperial usurpation of republican order. Sacri-
ficing to nothing while pretending it is something expresses the
truth while covering it up; it is a "fetishistic disavowal" of col-

[64] Ibid., 131-132.
[65] Lacan, *Ecrits*, p. 68.
[66] Ibid., 199.
[67] Ibid., 68.
[68] Ibid., 67.

lective guilt *par excellence*. Such cynical charades constitute a powerful social bond - just like the deference paid in Victorian England to "twelve good men and true," or the Articles of Religion. As Ian Ker has shown, "what gives [*Callista*] so much of its interest, is the largely unexpressed analogy between [the Roman world and] ... nineteenth-century Protestant England"[69] - the world of *Present Position of Catholics* and *Who's to Blame?* Except, of course, that Rome had a more extreme way with nonconformists than six months in quod.

So much for Rome, but what does Callista want instead of her role in the Roman Big Other? Further consideration of Lacan's Imaginary Order will help to elucidate this question, specifically his account of a still-uncoordinated baby recognizing its image in a mirror, *seeing* itself as whole but *feeling* its immature body as disordered. Like so much else in the Lacanian system, the infant's sense of self is thus split - "that there," the ideal self in the mirror, is better than "this here," the felt self which is physically out of control. This produces, Lacan maintains, a "narcissistic fear of damage to [the] body," "a neurosis of self-punishment,"[70] and images "of ... mutilation, dismemberment, dislocation, evisceration"[71] - just what Callista can expect from Roman justice.

Callista, therefore, chooses our oldest, worst nightmare. Why? Can we interpret her choice as compulsive infantilism, a deeply neurotic decision to allow her felt self to be dismembered merely to protect the fantasy of an ideal self formed when she was eighteen months old? Or, worse, does she choose, in Žižek's words, an "attitude of radical self- instrumentalization, of turning [herself] into the pure instrument-object of the Other's *jouissance*"[72] - the

---

[69] Ker, *John Henry Newman*, 420.

[70] Lacan, *Ecrits*, 28.

[71] Ibid., 11.

[72] Žižek, *The Plague of Fantasies*, 232.

good pleasure, that is, of her God and of the people of Sicca? This is the position Lacan identifies, not as neurotic, but as *perverted*; and Newman's less sympathetic readers might want to interpret Callista's behaviour in just such terms.

But we are still only at the level of signifiable motives, of the partial objects of desire in the metonymic chain. According to Lacan, however, there is another, unspecifiable energy, into which desire resolves itself, once it is freed from attachment to partial objects - whether they are "healthy" like harvest and pearl, or "perverted" like *barathrum* and rack. This he calls blind drive.

Blind drive emerges in a third key moment in our psychic formation. In addition to seeing its reflected image, and learning the word "Father," the child discovers how to play with death in the game, famously observed by Freud and called in German '*Fort! Da!*' - 'All gone! Back again!'. In making things disappear and return, the child learns about extinction as an experience of power: "desire becomes human" when it is spoken. The words "All gone! Back again!" make *what* comes and goes unimportant. The action becomes "its own object" and this eliminates compulsive attachment to partial objects.[73] This is blind drive, and it is linked to a disclosure that none of us wishes to confront: the path of desire is always absent and is never me or mine. Ultimately there is nothing for any of us to desire, just drive without content, indistinguishable from death, from nothing.

The Lacanian answer to the question, "What is to be desired?" is, then, "Nothing." But who or what does this blind desiring? What is the me or mine from which the path of desire is always absent? Žižek summarises the Lacanian answer. I am constituted when my infant self first says, "Me!," when "I posit my unity ... in a signifier which represents me." But this "positing,"

---

[73] Lacan, *Ecrits*, 103.

he insists, is "blind" because the word "Me!" is "outside myself" - I have had to learn it. Moreover it does not signify anything that can be observed; rather it is the assumption that makes observation possible, another instance of the foundational gap or fissure on which all signifying systems depend. "Me!," Žižek declares, is "*a signifier ... which stands for 'nothing'*,"[74] another "fundamental, constitutive, primordial *lie*." [75]

In Lacanian logic, therefore, the answer to both our questions is the same - Nothing. Callista must stop "yearning after some object that may possess [her]," and surrender to "the purity of Non-Being."[76] This is not a counsel of despair, however - something comes of the Lacanian nothing, or if not "something," at any rate, "*jouissance*." I cannot begin to summarise what "*jouissance*" entails for Lacan, but it is at once close to the vision driving Callista and Newman, and profoundly *heretical*. Newman could have accepted Lacan's assertion that as long as we function in a signifying process, that is, in "the world," we "cannot aim at being whole"[77] - our socially constructed identities must indeed fall upon the ground and die. He might have also agreed that an absence of "*jouissance*" "makes the universe vain."[78]But what would surely have been intellectually and morally intolerable for him would have been Lacan's conclusion, that "*jouissance*" entails "the purity of Non-Being" - an *enthusiastic* denial of ontological status to the self and to the Other.

It is of some importance, therefore, to be able to demonstrate that Callista's martyrdom does not even implicitly illustrate this nihilistic logic. This is difficult to accomplish, however, because

[74] Slavoj Žižek, *The Indivisible Remainder: An Essay on Schelling and Related Matters* (London, New York: Verso, 1996) 43.

[75] Ibid., 1.

[76] Lacan, *Ecrits*, 317.

[77] Ibid., 287.

[78] Ibid., 317.

Newman treats her inner life with such reserve. For "the novel-ist," Lacan writes, "... situations ... [make] possible the emer-gence of 'depth psychology';"[79] but Callista is never *situated*. From the start she has lost interest in tangible objects of desire - we don't see any young Greeks compete with Agellius for her attention. Her "depths" are therefore invisible - as a heroine, she is uninteresting compared, say, with Charlotte Brontë's Lucy Snowe or Henry James's Isabel Archer. She is simply driven and consumed with anxiety in case what drives her is without value. We do not go with her into the *barathrum* - who except Kingsley would wish to? - but the narrative also remains aloof from the path of her desire; it leaves us to find our own explanation for her behaviour. The question *"Que voulez-vous?"* - "What do *you* want from the story of Callista?" - is returned to us with exem-plary reticence.

4. *"Ergo sum"* : The Philosophical Notebook *again*

Callista, then, presents us with a problem. I used the word "heretical" of Lacan's "*jouissance,*" and it is clear that the eco-nomical principle leads logically in this direction. As we have noted, Newman himself sensed that theologians might regard it as compromising the doctrine that "our Lord took His flesh from Mary." Be that as it may, the Lacanian tradition does explicitly subvert, or rather invert, the Joannine doctrine of the Word.

According to Žižek, Lacanianism goes back at least to the German Romantic philosopher, Friedrich Wilhelm Schelling; and for Schelling, the "Word" is not a Person, but merely the act by which "God" posits "Himself as Reason."[80] Although this posit-ing is understood by Schelling to take place "in the beginning,"

---

[79] Ibid., 217.
[80] Žižek, *The Indivisible Remainder,* 16.

there is, he thinks, a phase which somehow precedes it, "when God ... was ... at the mercy of the antagonism of matter, without any guarantee that ... Light ... would eventually prevail over ... Ground."[81] However, this mysterious state of divine helplessness is no less mysteriously "*preontological*"[82] - in the fashionable phrase, always already. Žižek's updated version of what he calls this "basic insight" is that it is not the Absolute but the human subject that begins as the pure "night of the Self," and then generates "the symbolic order, the universe of the Word, *logos*."[83]

Either way, of course, St. John's Prologue is being turned on its head. St. John writes of the Word being made flesh, while Schelling and Zizek both represent the Flesh (Ground) becoming (or positing) Word. Besides, their version of the "*logos*," the rationality of language, is self-evidently multiple and contingent, and so, finally, nothing. They agree, in effect, with St. Athanasius that "Men have many words, and after those many, not any one ... for the speaker has ceased and thereupon his word fails."[84]

"But," St Athanasius continues, "God's Word is one and the same, and ... *remaineth for ever*;" and the Johannine teaching is that "flesh" is something this Divine Word could *become*. From the first Epistle to the Thessalonians, therefore, to the condemnation of the Monothelites over six hundred years later, the mind of the Church, though principally concerned with expressing the

---

[81] Ibid., 32.

[82] Slavoj Žižek / F. W. Schelling, *The Abyss of Freedom / Ages of the Word: An Essay by Slavoj Žižek with the text of Schelling's* Die Weltalter *(second draft, 1813) in English translation* by Judith Norman (Ann Arbor, MI: The University of Michigan Press, 1997) 6.

[83] Ibid., 8-9.

[84] John Henry Newman, *Select Treatises of St. Athanasius in Controversy with the Arians*, freely translated by John Henry Cardinal Newman, 2 vols., 2nd ed. (London: Pickering and Co., 1881) 2:339.

mystery of the Word, had necessarily to think about the flesh; and in finally affirming that the human being has a "natural will," she completed her understanding of what being "made flesh" amounts to. The result was a radically new conception of the human subject, a conception to which, in the West, we have given the name "person." Insofar as this word is applied to the Triune God, Newman insists in the *Notebook* (as elsewhere), it "adds nothing to what we knew before using it."[85] But the concept "person" did add considerably to what we know about human beings. As Newman puts it in the *Notebook*, the "very idea of a person, is a being who is beyond [scientific] law."[86] It was an idea unknown to the pre-Christian world. In both Greek and Latin, the term coming nearest to it was a metonymy, "head."[87] Yet it is this conception, so fundamental to theology and anthropology alike, that the Lacanian tradition in general, and the economical principle in particular, apparently subvert.

The question which Newman, therefore, needs above all to address is how creatures of flesh like ourselves, circumscribed as we are by the economical principle, can nevertheless enjoy the "unity ... individuality ... and ... independent existence" explicitly and authoritatively attributed to us by the Church Fathers and the early Councils. His answer is to be found in his impatient and repeated rejection in the *Notebook* of the suggestion that reasoning is founded on "an act of foi aveugle," of blind faith[88] - in effect Žižek's blind positing. Just as Wittgenstein insists that "I can

---

[85] Newman, *Philosophical Notebook*, 2:105.

[86] Ibid., 2:173.

[87] Hermann Frankel, *Early Greek Poetry and Philosophy: A History of Greek Epic, Lyric, and Prose to the Middle of the Fifth Century*, trans. Moses Hadas and James Willis (New York and London: Harcourt Brace Jovanovich, A Helen and Kurt Wolff Book, 1973) 77 n.

[88] Newman, *Philosophical Notebook*, 2:31.

know what someone else is thinking, not what I am thinking"[89] - the word "know" with respect to one's own experience adding nothing to the sentence - so for Newman it is meaningless to speak of "faith in [the] reasoning process,"[90] for even though our unity, individuality and independent existence are not *immediately* obvious, the *"ergo"* with which we infer them is, quite simply, ours. Newman's analysis differs from Wittgenstein's, however, in so far as the latter is an insight into language - a "whole cloud of philosophy condensed into a drop of grammar" - because Newman's is an insight into himself. *He takes intellectually responsible possession of the gap between his* "sentio*" and his"*sum." The word "therefore" signifies not a self-constituting moment - the human being is always already a person - but a moment of discovery. Obviously, no baby ever said "therefore" before saying "me." But even in Lacan's account, the infant mind makes an inference about its own image before it says anything about itself; so even if the word "me" is "outside myself," as Zizek argues, the power to make inferences is not; and such a power may be predicated of every emergent human consciousness, including that of the Eternal Word made flesh.

The speculations in the *Notebook* have, therefore, incalculable philosophical importance. The "phenomena to which [the metaphysician] appeals," Newman observes, "and the principles which he assumes [are] within his own [breast] ... His hermit spirit dwells in his own sphere."[91] Two great intellectual traditions converged in his own hermit spirit. First, of course, there was the theology of the Fathers. But second there was the great achievement of modern self-analysis - the relativist understanding of our condition, inscribed in the economical principle. Newman's crucial

[89] Wittgenstein, *Philosophical Investigations,* 222.

[90] Newman, *Philosophical Notebook*, 2:35.

[91] Ibid., 2:87.

contribution was to bring these two apparently incompatible streams of thought into fruitful union.

Two consequences of his *"ergo"* will indicate how fruitful. The first concerns his ability to hold back from complete explanation. When he read H. M. Chalybäus' account of the German philosophers, he was pleased to find that they too had practised his introspective method. He was particularly gratified by Schelling's assertion that conclusions "can never be demonstrated;" one can only find "corroboration" by self-attention.[92] But he was not otherwise impressed with Schelling because, as Chalybäus notes, there are "no less than three or four, and even five modifications of his system,"[93] each involving what Žižek calls "a highly reckless premiss that the two series (of experiential reality and of the conceptual framework) will be fully correlated."[94] Newman would have agreed about the recklessness of the premiss. "Of course truth is always consistent with itself," he writes in the *Notebook*, "but that does not prove that we can always show that consistency."[95] He accordingly indulges in a kind of intellectual "negative capability," going "the whole hog with Darwin,"[96] accepting the Church's teaching on the Incarnation, and defending economy, without feeling any requirement to "refer everything to *one* principle."[97] In Wittenstein's terms, he made the "radical break with the idea that language always functions in one way."[98]

Philosophers like Schelling, however, are denied this freedom.

---

[92] H. M. Chalybäus, *Historical Development of Speculative Philosophy from Kant to Hegel* (Edinburgh: T. & T. Clark, 1854) 250; *Philosophical Notebook*, 1:321.

[93] Chalybäus, *Historical Development of Specualtive Philosophy*, 262.

[94] Žižek, *The Indivisible Remainder*, 16.

[95] Newman, *Philosophical Notebook*, 2:177.

[96] Ibid., 2:158.

[97] Ibid., 1:232.

[98] Wittgenstein, *Philosophical Investigations*, p.102e.

For them, everything *must* arise within a single field - "matter" or "ground" or the "night of the Self," or alternatively 'spirit" or "reason." Schelling, for example, has to describe "the causal chains of Reason"[99] arising from the random irrationality of material Ground, Lacan how Desire gets to be boxed in by Language. They are both locked into the logically arbitrary and self-defeating task of describing the pre-history of description, of putting into words the generation of words - hence Schelling's endless revisiting of the same problem.

Žižek sees this revisiting as a strength: the "great works of *materialist* thought, from Lucretius ... to ... Lacan," he suggests, " ... tackle the same nodal problem again and again ... [but] although they ultimately fail ... their very failure is theoretically extremely productive."[100] An alternative description of these endless reconsiderations, however, might be what Lacan calls "the ever avoided encounter ... the missed opportunity ... the vanity of repetition."[101] Newman certainly would have thought so. Secure in his "*ergo*," he knew that the foundation of all being is not ground, or matter, or spirit, but person. He had no need to construct a single, systematic view the world outside his hermit spirit; as a person, he could live with disparate economies. And so, therefore, can we.

Finally there is the argument for the existence of God from Conscience. Newman copied back into the *Notebook* Callista's assertion that conscience is no "mere law of my nature, as is to joy or to grieve ... [but] the echo of a person speaking to me."[102] In itself, this is hardly an argument. But, Newman points out, "if one external unexperienced fact" - my existence - "may be

---

[99] Žižek, *The Indivisible Remainder*, 16.

[100] Ibid., 6-7.

[101] Lacan, *The Four Fundamental Concepts of Psycho-analysis*,128.

[102] Newman, *Philosophical Notebook*, 2:59; *Callista*, 314.

known by *reasoning upon* experience, perhaps another may. Therefore the idea is not absurd that as from 'sentio' ['I feel'] I infer the existence of myself, so from 'conscientiam habeo' ['I have a conscience'], I infer the existence of God, and again from the phenomena of sense I have the existence of matter."[103] This, it should be noted, is not, strictly, a "proof." It only suggests that, provided my experience of moral accountability is as closely "bound up with ... the idea & the fact of my being"[104] as the *sentio* itself, then my *"ergo* a Divine Person" is as rational as my *"ergo* me" or my *"ergo* the world." Certitude of God's existence, therefore, is not *in principle* irrational; so Callista is not by definition mad to live and die as if in the presence of the Divine Person which her intelligence infers from her conscience and then corroborates in the only way possible by self-attention, (and, of course, the illuminations of Grace). It follows that even a sceptical reader is under an obligation at the least to take her choice seriously.

It is a choice which puts her into a different universe from that envisaged by Schelling and Lacan. There can be no distinction of Persons in Schelling's understanding of "God," only distinction of moments - the Word is merely an *event* in the history of the Absolute. And there is no distinction of persons either when Schelling's Romantic, quasi-theological metaphysic is revisited by tough-minded materialists like Lacan and Žižek. In their account, the self struggles to define itself in and against the non-self, and can only gain release from its solipsistic compulsions by relinquishing all claim to Being. Unlike the Lacanian "subject," however, Callista can ask "What do you want?" and expect an answer.

By the same token, we too can say what we want from her

---

[103] Ibid., 2:78.
[104] Ibid., 2:59.

story. We want Callista, *in extremis*, to have her question returned without conditions and with unqualified love. We want her to hear the "*Que voulez*-vous?" of the Eternal Word, one and the same and abiding for ever, welcoming her into the joy of her Lord - *la Jouissance de son Seigneur*.

NEWMAN ON THE BIBLE:
A *VIA MEDIA* TO POSTMODERNITY?

T.R.WRIGHT

Among "the things Newman stood for" which were "brought forward" by Vatican II, in a list compiled by Stephen Dessain and quoted by Nicholas Lash (himself more sceptical of the myth of Newman as the father of that council), is "a return to Scripture."[1] *Dei Verbum* urges all "engaged in the ministry of the Word" to "immerse themselves in the Scriptures by constant sacred reading and diligent study," looking forward, in its final words, to "a new impulse of spiritual life" which "may be expected from increased veneration of the Word of God."[2] *Dei Verbum,* in its final draft, omitted the stress on "inerrancy" of earlier draft schemas,[3] recognising that "in sacred Scripture, God speaks through men in human fashion," employing a variety of "literary forms" for the interpretation of which the exegete should deploy a sensitivity to "the circumstances of his [the writer"s] time and culture."[4] It can be seen to have given the seal of approval to a way of reading the Bible, not only regularly but critically, openly, and historically. I want to suggest that it was indeed indebted to Newman for this. It could have gone further (with him) in recognising the multiplicity

[1] Nicholas Lash, "Tides and Twilight: Newman since Vatican II," in Ian Ker & Alan G. Hill (eds.), *Newman After a Hundred Years* (Oxford: Clarendon Press, 1990) 460.

[2] Austin Flannery (ed.), *Vatican Council II: The Conciliar and Post-Conciliar Documents* (Collegeville, MN: Liturgical Press, 1984) 764-765.

[3] Bruce Vawter, *Biblical Inspiration* (London: Hutchinson, 1972) 144-146.

[4] Flannery (ed.), *Vatican Council II*, 764-765.

of meanings to which such reading gives rise, the inexhaustibility of Scripture to fresh reading and interpretation. But at least it recognised (as he did) the extent to which the Church is characterised and given energy by its reading of the Bible.

My concern now is not with the extent or manner of Newman's influence upon the council (interesting though that would be) but with an attempt to clarify his own extremely complex position. Surprisingly, given the importance of the Bible for Newman and for the Church, the subject has been given little attention by the Newman critical industry. Jaak Seynaeve's study, *Cardinal Newman's Doctrine on Holy Scripture,*[5] published in 1953, is, so far as I know, the only book-length study of the subject. Francis McGrath has written on the related topic of *Universal Revelation*[6] while Derek Holmes edited two volumes of Newman's papers on biblical inspiration (and wrote an article on the topic). But these are the only sustained book-length discussions of a subject of central importance both to Newman and the Church.

An article by Seynaeve on "Newman's Biblical Hermeneutics" in the special issue of *Louvain Studies* marking the centenary of Newman's death, begins with the declaration on the opening page of the *Apologia,* "I was brought up as a child to take great delight in reading the Bible," and notes "his practice of learning large sections of the Bible by heart." Seynaeve continues,

> Newman read the Bible constantly. Allusions to, and applications of, Holy Scripture are scattered throughout his works. Practically all his sermons draw their main inspiration from Scripture. There is almost no part of the inspired volumes which Newman did not use.[7]

[5] Jaak Seynaeve, *Cardinal Newman's Doctrine on Holy Scripture* (Louvain: Publications Universitaires de Louvain, 1953).

[6] Francis McGrath, *Universal Revelation* (Tunbridge Wells: Burns and Oates, 1997).

[7] Jaak Seynaeve, "Newman's Biblical Hermeneutics," *Louvain Studies* 15 (1990) 282.

His sermons, according to Seynaeve, are "such a mosaic of biblical texts ... that one can hardly tell the difference between the language of the Bible and his own,"[8] a tribute to his deep internalisation not only of its subject-matter but of its style.

Newman's Anglican Sermons, Eric Griffiths observes in another centenary essay, hardly ever quote anything but the Bible. As a Catholic he would throw in a few Fathers and saints "but not often."[9] His fellow Oratorians noticed a difference of tone when it came to reading the Gospels in particular, "the increased reverence in the reader's voice which culminated when he came to the words of our Saviour," preceded by "a kind of hush" and accompanied by "the complete elimination of the personality of the reader."[10] Less charitable listeners timed the pauses between sentences at thirty seconds each, which, as Griffiths calculates, would (if true) have brought some of his sermons over the five-hour mark. The point, however, is the reverence with which he treated scripture and the depth of meaning he found within it. Griffiths culls from the *Parochial and Plain Sermons* a number of passages which celebrate the multiplicity of voices to be found in the Bible:

> The All-wise, All-knowing God cannot speak without meaning many things at once ... Every word of His is full of instruction, looking many ways...Look at Christ's words, and this same character will strike you; whatever He says is fruitful in meaning, and refers to many things.[11]

Newman expresses utter contempt for those who believe the Bible easy to understand:

---

[8] Ibid., 282.

[9] Eric Griffiths, "Newman: The Foolishness of Preaching", in Ker & Hill, *Newman After a Hundred Years*, 74-75.

[10] Ibid., 77.

[11] John Henry Newman, *Parochial and Plains Sermons,* 8 vols. (London: Rivingtons, 1870 [1834-1843]) 1:152.

> The Eternal Wisdom of God did not utter His voice that we might at once catch up His words in an irreverent manner, think we understand them at a glance, and pass them over. But his word endureth for ever; it has a depth of meaning suited to all times and places , and hardly and painfully to be understood in any. They, who think they enter into it easily, may be quite sure they do not enter into it at all.[12]

Less felicitously perhaps, in the *University Sermons,* Newman characterises the role of readers of the Bible "as worms in an abyss of divine works."[13]

Postmodern bookworms, of course, have no difficulty with this image, happily celebrating the joyous affirmation of the play of the word as Derrida does at the end of "Structure, Sign and Play."[14] Not for them the nostalgia to be found in Newman as in Rousseau for the lost security or self-presence of the Word in language. Postmodernism, like modernism, is notoriously difficult to define, having, as Gabirel Daly has shown of the earlier term, a variety of meanings dependent on context. In architecture, for example, it stands for a playful intertextuality, a pastiche of earlier styles; in philosophy a suspicion of all master-narratives, especially the modernist belief in progress; in literature it involves a certain self-reflexivity, a deliberate playing with conventions. Play is a constant factor, although not merely in the sense of having fun, more with the stretching of previous limits placed upon meaning. Perhaps the most helpful indication of what postmodernism brings to a reading the Bible is given by the collective authors of *The Postmodern Bible,* who explain their title with reference to a shared

[12] Ibid., 1:28.

[13] D.M.MacKinnon & J.D.Holmes (eds.), *Newman's University Sermons: Fifteen Sermons Preached before the University of Oxford* (London: S.P.C.K., 1970 [1843]) 28.

[14] Jacques Derrida, *Writing and Difference,* trans. Alan Bass (Chicago: University of Chicago Press, 1978) 292-293.

suspicion of the claim to mastery that characterizes traditional readings of texts, including modern biblical scholarship ... by sweeping
away secure notions of meaning, by radically calling into question
the apparently stable foundations of meaning on which traditional
interpretation is situated, by raising doubts about the capacity to
achieve ultimate clarity about the meaning of a text, postmodern
readings lay bare the contingent and constructed character of meaning itself.[15]

Newman, I want to claim, shared this suspicion, this scepticism
about the possibility of secure linguistic meaning, although he was
(understandably) less joyful, more anxious about its possible consequences.

Some recent commentators have been bothered about the multiplicity of meaning which Newman finds in Scripture and the postmodern abyss to which they fear this leads. Valentine Cunningham, in the final essay of that "alternative" centenary volume,
John Henry Newman: Reason, Rhetoric and Romanticism, picks
up on Newman's celebration of "the variability of meaning, the
copiousness of the mysteries and allegories in the Scripture, the
multivalences of metaphor and figure in the sacred writings."[16]
Cunningham quotes passages from Newman's *Essay on the
Development of Christian Doctrine* which attack literalism as
heresy, characterising Arians and Nestorians alike as immune to
"that fulness of meaning, refinement of thought, subtle versatility
of feeling and delicate reserve or reverent suggestion, which poets
exemplify" and which is characteristic of Scripture.[17] It is
"absolutely impossible," Newman insists, "for doctrinal truths to

---

[15] *The Postmodern Bible,* Bible and Culture Collective (New Haven and
London: Yale University Press, 1995) 2.

[16] Valentine Cunningham, "Dangerous Conceits or Confirmations Strong?,"
in David Nicholls & Fergus Kerr (eds.), *John Henry Newman: Reason,
Rhetoric and Romanticism* (Bristol: Bristol Press, 1991) 242.

[17] Ibid.

remain in the mere letter of Scripture, if they are to be more than mere words, or to convey a definite idea to the recipient."[18] Newman, like Derrida, celebrates both

> the structure and style of Scripture, a structure so figurative and indirect, that no one would presume at first sight to say what is in it and what is not. It cannot, as it were, be mapped, or its contents catalogued; but after all our diligence, to the end of our lives and to the end of the Church, it must be an unexplored and unsubdued land, with heights and valleys, forests and streams, on the right and left of our path and close all about us, full of concealed wonders and choice treasures.[19]

Cunningham is so incensed by what he sees as Newman's deviousness with language and his contempt for naive Protestant reading of the Bible that he omits to mention that the mapping and cataloguing of revelation, its oversystematisation, is an error which the Anglican Newman associated with "Romanism" in general and scholasticism in particular.

My concern, however, is not with inter-denominational wrangling but with Newman's sophisticated model of reading. The indeterminacy or undecidability of Scripture is a crucial part of his argument that the Church's understanding of its faith necessarily develops. Like the reception-theorist Wolfgang Iser, he insists that there are necessary gaps in the text both of Scripture and of credal formation, which take time to be filled: "the gaps, if the word may be used, which occur in the structure of the original creed of the Church, make it probable that those developments ... were intended to complete it."[20] The model here, of course, in

---

[18] John Henry Newman, *An Essay on the Development of Christian Doctrine,* (ed.) J.M. Cameron (Harmondsworth: Penguin, 1974 [1845]) 151.

[19] Ibid., 162.

[20] Ibid., 154.

both Newman and Iser, is of a very controlled indeterminacy, structured gaps, whose implicit meaning can be inferred by any competent reader. Newman recognises, however, that some of the gaps or indeterminacies of Scripture are far from clearly structured, requiring the teaching of the Church as "partly the interpretation, partly the supplement of Scripture."[21]

> We are told that God has spoken. Where? In a book? We have tried it, and it disappoints; it disappoints, that most holy and blessed gift, not from fault of its own, but because it is used for a purpose for which it was not given. The Ethiopian's reply, when St Philip asked him if he understood what he was reading, is the voice of nature: "How can I, unless some man shall guide me?"[22]

It is characteristic of Newman that he should invoke the Bible even while illustrating its limits. It is also characteristic of him, according to Cunningham, that he should take us right up to the deconstructive abyss, peer terrifyingly into it, and jump back into the arms of Mother Church.

The words "supplement" and "gift," interestingly, are favourite terms for Derrida as well as Newman. Cunningham picks up on the first, which can slide from merely completing, making good what is missing, bringing up to date, to supplanting or replacing (as Jewish scholars would argue of the christening of the Hebrew Bible the Old Testament). But he misses the second, "gift," which in German means poison. Like the Greek word *pharmakon*, another favourite Derridean term, which means either medicine or poison, depending on context, the Bible is seen by Newman as an ambivalent gift, open to misuse and misreading, which can harm as well as cure, mislead as well as lead to salvation. Newman cites St. Basil likening the Bible to "a dispensary which supplies various medicines against

---

[21] John Henry Newman, *Apologia pro Vita Sua* (London: Dent, n.d. [1864]) 166.

[22] Newman, *Essay on Development*, 175.

every complaint."[23] It is not, however, a well-ordered, neatly cata-
logued Chinese pharmacy of the kind mocked by Derrida in his
analysis of "Plato's Pharmacy" (and Newman in his awareness of
the limits of neoscholasticism). The most interesting "operations" of
language, for both Newman and Derrida, take place in "the back
room, in the shadows of the pharmacy," in those intuitive areas of
the imagination prior to the cataloguing process.[24]

It is because Newman was aware of the power of the Bible, its
multivalence, its ambiguities and indeterminacies, its openness to
a range of possible readings, that he was also alert to heresy, its
misreading. And because he came down so hard on the latter (in
his Anglican days, at least, when liberal opponents dictated the
context of his argument), it is easy to be misled, like Robert Pattison in *The Great Dissent: John Henry Newman and the Liberal
Heresy,* into portraying him as an anti-modernist, stamping out
anything that smacked of the forbidden L-word. But, as Stephen
Thomas shows, in his more subtle portrait of *Newman and
Heresy: The Anglican years,* Newman grappled not only with
questions later to be labelled modernist: "He comes to us as a
modern," the "child of British empiricism ... overlaid with
Romanticism," "hypersensitive to epistemological issues, concerned with the psychology of impressions and ideas, agnostic
about their object."[25] Towards the end of the book, Thomas
claims that Newman's scepticism about our obtaining objective
knowledge of ultimate truth brings him "remarkably close to what
may be termed a 'postmodern' perspective."[26]

[23] Newman, *Essay on Development*, 339.

[24] Jacques Derrida, *Dissemination,* trans. Barbara Johnson (Chicago:
University of Chicago Press, 1981) 23.

[25] Stephen Thomas, *Newman and Heresy: The Anglican Years* (Cambridge:
Cambridge University Press, 1991)182-183.

[26] Ibid., 256.

This, I want to argue, is nowhere more apparent than in his treatment of the Bible, his recognition of its gaps and indeterminacies, its multiplicity, its openness to many differing interpretations, seen not as a weakness (though it clearly invalidates it as an interpretive authority) but as a product of its inner life and creativity, its openness to the operations of grace. Newman remains orthodox, perhaps "neo-orthodox, even "radical orthodox" in today's terminology, because he gives the teaching authority of the Church the final say in determining what should count as Catholic truth. Even this, however, Newman insists, falls well short of absolute truth. In postmodernity, to quote John Milbank's short *Summa* in Graham Ward's *The Postmodern God*, "there are infinitely many possible versions of truth, inseparable from particular narratives."[27] In the case of Catholicism, these narratives are those of the Bible as interpreted by tradition. What Newman means by "Catholic truth" is clearly more solid than what Milbank has in mind but the point is that its linguistic expression remains inadequate to the Word itself. And there can be no shortcut or short-circuit of the complexity of the business of reading the Bible, even for the Church beacuse it has a duty to consider all the evidence produced by historical, critical and scientific research, all the arguments produced by biblical exegetes, before making definitive decisions. Even then, it does so pragmatically, resolving uncertainty without claiming absolute knowledge. Reading and interpretation don't work like that.

Newman's thinking on the Bible is not conveniently focussed in one text but must be gleaned from a range of writing over fifty years, from the products of his Anglican controversies, *The Arians of the Fourth Century, The Tracts for the Times* (in particular

[27] John Milbank, "Postmodern Critical Augustinianism: A Short *Summa* in Forty-Two Responses to Unasked Questions," in Graham Ward (ed.), *The Postmodern God: A Theological Reader* (Oxford: Blackwell, 1997) 265.

Tracts 73 and 85), *The Via Media* and the *Essay on the Development of Christian Doctrine* to his writings as a Catholic, among which the most relevant are *The Idea of a University,* the *Apologia, An Essay in Aid of a Grammar of Assent* and the essays on Biblical Inspiration he wrote either side of the First Vatican Council (the last in 1884). Even a novel such as *Callista* whose eponymous heroine comes to faith through reading a copy of St.Luke's Gospel, sheds light on the way in which Newman thought the Bible should be read. I will adduce evidence from all of these texts, focussing in particular on the *Via Media,* in whose pages Newman can be seen engaging in a dialogue with himself, the Catholic annotations of 1877 "correcting" his earlier Anglican speculations. It is the *Via Media,* I hope to show, which most clearly illustrates the ways in which Newman can be said to anticipate postmodernity in particular in his awareness of textuality, the limits of language, the phenomenologically peculiar status of written marks, seemingly objective on the page but only coming to life in the minds of their readers.

As Cunningham complains, Newman's writing never "fails to be obsessively preoccupied with the nature of textuality, of words, of reading and writing, of meaning, words about words, i.e. problems of interpretation."[28] Quite so; this is what makes him so interesting to a Derridean age, similarly obsessed with the ambiguous gift, the *pharmakon* of writing, the re-marks and grafting of an apostolic tradition and the supplement of interpretation.

This is not, of course, how Robert Pattison presents the Anglican Newman, the scourge of contemporary liberals such as Dr. Hampden. For Pattison it is Hampden who anticipates that scepticism about the capacity of language to represent reality characteristic of the late twentieth century. Pattison clearly enjoys locating the origins of "fashionable theories of deconstruction ... in the

---

[28] Cunningham, "Dangerous Conceits or Confirmations Strong?," 233.

detritus of nineteenth-century theology."[29] Again, as with Cunningham, I would accept his diagnosis but feel more optimistic about the symptoms. Hampden's Bampton lectures of 1832, which caused Newman so much heartache, were on *The Scholastic Philosophy Considered in Its Relations to Christian Theology* and one of the reasons they worried Newman so much, as Pattison himself recognises, is that their view of the inadequacy of doctrinal propositions and systematic theology was not dissimilar to Newman's own. Hampden emphasised "the truths of the gospel," which he called "facts" (divine truth) in opposition to linguistic propositions or ideas (human truth). Like the pragmatic reader-response theorist of our own age, Stanley Fish, Hampden emphasised the role of interpretive communities, what he called "the agreement of a community" in establishing what we take to be "reality," but such human truth, he insisted should not be mistaken for divine. For Hampden, only revelation, recorded in Scripture, could be regarded as "indisputably true ... nothing independent of these books, or not taken from them, can possess the same authority."[30] The Gospel records "revealed facts" while "theological propositions" simply connect "signs." Scripture acts as a catalyst provoking a response of faith and action; "Strictly to speak, in the Scripture itself there are no *doctrines*."[31]

This, according to Pattison, was what Newman found unacceptable in Hampden and what his early work in patristics set out to dispute, finding at the heart of the Arian heresy a similar scepticism about language. At times, however, as Pattison himself recognises, Newman can seem as sceptical as Hampden both in the *University Sermons*, which see words as "earthly images,

[29] Robert Pattison, *The Great Dissent: John Henry Newman and the Liberal Heresy* (Oxford: Oxford University Press, 1991) 90.

[30] Ibid., 89, citing *Scholastic Philosophy*.

[31] Ibid., 91-93, again citing Hampden.

which are infinitely below the reality,"[32] and in the *Grammar of Assent*, where even Scripture is limited: "God has condescended to speak to us so far as human thought and language will admit, by approximations."[33] Newman saw precision in language as "an act of Arian insolence," which is why his own language, as Perrone was to complain, was always rich in metaphor and ambiguity, complex and even "confused" (the term Perrone and Pattison share in describing Newman). Pattison argues that Newman "accepted his enemies' premises about interpretation" but "drove them home to orthodox conclusions."[34] In today's terminology, however, that makes him "neo-orthodox," the "neo" advertising an awareness of the limits of all doctrinal propositions.

'*Neologism*', of course, was the term used by the Tractarians of German Higher Criticism, described by Newman in *Arians* as a heresy which "has shown itself desirous and able to conceal itself under the garb of sound religion, and to keep the form, while it destroys the spirit, of Christianity."[35] The question then, as now, is how far you can go in applying secular reason to revealed religion, a question which Newman addressed directly in Tract 73 in 1835, "On the Introduction of Rationalistic Principles into revealed Religion," later included in the first volume of *Essays Critical and Historical*. By rationalism, Newman explains, he means "a certain abuse of Reason" which makes it "the standard and measure" of revelation,[36] an abuse characteristic not just of

---

[32] *Newman's University Sermons*, 268-9.

[33] John Henry Newman, *An Essay in Aid of a Grammar of Assent*, (ed.) I.T. Ker (Oxford: Clarendon Press, 1985 [1870]) 269.

[34] Pattison, *The Great Dissent*, 161.

[35] John Henry Newman, *The Arians of the Fourth Century* (London: Lumley, 1871 [1833]) 106.

Protestant pietists, exalting private judgement, but of scholastic theologians, failing to recognise the limits of their own systems. Newman anticipates the postmodern Catholic theologian Jean-Luc Marion in distinguishing between subjective truth, "that which each mind receives in particular" and objective truth, "that which we have but partially mastered or made subjective." He certainly shares the postmodern dislike of all claims intellectually to "grasp" or "master" revelation. Faith is "the reaching forth after and embracing what is beyond the mind," not truths "mastered by the mind" but "beyond it."[37] It is the difference, in Marion's terms, between an idol, claiming to represent the whole truth, and an icon, pointing beyond itself to what is not fully understood.

Tract 73 takes particular exception to the work of liberal protestant theologians such as Thomas Erskine, confidently refusing to believe anything he cannot understand and opposing "Manifestation" to "Mystery." Newman by contrast, sees revelation as deeply mysterious, "doctrine *lying hid* in language ... of depth unfathomable, and illimitable in its extent."[38] We should therefore be "reverent" in dealing with revelation, avoiding "all rash theorizing and systematizing as relates to it." We should also "religiously adhere to the form of words" in which it comes.[39] Erskine is found guilty of that ultimate sin against the Holy Spirit in the eyes of all postmodernists, excessive lucidity: "he speaks so clearly" about the Bible and the indications it gives of "the character of God," utterly failing to appreciate its otherness, in contrast with St Paul preaching Christ crucified as "a *strange* doctrine and a stumbling block" or St John, at the opening of his gospel,

[36] John Henry Newman, *Essays Critical and Historical,* 2 vols. (London: Pickering, 1873 [1871]) 1:31.

[37] Ibid., 1:34-36.

[38] Ibid., 1:41. Unless otherwise stated, the italics are Newman's.

[39] Ibid., 1:47.

recognising that the light of the Word "was too glorious for men"
and *"shone in darkness."*[40] Jacob Abbott, a popular and prolific
writer of religious books for young people, including *the Corner
Stone, or a Familiar Illustration of the Principles of Christian
Truth,* is also held up for ridicule for claiming to know too much,
to be able to make an *"exhibition* of the Gospel," a *"Manifestation of the Divinity"*).[41] Abbott, like Renan after him, goes into
raptures about Christ's love of nature, his midnight rambles in the
Galilean hills, his love of lilies and so on. Newman, in response,
waxes apocalyptic on "that scornful, arrogant, and self-trusting
spirit, which has been unchained during these latter ages," and
presumes to make itself the judge of divine revelation.[42] A "Postscript" on Schleiermacher sees the founder of liberal Protestantism as the origin of this impiety (although Newman had probably read even less of Schleiermacher than he had of Luther).

Again, however, it is important to recognise that Protestantism
is not the only target of Newman's attack on theological over-
confidence in the capacity of language to do justice to revealed
truth. His 1837 *Lectures on the Prophetical Office of the Church
Viewed Relatively to Romanism and Popular Protestantism,*
republished forty years later as the *Via Media of the Anglican
Church,* make this abundantly clear. The Anglican Church, or at
least the theoretical version of it which Newman propounded in
the late 1830s, attempts to steer a middle course between two
extremes, one of which places too much emphasis on reason and
the other on tradition as the authoritative interpreter of Scripture.
As Newman explains in a characteristically complex sentence
which includes a fair sprinkling of the buzzwords of postmodernity, complexity versus mastery, multiplicity and indeterminacy

[40] Ibid., 1:57-58 (Newman's italics).
[41] Ibid., 1:73.
[42] Ibid., 1:91.

versus univocity,

> the middle path adopted by the English Church cannot be so easily
> mastered by the mind, first because it is a mean, and has in conse-
> quence a complex nature, involving a combination of principles, and
> depending on multiplied conditions; next, because it partakes of that
> indeterminateness which...is to a certain extent characteristic of
> English theology; lastly, because it has never been realized in visi-
> ble fulness in any religious community.[43]

Of the various possible authorities to which men turn in matters of
religion (Reason, Tradition, Scripture and Antiquity) Roman
Catholics are accused of "simplifying matters by removing Reason,
Scripture, and Antiquity, and depending mainly upon Church authority." Latitudinarians exalt reason, Mystics rely too much on the heart
and Protestants "consider ... Scripture to be all in all." The "true
Catholic Christian," however, "uses all duly and to God's glory."[44]

Most of the *Via Media*, in fact, turns upon the question of Scripture and its interpretation. Newman recognises that "apparent contradictions" will arise, for instance between "Scripture and Reason as
regards miracles" (he hadn't read Strauss but he had talked to Pusey
and encountered Strauss's principles in Milman, as we shall see) or
between "Antiquity and Scholarship, as at times perhaps in the interpretation of Scripture. When this happens, Newman insists, at this
stage of his career, "we must follow Scripture."[45] "Romanists"
(amended in 1877 to "the controversialists of Rome") may object
that "the right of free judgment upon the text of Scripture" inevitably
leads to "various discordant opinions" but Newman in 1837 is

> not willing to grant this of the Holy Scriptures ... There have been

---

[43] John Henry Newman, *The Via Media of the Anglican Church*, (ed.)
H.D.Weidner (Oxford: Clarendon Press, 1990 [1837, 1877])166.

[44] Ibid., 169.

[45] Ibid., 170.

writers of their communion, indeed, who have used the most disparaging terms of the inspired volume, as if it were so mere a letter that it might be molded into any meaning which the reader chose to put upon it.[46]

Newman accepts that "men continually misinterpret Scripture" but believes that such misreadings are occur only in "the adjuncts and details of faith, not in fundamentals." If there are differences within the Church, even schism, "it is not that Scripture speaks variously, but that the Church of the day speaks not at all," failing to resolve questions of interpretation.[47]

Such questions, Newman acknowledges, are bound to arise. The sixth lecture of the series, "On the Abuse of Private Judgment," again accepts that the Bible is a difficult book to read, pouring scorn on the "popular view" that "every Christian has the right of making up his mind for himself what he is to believe, from personal and private study of the Scriptures."[48] Some of Newman's own prejudices and limitations emerge in the manner in which he blusters against the "preposterous" notion that "every individual Christian, rich and poor, learned and unlearned, young and old, in order to have an intelligent faith, must have formally examined, deliberated, and passed sentence upon the meaning of Scripture."[49] He concedes that even "one of the common run of men," otherwise riddled with "prejudice" and "inaccuracy of mind," "may gain religious impressions and practical guidance from Scripture" but disputes his capacity to formulate sound doctrine from it: "Scripture is not so clear - in God's providential arrangement, to which we submit - as to hinder ordinary persons, who read it for themselves, from being Sabellians" (i.e., failing to

---

[46] Ibid., 173.
[47] Ibid., 174-177.
[48] Ibid., 179.
[49] Ibid.

achieve a full understanding of the Trinity). Orthodoxy may be "the one and only sense of Scripture" but "is all that is contained in Scripture clearly stated, and may all that is but implied be rejected?"[50] Newman's implied answer is clearly "no."

The more Newman explores the complexities of the reading process, the "prejudices" and "prepossessions" which people bring to texts, the more he sounds like Stanley Fish, the guru of postmodern pragmatic Reader-Response theory. The "mass of men," Newman insists, cannot "contemplate Scripture without imparting to it the colouring which they themselves have received in the course of their education." There is a huge range of competence among different readers: "At times the commentator is sensitively alive to the most distant allusions, at times he is impenetrable to any."[51] He proceeds to play Fishy games with key passages from Scripture, bringing out their potential ambiguities. When Christ says to the Apostles, "Drink ye *all* of this" (Newman's emphasis), is this to be read as an injunction for the laity to be admitted to both kinds of the eucharist? Does the "all," in other words, refer to all the people in the room or all the wine in the cup? Anticipating a low Anglican response (the former), Newman proceeds, "yet when He said to them, I am with you *always*," he is understood (by Protestants) to have spoken

> to the original Apostles, exclusively of their successors in the ministry. When St Paul speaks of "the man of sin," he meant a succession of sinners; but when Christ said, "I give unto thee the keys of the kingdom of heaven," He does not mean a line of Peters ... "Do this in remembrance of Me," is to be understood as a command; but, "Ye also ought to wash one another's feet," is not a command.[52]

[50] Ibid., 183.
[51] Ibid., 184.
[52] Ibid., 185.

There is something quite shocking about the flippant and almost "cruel" manner (to use Hutton's adjective) in which Newman piles up these difficulties, bamboozling his audience out of their self-confidence in their habitual modes of reading. The point he is proving, however, is quickly established: to read and interpret the Scriptures is no easy matter. It is "sometimes literal and sometimes figurative" and to judge when it is which is difficult; "the mass of men, if left to themselves, will not possess the faculty of reading it naturally and truly."[53] To rely upon "the *private* reading of *Scripture*" as "the *one* essential requisite ... rejecting all other helps" is therefore "presumptuous."[54] Newman provides a number of "instances of the abuse of private judgment" or misreadings of Scripture even by eminent fathers, including Irenaeus on Jesus living to forty or fifty, Justin on him being deformed, and Clement on Paul being married. If they can get it wrong, what hope can there be for us?

Newman insists that he is not setting up "the Church against Scripture" but simply making her "the keeper and interpreter of Scripture," a role whose charter can be found in Scripture itself in the many instances where the apostles are described as being "of one accord." Even when they are not, St. Paul insists that they should be. The Catholic Newman adds a footnote to the effect that it was by "a happy coincidence, a providential disposition," that the divisions within Christianity occurred only *after* "the complete enunciation by the Church of all the 'fundamentals' of faith."[55] The Anglican Newman forty years earlier was more concerned about "those points in the superstructure of faith" in which differences had arisen, attributing the problem to the Roman tendency to "increase" doctrine, a process later to be welcomed as develop-

---

[53] Ibid., 186.
[54] Ibid., 195-197.
[55] Ibid., 229.

ment.[56] The Catholic annotator of the *Via Media* explains, "Doctrines remain implicit till they are contravened; they are stated in
explicit form" in answer to new questions and variant readings,
misreadings or heresies.[57] For the Anglican Newman, the deposit
of faith cannot admit of "increase;" for the Catholic Newman,
following Vincent, "though unalterable, it admits of growth."[58]
The *Via Media*, to use another postmodern buzz- word, is a dia-
logical text, its two principle voices being the Anglican Newman
of 1837 and the Catholic Newman of 1877.

The central issue, as ever, is language. The Anglican Newman
insists that the early Church struggled to express its faith, only
gradually coming to increasingly acceptable formulations:

> The words of the creed were not inspired; they were only valuable
> as expressing a certain sense, and if they were found deficient in
> expressing that sense, there was as little interference with things
> sacred, as little real change, in correcting or supplying what was
> needful, as in completing the lines of a chart or map by the origi-
> nal.[59]

Here, notice, mapping is all right, so long as it is accurate, prepared to modify itself in the face of empirical evidence. Newman,
for the moment at least, plays down the difficulty of establishing
"reality" independent of language. The early Christians, he
claims, knew what they meant by titles such as "Son of God":
"they did not use a dead letter; they knew what they meant by it,
and they one and all had the same meaning." So when the phrase
"consubstantial with the Father" was added, "they did but fix and
perpetuate that meaning, as it had been held from the beginning,
when an attempt had been made to put a new sense upon it." Forty

---

[56] Ibid., 237.
[57] Ibid., 246.
[58] Ibid., 247.
[59] Ibid., 248.

years on, I am glad to say, Newman was less convinced (for this
earlier view represents either a naive view of language or an over-
estimation of the education of the apostles, for the title "Son of
God" is surely the most difficult of all Jesus's titles). The footnote
on this passage recognises, "New questions, new opinions are
ever rising in the Chruch" and require authoritative answers.[60] A
little later, another note by the older and wiser Newman opposes
the high Anglican view of tradition with the question, "How can
history, that is, words and deeds which are dead and gone, act as
an effectual living decider of quarrels between living men?"[61]
How can the Fathers be expected to answer Luther?[62]

The Anglican Newman's answer to this question is that "the
Church necessarily has less power over the Creed now than
anciently." Again, it is a matter of the status of the language in
which faith found expression: "for at first it [the Creed] was but a
form of sound words, subservient to a Faith vividly and accurately
engraven on the heart of every Christian." Interestingly, Newman
uses a metaphor of writing (or is engraving on the heart a form of
sculpture) to describe a privileged state before writing was necessary, when their words were "of secondary value." Now that "the
living power of truth has declined," he argues, these early creeds,
"instead of being a mere summary of an existing Faith," become
"almost sacred from being the chief remains left us of an Apostolical truth; as the likeness of a friend, however incomplete in
itself, is cherished as the best memorial of him, when he has been
taken from us."[63] Perhaps this is a reference to Hurrell Froude,
whose written *Remains* Newman had helped publish the previous
year. But if it refers to Christ, it might be objected the argument

[60] Ibid., 248.
[61] Ibid., 285.
[62] Ibid., 287.
[63] Ibid., 253-254.

has rather more strength applied to the Gospels than to the creeds. It is the gospels, surely, "however incomplete," which give us our best "likeness" of Jesus.

Newman, however, insists that it is the Creed, "not in its mere letter, but in its living sense" which is "the engrafted word, which is able to save our souls,"[64] although neither he nor his modern editor indicate that the quotation here is scriptural (from James 1:21). James is instructing his readers to lay aside "all superfluity of naughtiness" and receive the word "with meekness" but his metaphor of grafting is ripe for deconstruction.The graft is one of Derrida's favourite metaphors, himself keen to "liberate theology from what has been grafted on to it, to free it from its meta-physico-philosophical super-ego, so as to uncover an authenticity of the 'gospel'," returning to a faith "very close to Scripture, a faith lived in a venturous, dangerous, free way."[65] The Anglican Newman, however, perpetually struggles to escape from the conditions of language, its reliance on writing in the sense of previous codes which determine the sense of words. The early Christians, he feels, must have been liberated from textuality, intuitively, unmediatedly understanding what the meaning of the phrase "Son of God." The historical argument (as opposed to the linguistic one) has a certain validity: the creeds, like the gospels, have a special "sacred" status as a result of their closeness to Christ himself. But can they escape the conditions of writing?

Well, Newman gives it a go, turning in the tenth lecture of the *Via Media* to meditation "On the Essentials of the Gospel." He is bothered by the fact that the Creed makes no mention of the Scripture as "the word of God,"[66] although he argues that the

[64] Ibid., 254.

[65] Kevin Hart, "Jacques Derrida (b.1930): Introduction", *The Postmodern God*, 162.

[66] Newman, *Via Media*, 260.

Bible is not only "fundamental of faith" but "the foundation of the fundamentals;" it is "passed over in the Creed, as being presupposed and implied in it."[67] But this metaphor too (of foundations) shows distressing signs of being *mis en abyme*, that is, opening up to an infinite deferral, each new foundation resting upon an earlier one. Newman attempts to cut this process short: "Now what is the Bible," he asks "but the permanent voice of God, the embodied and continuous sound, or at least the specimen and symbol of the message once supernaturally delivered?"[68] Each succeeding phrase, unfortunately (or fortunately, depending on whether you deplore or welcome textuality), cuts the ground from under the supposed fixing of meaning. Newman, aware that a voice cannot be "permanent" or "continuous," cannot go on simply repeating itself, reverts to a notion of language symbolising, re-presenting a "message once ... delivered." He proceeds to ridicule the popular phrase "Bible-Christians" since if it is not simply a truism ("We are all of us Bible-Christians in one sense") it must be meant to imply that "doctrines of whatever sort" are "of but secondary importance." Having called the Bible the foundation of doctrine, he now returns to his insistence that the "Bible does not carry with it its own interpretation" but requires a living authoritative interpreter.[69] So where is the final foundation, the ultimate ground?

Another question, lurking behind this one, is that raised by the sixth of the 39 Articles, quoted at the beginning of the following lecture "On Scripture as the Record of Faith." This claims that "Holy Scripture containeth all things necessary to salvation."[70] Again, Newman anticipates Stanley Fish in recognising the sheer

[67] Ibid., 261.
[68] Ibid., 262.
[69] Ibid., 264.
[70] Ibid., 282.

difficulty of deciding what is or is not in a text. There is, Fish argues, always a text (in the sense of words on a page) but "what is in it can change, and therefore at no level is it independent of and prior to interpretation."[71] Similarly, Newman too asks, "who is to be the *judge* of what is and what is not contained in Scripture"?[72] The Anglican Newman calls on Tradition to help the Church in deciding, but the Catholic Newman objects, "Is it not as difficult, and just as much and as little of a usurpation, to judge of what Tradition says, as of what Scripture says?" The Anglican Newman complains that both Romanists and Latitudinarians have "a tendency to deny that Scripture has one definite unalterable meaning."[73] The Catholic replies that although the Council of Trent "forbids any interpretation of Scripture which runs counter to the unanimous consent of the Fathers," it recognises and accepts the responsibility of making a final decision: "The facts of Antiquity are not too clear to dispense with the exercise of a judgment upon them."[74] The Catholic Newman is happy to give this final authority to the Church.

Interestingly, however, the Catholic Newman feels no need to qualify the emphasis his Anglican self places upon the importance of the Church regulating itself, forming and moulding itself, refining its capacity to make these interpretive decisions, by the constant reading of Scripture:

> The Church is bound over to test and to verify her doctrine by Scripture throughout her course of instruction. She must take care to show her children that she keeps Scripture in mind, and is ruling, guiding, steadying herself by it. In Sermons and Lectures, in cate-

---

[71] Stanley Fish, *Is There a Text in this Class?* (Cambridge, MA.: Harvard University Press, 1980) 272.

[72] Newman, *Via Media*, 282.

[73] Ibid., 284.

[74] Ibid., 285.

chizings and controversy, she must ever appeal to Scripture, draw her arguments from Scripture, explore and develop Scripture, imitate Scripture, build up her form of doctrine on Scripture rudiments; and though individuals have no warrant to set themselves against her particular use of Scripture, yet her obligation to use it is surely a great practical limitation of her power.

For the Anglican Newman, the sceptical abyss opened up by seemingly irresolvable hermeneutic difficulties could be said to be closed pragmatically by a combination of regulating influences. He disputes Chillingworth's minimising principle that "*nothing is necessary to be believed but what is plainly revealed.*"[75] He does not see why revelation should be "plain, or that faith requires clear knowledge," launching into another diatribe against "literal" reading. We do not go around cutting off our right hands or plucking out our right eyes or even washing one another's feet.[76] That there are four gospels, "four lives of Christ, written for different portions of the Church, and not tending to make up one whole,"[77] supports such a perspectivist position (perspectivism being distinguished from relativism in that it recognises different points of view from which an object can be seen without doubting that there is a single object being observed). The incompleteness of the scriptural record makes even the Anglican Newman recognise that the Church is left "to interpret, perhaps to supply what Scripture left irregular and incomplete."[78]

The Anglican Newman remains content with this somewhat messy position, the sliding between tradition as the interpreter and as the supplement of scripture, seeing it as part and parcel of "the special way in which Truth is struck out in the course of life," a

[75] Ibid., 289.
[76] Ibid., 292.
[77] Ibid., 294.
[78] Ibid., 295.

combination of "common sense, chance, moral perception, genius" and other not altogether controllable forces, whether in the scriptures themselves, in the Fathers or later in the early Anglican divines responsible for the articles[79], which are not to be read as "a system of theology ... but a protest against certain specific errors."[80] A long editorial note on this whole lecture by H.D.Weidner, editor of the Clarendon edition of the *Via* Media, explains that Newman's position as a Catholic, initially accepting that Trent had taught that "Scripture was materially insufficient and needed the supplement of tradition," later became less clearcut. Both the revised *Via Media* and the revised *Essay on Development* of 1878 argue that the "Tridentine formulas allowed for tradition as interpretative but not necessarily supplementary."[81] A mind as subtle and supple (some would say as Fishy) as Newman's is never going to be tied down to one interpretation for long, nor one interpretation of an interpretation.

The Newman of 1837, however, continued to stress the importance of the Scriptures. Lecture XII, "On Scripture as the Record of Our Lord's Teaching," begins with a moving celebration of the power of the Gospels, "the nearest possible approach to the perpetual presence of the Apostles in the Church,"[82] the qualifying phrase "nearest possible" granting that all representation implies the actual absence of the object of which any description remains an approximation. Nevertheless, such is the power and, Newman assumes, accuracy of the Gospels that they afford us "literally the sight of Almighty God in His judgments, thoughts, attributes, and deeds."[83] His teaching has a self-authenticating genius, a "peculiar character"

---

[79] Ibid., 296.
[80] Ibid., 300.
[81] Ibid., 408.
[82] Ibid., 304.
[83] Ibid., 305.

that marks it as His, the style of "One who spake as none other man could speak." Newman makes a virtue of what might, from a literary perspective, appear weaknesses: "the Evangelists heap his words together, though unconnected with each other, as if under a divine intimitation"[84] (*sic*, possibly an innocent misprint but more interestingly read as a Freudian slip combining intimidate and imitate: they were terrified into accuracy, representing the *ipsissima verba*). Newman marvels at the "short and expressive sentences" in which Christ is recorded as speaking, most evident in the seven last words. There is no rhetoric, "no diffuse and lavish communications," nothing "exuberant, various, or vague;" "our Lord was sparing in His words and actions."[85] There is the same terseness, in other words, in Christ's language as Auerbach in *Mimesis* noticed in the Bible as a whole, forcing readers to extract deeper meaning. Similarly, Christ's teaching, Newman claims, was like "a seed deposited in their [the disciples"] hearts, which, under the influences of heavenly grace, would, in due season, germinate, and become "the power of God unto salvation" to all that believed."[86] Newman recognises that the fourth gospel is already half-way to tradition, St John writing "what might be considered a supplement to the three preceeding Gospels."[87] Yet even he, according to Newman, treasures the actual words of Jesus, recording and "contemplating them even in ignorance, rather than superseding them." The fact that the Synoptic Gospels record exactly the same words at the institution of the Eucharist, is seen by Newman as confirmation of their principle that, in matters of crucial importance, accuracy mattered. The inscription on the cross, by contrast, varies, since not regarded as vital.

[84] Ibid., 307.
[85] Ibid., 309.
[86] Ibid., 315.
[87] Ibid., 311.

The Scriptures remained for the Anglican Newman, as he explains in the penultimate lecture of the *Via Media*, "On Scripture as the Document of Proof in the Early Church," "the document of all appeal," "the touchstone of all doctrine."[88] He waxes lyrical on the way the Fathers "guided themselves by the notices of the written word, as by landmarks in their course," only for his older Catholic self to comment, somewhat tetchily, "This is incorrect, and I cannot guess whence the author got such a statement."[89] The Fathers cited by the Anglican Newman use a range of metaphors of the Bible, all of them stressing its creative nature, Origen calling it "God's One Perfect and Complete Instrument, giving forth, to those who wish to learn, its one saving music from many notes combined," Cyprian revelling in the "fountains of divine fulness" and Optatus developing the traditional image of a testament: "when a father feels himself to be dying, and fears lest after his death his sons should quarrel and go to law, he summons witnesses, and transfers his will from his heart, which is soon to fail, to tablets which shall endure."[90]

The problem about wills, however, as Derrida noted in attempting to read Marx's legacy to mankind in *Specters of Marx*, is that they too require interpretation.[91] The wiser Newman of 1877 accepts that the Scriptures were of "first importance with the early Church but that was because

> The early Christians, when teaching and proving Christianity, had nothing tangible to appeal to but the Scriptures. As time went on, and a theological literature grew up, the appeal exclusively to Scripture ceased. Intermitted it could never be. Scripture had the prerog-

---

88 Ibid., 319.
89 Ibid., 321.
90 Ibid., 323-325.
91 Jacques Derrida, *Specters of Marx*, trans. Peggy Kamuf (London: Routledge, 1994) 16-17.

ative of inspiration, and thereby a sacredness and power *sui generis*; but, from the nature of the case, it was inferior as an instrument of proof, in directness and breadth, to Councils, to the Schola, and to the Fathers, doctors, theologians, and devotional writers of the Church.[92]

Only as an "instrument of proof," Newman is saying. His love of the Bible, as we shall see, in no way diminished as a Catholic, but he became even more aware of its limitations as a vehicle for "proving doctrine."

These limitations come to the fore in Tract 85, "Holy Scripture in Its Relation to the Catholic Creed," first published in 1838 and reprinted in *Discussions and Arguments* in 1872. Here Newman meets the demand for "more adequate *Scripture proof*" of the tractarian emphasis on the authority of the Church with what he admits is "a kill-or-cure argument." It is true that the doctrine of "Apostolical Succession is "not clearly taught in Scripture" but then neither are a number of other doctrines he proceeds to enumerate, beginning with "the divinity of the Holy Ghost, which is nowhere literally stated in Scripture." There is nothing in the Bible about its own inspiration, nothing which "proves" Original Sin, justification by faith alone or even the divinity of Christ.[93] None of these doctrines are "clearly stated" in a manner which defies alternative interpretations.

Newman proceeds to spell out three possible conclusions to be drawn from this: first, that "Christianity contains no definite message, creed, revelation" (the Latitudinarian position), second, "there really is a true creed or system in Scripture, still it is not on the surface of Scripture, but is found latent and implicit within it" (the Anglican position as Newman holds it) or third, that revela-

---

[92] Newman, *Via Media*, 328-329.

[93] John Henry Newman, *Discussions and Arguments on Various Subjects* (London: Longmans, Green and Co., 1885 [1872]) 110-124.

tion "must be learned collaterally from other sources" (the Roman position). Newman rejects the first position as "extravagant": "Why should God speak unless He meant to say something?"[94] If Scripture were really "so obscure that nothing can be made of it," he would be driven to Romanism. He delivers a thunderous attack on those who luxuriate in the literary complexities of the Bible (among whom I suspect is part of himself):

> It is very well for educated persons, at their ease, with few cares ... to argue and speculate about the impalpableness and versatility of the divine message, its chameleon-like changeableness, its adaptation to each fresh mind it meets; but when men are conscious of sin, are sorrowful, are weighed down, are desponding, they ask for something to lean on, something external to themselves.[95]

Since religion must be definite, objective and "dogmatic" in order to provide such help, Newman concludes that the Church has a duty to teach "things but indirectly taught in Scripture," not adding to it as the Romanists but drawing out what is "indirectly and covertly recorded there."[96]

The third and fourth chapters of Tract 85 spell out the complex nature of the Bible, inspired by God but written by men, not really "one book" but "a great number of writings, like the world itself full of riches, fertile areas, but also subject to accidents, "a long history of change and chance." It is neither complete nor systematic, though God has "over-ruled matters so far as to make the apparently casual writings of the Apostles a complete canon of saving faith."[97] Among the illustrations of the "unstudied" and "perplexed" nature of Scripture Newman gives are the well-known discrepancies between the two accounts of creation in the

---

94 Newman, *Via Media*, 126-130.
95 Ibid., 133.
96 Ibid., 141-142.
97 Ibid., 149-150.

opening chapters of Genesis, "an instance of the unsolicitous free-dom and want of system of the sacred narrative,"[98] the omission of the raising of Lazarus from the Synoptic Gospels, the variant accounts of Our Lord's resurrection and the different versions of the death of Judas in Matthew and Acts.

Chapter five of Tract 85 explores "The Impression made on the Reader by the Statements of Scripture," a phenomenological approach which again anticipates modern Reader-Response Criticism. Like Auerbach again, Newman stresses the simplicity and depth of the Bible, its lack of ornament and rhetoric; and like Iser, he notices that readers themselves are left to make their own judgments. We are often not told "whether the events recorded are presented for praise or blame ... We are left to a comment, the comment of our own judgment, external to the inspired volume."[99] The impiety of Ahaz in 2 Kings 16 passes with "no epithet, no turn of sentence, which betrays the divine judgment," the martyrdom of St John the Baptist with not "a word of indignation, of lament, or of triumph." The facts of St Paul's journey to Jerusalem are related "nakedly, leaving us "continually perplexed what to think."[100] The first three Gospels "contain no declaration of our Lord's divinity, and there are passages which tend at first sight the other way."[101] "Is it possible," Newman asks, that they were unaware of this "great and solemn truth"? No, we can, "knowing the doctrine" ... discern in them a feeling of reverence towards our Lord, which fully implies it."[102]

Newman, as is his wont, concedes a great deal, for instance the plausibility of the argument that "the divinity of Christ was an

[98] Ibid., 154.
[99] Ibid., 174-175.
[100] Ibid., 176-178.
[101] Ibid., 184.
[102] Ibid.

after-thought, brought in by the Greek Platonists and other philosophers upon the simple and primitive creed of the Galilean fishermen."[103] He anticipates Renan's emphasis on the "oriental imagination:

> Let it be borne in mind, that a figurative, or what may be called a sacramental style, was the very characteristic of oriental teaching; so that it would have been a wilful disrespect in any hearer who took the words of a great prophet in their mere literal and outside sense.[104]

He predicts the unsettling of minds over biblical criticism, over questions of the canon. He even appears to have anticipated the coming of Alter and Kermode, the appropriation of the Bible "as a sort of literature," not to mention the Jesus Seminar, the selection of certain portions of Scripture as more authentic than others. He accepts there may be "error" in Revelation but only in "matters of detail," "not in principles." If there is an air almost of desperation in his resolve to stay firm, to accept the "hidden" truth of the Bible (he ends chapter 7, "God will not deceive me," and chapter 8 asserting his love and loyalty for the Church and "her Bible"), it is because he recognises the difficulties involved in reading it. He might wish that God had "spoken more distinctly" but "God's ways surely are not as our ways." He chooses to give us "doctrines which are but obscurely gathered from Scripture, and a Scripture which is but obscurely gathered from history" and we must make the best of it.[105]

There were, of course, limits on how much of the Higher Criticism Newman would accept, limits that appear in his 1841 review of Henry Milman's *History of Christianity*, reprinted in *Essays*

---

[103] Ibid., 187.
[104] Ibid., 192.
[105] Ibid., 244.

Critical and Historical in 1871. He is not bothered by the evidence Milman adduces of Christianity appropriating material from other religions, seeing the "great characteristic of Revelation" as "addition, substitution," the use of the "existing system" of human signification.[106] He is concerned, however, by Milman's arbitrary reduction of the miraculous or supernatural elements in the New Testament, his rejection of all private miracles such as visions of angels. Like Strauss, Milman sees myth as a "vehicle" for truth, *"a kind of language"* appropriate for the age in which revelation was made. Appearances of angels, he argues, "are imaginative, not fictitious," true for the beholders but not to be taken literally by a later more "rational age."[107] This for Newman is an unholy compromise, an abandonment of tradition, an ignoble attempt to "reconcile the faith of eighteen centuries" with "the infidelity of the nineteenth." He cannot accept that the Virgin Mary only thought she saw an angel, that the devils were only in the minds of the Gadarene swine. "What limits are we to put to this denial of historical truth?", asks Newman. "Where is theory to stop, if it is once allowed?"[108] If the angels at the tomb are to be explained as the "impressions" of *"highly excited* and *bewildered"* women, why should we accept the resurrection itself (as Milman did)? The admission of rationalistic principles into revelation, Newman claims, will not only cause angels to "melt into impressions" but Christianity to "melt away in our hands like snow."[109] Newman quickly closes the hermeneutic door (or window) opened by the *Via Media*.

Newman's rejection of Milman's compromise with the more radical Higher Criticism of Germany (with which Newman never

---

[106] Ibid., 194.
[107] Ibid., 218-219.
[108] Ibid., 223-224.
[109] Ibid., 242.

fully engaged) is out of keeping, I would argue, with the otherwise subtle and sophisticated hermeneutics evident in his other Anglican writings from *Arians* to the *Essay on Development*. Newman's writing on the Bible as a Catholic, by contrast, lacks either the urgency or interest of this earlier writing, perhaps because of his greater sense of security in the authority of the Church as the interpreter of revelation. He has jumped into the arms of Mother Church, who knows best. The *Apologia* announces rather blandly, as a side issue, "I now consider my Anglican interpretations of Scripture to be erroneous."[110] *The Idea of a University* announces,

> he who believes Revelation with that absolute faith which is the prerogative of a Catholic, is not the nervous creature who startles at every sound, and is fluttered by every strange or novel appearance which meets his eyes. He has no sort of apprehension, he laughs at the idea, that any thing can be discovered by any other scientific method, which can contradict any one of the dogmas of his religion.[111]

Such confidence, however, is as disturbing as his earlier anxiety, betraying as it does the imperviousness to evidence characteristic of neo-orthodoxy at its most solipsistic, happily cocooned in its own self-enclosed system, immune either to criticism or experience.

In practice, Newman did continue to work on the Bible and to worry about the challenges to its authenticity emerging from various sciences. It was to Newman that the Bishops turned for their projected new English translation of the Bible in 1857, and, according to Ward, he worked on an "elaborate introduction - *Prolegomena* was to be its title - to be prefixed to his translation of the Scriptures." The project, unfortunately, was abandoned and

---

[110] Newman, *Apologia pro Vita Sua*, 97.

[111] John Henry Newman, *The Idea of a University*, (ed.) Martin J. Svaglic (San Francisco: Rinehart Press, 1960 [1852-9]) 353.

the unfinished manuscript destroyed in 1877.[112] Other notes, apparently prepared in response to the publication of *Essays and Reviews* in 1860, have since been edited as *The Theological Papers of J.H.Newman on Biblical Inspiration and Infallibility*. Fragmentary and not intended for publication, they indicate a continuing awareness on Newman's part of the limits of the Bible. They also display a somewhat mellower attitude to Higher Criticism, an openness to the findings of science and history.

The first of the papers on "The Problem of Inspiration" accepts that the Bible has "two aspects: it is both the work of God, and the work of man" (there is a latent incarnational analogy throughout). As revelation, it needs to be accepted as infallible in matters of faith and morals but as the work of human beings it is liable to error. Luke is not necessarily infallible on the distance between Jerusalem and Emmaus while Matthew's list of forty generations between Abraham and Christ is not to be taken literally. The Bible, Newman still recognises, is not "one whole book" but "a miscellaneous collection of books written independently ... accidentally written ... and accidentally preserved.[113] It is neither equally inspired nor "of equal preciousness [value]."[114] The writers differ greatly, writing in "various languages, in various styles, some hardly grammatical, others correct and elegant."[115] Newman tries to argue that Scripture is "inspired" in the sense of being infallible in its supernatural aspect , even announcing the principle that "*What protects any part of Scripture from scientific and historical criticism is the profession or the claim to be religious*

---

[112] Wilfrid Ward, *The Life of John Henry Cardinal Newman,* 2 vols. (London: Longmans, Green and Co., 1927 [1912]) 1:423.

[113] John Henry Newman, *The Theological Papers of John Henry Newman on Biblical Inspiration and on Infallibility,* (ed.) J. Derek Homes (Oxford: Clarendon Press, 1979) 23.

[114] Ibid., 22.

[115] Ibid., 24.

[supernatural]" but the fact that he immediately promises to return to the question how this is to be decided in "another chapter" suggests his awareness of problems here.

Many of the papers tail off precisely at the point when they reach a difficult question, or provide answers to these questions that are patently inadequate. The "Revised Introduction" of 1861, for example, attempts to establish science and religion as separate worlds, another familiar neo-orthodox gambit. There is no need to reconcile Scripture and science, Newman claims,

> because there is as little as possible common to them...theology sits easy...in its own domain, without any fear...of any collision between itself and secualr knowledge...provided each party will but consent to remain within its own boundaries.[116]

For the Catholic Newman the "only sovereign and decisive authority" in matters of faith and morals is "the direct decision of the Church." He recognises the difference in language-use between dogmatic decisions of Popes and Councils, which are "precise, ... measured and circumscribed," and the teachings of Scripture,which "are ever open, free, various, exuberant, but ... with little of method and definiteness. The first guard us from falling into error;" the latter "draw us on to the spontaneous love of what is highest, truest, and best."[117] It is clear which makes the more interesting reading, but formal definitions are necessary safeguards against the very freedom of the Scriptures.

Newman's theological papers on the Bible reveal a continuing awareness of biblical criticism. He imagines a number of Catholic interlocutors bringing their problems to him:

> "People come and tell me that the book of Genesis is made up of

[116] Ibid., 36.
[117] Ibid., 39.

various documents; am I called on *de fide* to believe that it is all written by one author, and him Moses?" No: - "then I need not fret myself about the chance of some collision ... on this matter between criticism and faith."[118]

Catholics are not required to believe that David was the author of all the Psalms or Solomon of the book of Ecclesiastes: "I need not fear to open my mind to such principles of investigation and sources of knowledge as prove or assume that they [the Psalms] are written in successive centuries."[119] Newman is more protective of the New Testament, seeing "the mere fact of writing" at the time of the Apostles "when the materials of writing were not easy" as implying "a formal act." Furthermore, "an authoritative account of the life and actions and sayings of our Lord and Saviour, in whom the whole revelation centres, is naturally the sort of writing for which divine inspiration would be given."[120] Newman remains constantly aware of the complexity of language, which "involves a vast *entourage* of human ideas, associations, memories, sympathies, media of judgments." For these reasons he is sure that the Fathers would have recognised that Scripture, "though the writing of God, though sacred in its separate words, though full of profound meanings and spiritual mysteries" remained "the word of man ... and in this aspect necessarily imperfect."[121]

Newman returned to the question of the Bible in an article "On the Inspiration of Scripture" in the *Nineteenth Century* in 1884, after the First Vatican Council had pronounced on the subject: *Deum habent Auctorem.*[122] Newman points out that the Latin *auctor* is not identical with the English author, suggesting a number

---

[118] Ibid., 50.
[119] Ibid.
[120] Ibid., 65.
[121] Ibid., 88.
[122] Vawter, *Biblical Inspiration,* 70.

of preferable translations (authority, originator, inventor, founder, primary cause) and reiterating his view that there are "two writers of the Scriptures, the divine and the human."[123] As Owen Chadwick acknowledges, it is tempting for a modern reader of this essay to dismiss it as "obsolete: an old man tackling a non-problem with out-of-date principles." Read with "historical understanding," however, it represents an important step in prising open the Catholic mind to the findings of historical criticism, if "only a chink."[124] Newman altogether rejects the notion that Catholics are required to "assent to the views and interpretations of Scripture which modern science and historical research have utterly discredited."[125] He once more asserts that the Bible is "a document, multiform and copious in its contents,"[126] whose human authors were not always aware what they were writing. He accepts scholarly arguments about the dubious authorship of the ending of Mark's Gospel, the two Isaiahs, the Letter to the Hebrews and so on. He sees no need to believe in the infallibility of *obiter dicta*, "unimportant statements of fact."[127] It is altogether unremarkable by modern standards but it did at least help to bring Catholics in touch with the world of historical scholarship.

Newman's writing on the Bible is important, I would claim, both because of the subtlety of his grappling with hermeneutic problems and because of his awareness of the centrality of the Bible in the whole process of faith, a process of the imagination and the heart as well as the intellect. This, of course, is spelt out in detail in the *Grammar of Assent*, especially in the long section on

---

[123] John Henry Newman, "On the Inspiration of Scripture," *Nineteenth Century* 15 (1884) 189.

[124] Owen Chadwick, *Newman* (Oxford: Oxford University Press, 1983) 75.

[125] Newman, "On the Inspiration of Scripture," 185.

[126] Ibid., 190.

[127] Ibid., 196-197.

"Revealed Religion" with which that book ends. It is also cap-
tured imaginatively in his novel *Callista,* the story of a third-cen-
tury convert for whom the key moment is her reading in prison of
a copy of St Luke's Gospel. Newman describes the act of reading,
analysed so subtly in his Anglican works, the complex process by
which material at first strange and unfamiliar can overturn an individual's whole perception of the world, her whole personality:

> It was the writing of a provincial Greek; elegant, however, and
> marked with that simplicity which was to her taste ... It was
> addressed to one Theophilus, and professed to be a carefully
> digested and verified account of events which had already been
> attempted by others. She read a few paragraphs, and became inter-
> ested, and in no long time she was absorbed in the volume. When
> she had once taken it up, she did not lay it down. Even at other
> times she would have prized it, but now, when she was so desolate
> and lonely, it was simply a gift from an unseen world. It opened a
> view of a new state and community of beings, which only seemed
> too beautiful to be possible. But not into a new state of things alone,
> but into the presence of One who was simply distinct and removed
> from any thing that she had, in her most imaginative moments, ever
> depicted to her mind as ideal perfection.[128]

Newman follows the way in which Callista kindles to the person of Christ, even her imaginative identification with "the poor
girl at the feast, who would anoint His feet." He traces too the
way in which she enters "a new world of thought," a world in
which she finds herself astonishingly different.[129]

I want to suggest that this is Newman at his best, imaginatively
representing the creative capacity of language, its power to open
up new worlds. The other side of Newman, however, his awareness of the dangers and limits of language, needs also to be

---

[128] John Henry Newman, *Callista: A Sketch of the Third Century* (London:
Burns and Oates, n.d. [1855]) 252-253.
[129] Ibid., 253-254.

acknowledged. Both aspects of language, its exuberant playfulness, forever generating new meaning, and its potentially dangerous excess, its problematic relation to "reality," have featured in postmodern debates, some of which Newman anticipates. One of the reasons that Newman continues to appeal to both sides of the constant and necessary debate within the Church between "progressives" and "traditionalists" (whether in the times of the modernists or the postmodernists) is that he sees (and in the *Via Media* expresses) both sides of the question. He sees that the Church needs both to engage freely and imaginatively with its foundational texts and to impose certain limits upon this freedom in order to maintain its living tradition. He celebrates the richness and inexhaustibility of language, the words engrafted in that tradition, but he recognises too the inadequacy of all our words in the face of the Word, the difference between our grasp of truth and Truth itself.

NOTES ON THE CONTRIBUTORS

Gabriel Daly is Lecturer in Systematic and Historical Theology, Trinity College, Dublin. His writings include *Transcendence and Immanence: A Study in Catholic Modernism and Integralism* (1980) and *Creation and Redemption* (1988).

Louis Dupré is the T. Lawrason Riggs Professor in Religious Studies at Yale University. His books include *Passage to Modernity* (1993) and *Metaphysics and Culture* (1994).

Sheridan Gilley is Reader in Theology at the University of Durham. His writings include *Newman and His Age* (1990).

Ian Ker is Tutor at Campion Hall, and a member of the Faculty of Theology of the University of Oxford. His books include *John Henry Newman: A Biography* (1988), *Newman and the Fullness of Christianity* (1993) and *Healing the Wound of Humanity: The Spirituality of John Henry Newman* (1993).

Fergus Kerr is Regent of Blackfriars, Oxford and Honorary Senior Lecturer in Theology at the University of Edinburgh. He is the author of *Theology after Wittgenstein* (1986, 1997) and *Immortal Longings: Versions of Transcending Humanity* (1997).

Alister E. McGrath is the Principal of Wycliffe Hall, Oxford and a Research Lecturer in Theology at the University of Oxford. His books include *The Genesis of Doctrine* (1990) and *Iustitia Dei: A History of the Christian Doctrine of Justification* (1986, 1998).

Terrence Merrigan is Professor of Christology at the Faculty of Theology, Katholieke Universiteit Leuven, Belgium. He is the author of *Clear Heads and Holy Hearts: The Religious and Theological Ideal of John Henry Newman* (1991), and the editor of *The Myriad Christ: Plurality and the Quest for Unity in Contemporary Christology* (2000).

William Myers is Professor of English Literature at the University of Leicester, England. He has published studies of Dryden, Milton, George Eliot and Evelyn Waugh. His latest book is *The Presence of Persons* (1998).

Terence R. Wright is Professor of English at the University of Newcastle. His books include *The Religion of Humanity* (1986) and *Theology and Literature* (1988).

INDEX OF NAMES

The use of italics indicates that the reference is contained in a footnote on the relevant page

INDEX OF SUBJECTS

The use of italics indicates that the reference is contained in a footnote on the relevant page

PRINTED ON PERMANENT PAPER • IMPRIME SUR PAPIER PERMANENT • GEDRUKT OP DUURZAAM PAPIER - ISO 9706

ORIENTALISTE, KLEIN DALENSTRAAT 42, B-3020 HERENT